MORE PRAISE FOR *BETTER THAN BEFORE*

"Grab this now! *Better Than Before* is essential reading. In this generous and actionable book, Gretchen Rubin helps us make sense of how privilege and opportunity make so many of us unhappy, and shows how basic daily choices can free us to make the most of what we have."

—Seth Godin, bestselling author of *Linchpin*

"Almost everyone wants to be 'better'—slimmer, smarter, better looking, more interesting, more productive—and we want to know we're improving, we want the reinforcing evidence. Gretchen Rubin's new masterpiece, *Better Than Before*, shows us how. Unlike other books on habits, Rubin's book gives us the specific tools and a blueprint for getting back on track—the fast track."

—Brian Wansink, Ph.D., bestselling author of *Mindless Eating*

BETTER THAN BEFORE

BETTER THAN BEFORE

Mastering the Habits of

Our Everyday Lives

GRETCHEN RUBIN

CROWN PUBLISHERS

NEW YORK

Copyright © 2015 by Gretchen Rubin

Published in the United States by Crown Publishers, an imprint of the
Crown Publishing Group, a division of Random House LLC,
a Penguin Random House Company, New York.

www.crownpublishing.com

CROWN is a registered trademark and the Crown colophon is
a trademark of Random House LLC.

Library of Congress Cataloging-in-Publication Data
Rubin, Gretchen Craft.
Better than before / Gretchen Rubin.
pages cm
1. Habit. 2. Change (Psychology) I. Title.
BF335.R82 2054
153.1—dc23
2014031703

ISBN 978-0-385-34861-4
eISBN 978-0-385-34862-1

Printed in the United States of America

Book design by Lauren Dong
Jacket design by Christopher Brand and Ben Wiseman

10 9 8 7 6 5 4 3 2 1

First Edition

For my family, again

The greatest of empires, is the empire over one's self.

—PUBLILIUS SYRUS

Contents

DESIRE, EASE, AND EXCUSES

UNIQUE, JUST LIKE EVERYONE ELSE

A Note to the Reader

Better Than Before tackles the question: *How do we change?* One answer—by using habits.

Habits are the invisible architecture of daily life. We repeat about 40 percent of our behavior almost daily, so our habits shape our existence, and our future. If we change our habits, we change our lives.

But that observation just raises another question: *Okay, then, how do we change our habits?* That's what this book seeks to answer.

But while *Better Than Before* explores how to change your habits, it won't tell you what particular habits to form. It won't tell you to exercise first thing in the morning, or to eat dessert twice a week, or to clear out your office. (Well, actually, there is *one* area where I do say what habit I think is best. But only one.)

The fact is, no one-size-fits-all solution exists. It's easy to dream that if we copy the habits of productive, creative people, we'll win similar success. But we each must cultivate the habits that work for *us*. Some people do better when they start small; others when they start big. Some people need to be held accountable; some defy accountability. Some thrive when they give themselves an occasional break from their good habits; others when they never break the chain. No wonder habit formation is so hard.

The most important thing is to *know ourselves*, and to choose the strategies that work for us.

Before you begin, identify a few habits that you'd like to adopt, or changes you'd like to make. Then, as you read, consider what steps you want to try. You may even want to note today's date on your book's flyleaf, so you'll remember when you began the process of change.

To help you shape your habits, I regularly post suggestions on my blog, and I've also created many resources to help you make your life better than before. But I hope that the most compelling inspiration is the book you hold in your hands.

I see habits through the lens of my own experience, so this account is colored by my particular personality and interests. "Well," you might think, "if everyone forms habits differently, why should I bother to read a book about what someone else did?"

During my study of habits and happiness, I've noticed something surprising: I often learn more from one person's idiosyncratic experiences than I do from scientific studies or philosophical treatises. For this reason, *Better Than Before* is packed with individual examples of habit changes. You may not be tempted by Nutella, or travel too much for work, or struggle to keep a gratitude journal, but we can all learn from each other.

It's simple to change habits, but it's not easy.

I hope that reading *Better Than Before* will encourage you to harness the power of habits to make change in your own life. Whenever you read this, and wherever you are, you're in the right place to begin.

BETTER THAN BEFORE

DECIDE NOT TO DECIDE

Introduction

It is a profoundly erroneous truism that we should cultivate the habit of thinking of what we are doing. The precise opposite is the case. Civilization advances by extending the number of operations we can perform without thinking about them.

—ALFRED NORTH WHITEHEAD,
An Introduction to Mathematics

For as long as I can remember, one of my favorite features in any book, magazine, play, or TV show has been the "before and after." Whenever I read those words, I'm hooked. The thought of a transformation—any kind of transformation—thrills me. Whether the change is as important as quitting smoking, or as trivial as reorganizing a desk, I love to read about how and why someone made that change.

"Before and after" caught my imagination, and it also provoked my curiosity. Sometimes, people can make dramatic changes, but more often, they can't. Why or why not?

As a writer, my great interest is human nature, and in particular, the subject of happiness. A few years ago, I noticed a pattern: when people told me about a "before and after" change they'd made that boosted their happiness, they often pointed to the formation of a crucial *habit*. And when they were unhappy about a change they'd failed to make, that too often related to a habit.

Then one day, when I was having lunch with an old friend, she said something that turned my casual interest in habits into a full-time preoccupation.

After we'd looked at our menus, she remarked, "I want to get myself in the habit of exercise, but I can't, and it really bothers me." Then, in a brief observation that would absorb me for a long time to come, she added, "The weird thing is that in high school, I was on the track team, and I never missed track practice, but I can't go running now. Why?"

"Why?" I echoed, as I mentally flipped through my index cards of happiness research to find some relevant insight or useful explanation. Nothing.

Our conversation shifted to other topics, but as the days passed, I couldn't get this exchange out of my mind. Same person, same activity, different habit. *Why?* Why had she been able to exercise faithfully in the past, but not now? How might she start again? Her question buzzed in my head with the special energy that tells me I've stumbled onto something important.

Finally, I connected that conversation with what I'd noticed about people's accounts of their before-and-after transformations, and it struck me: *To understand how people are able to change, I must understand habits.* I felt the sense of joyous anticipation and relief that I feel every time I get the idea for my next book. It was obvious! *Habits.*

Whenever I become gripped by a subject, I read everything related to it, so I began to plunder the shelves in cognitive science, behavioral economics, monastic governance, philosophy, psychology, product design, addiction, consumer research, productivity, animal training, decision science, public policy, and the design of kindergarten rooms and routines. A tremendous amount of information about habits was floating around, but I had to divide the astronomy from the astrology.

I spent a lot of time delving into treatises, histories, biographies, and in particular, the latest scientific research. At the same time, I've learned to put great store in my own observations of everyday life, because while laboratory experiments are one way to study human nature, they aren't the only way. I'm a kind of street scientist. I spend most of my time trying to grasp the obvious—not to see what no one has seen, but to see what's in plain sight. A sentence will jump off the page, or someone's casual comment, like my friend's remark about the track team, will strike me as highly significant, for reasons that I don't quite understand; then, as I learn more, these loose puzzle pieces begin to fit together, until the picture comes clear.

The more I learned about habits, the more interested I became—but I also became increasingly frustrated. To my surprise, the sources I consulted made little mention of many of the issues that struck me as most crucial:

- Perhaps it's understandable why it's hard to form a habit we *don't* enjoy, but why is it hard to form a habit we *do* enjoy?
- Sometimes people acquire habits overnight, and sometimes they drop longtime habits just as abruptly. Why?
- Why do some people dread and resist habits, while others adopt them eagerly?
- Why do so many successful dieters regain their lost weight, plus more?
- Why are people so often unmoved by the consequences of their habits? For instance, one-third to one-half of U.S. patients don't take medicine prescribed for a chronic illness.
- Do the same strategies work for changing simple habits (wearing a seat belt) and for complex habits (drinking less)?
- Why is it that sometimes, though we're very anxious—even desperate—to change a habit, we can't? A friend told me, "I have health issues, and I feel lousy when I eat certain foods. But I eat them anyway."
- Do the same habit-formation strategies apply equally well to everyone?

- Certain situations seem to make it easier to form habits. Which ones, and why?

I was determined to find the answers to those questions, and to figure out every aspect of how habits are made and broken.

Habits were the key to understanding how people were able to change. But *why* did habits make it possible for people to change? I found the answer, in part, in a few sentences whose dry, calm words disguised an observation that, for me, was explosively interesting. "Researchers were surprised to find," write Roy Baumeister and John Tierney in their fascinating book *Willpower*, "that people with strong self-control spent *less* time resisting desires than other people did. . . people with good self-control mainly use it not for rescue in emergencies but rather to develop effective habits and routines in school and at work." In other words, *habits* eliminate the need for *self-control*.

Self-control is a crucial aspect of our lives. People with better self-control (or self-regulation, self-discipline, or willpower) are happier and healthier. They're more altruistic; they have stronger relationships and more career success; they manage stress and conflict better; they live longer; they steer clear of bad habits. Self-control allows us to keep our commitments to ourselves. Yet one study suggests that when we try to use self-control to resist temptation, we succeed only about half the time, and indeed, in a large international survey, when people were asked to identify their failings, a top choice was lack of self-control.

There's some debate about the nature of self-control. Some argue that we have a limited amount of self-control strength, and as we exert it, we exhaust it. Others counter that willpower isn't limited in this way, and that we can find fresh reserves by reframing our actions. As for me, I wake up with a reasonable store of self-control, and the more I draw on it, the lower it drops. I remember sitting in a meeting and resisting a cookie plate for an hour—then grabbing two cookies on my way out.

And that's why habits matter so much. With *habits*, we conserve our self-control. Because we're in the habit of putting a dirty coffee cup in the office dishwasher, we don't need self-control to perform that action; we do it without thinking. Of course, it takes self-control to establish good habits. But once the habit is in place, we can effortlessly do the things we want to do.

And there's one reason, in particular, that habits help to preserve our self-control.

In ordinary terms, a "habit" is generally defined as a behavior that's recurrent, is cued by a specific context, often happens without much awareness or conscious intent, and is acquired through frequent repetition.

I became convinced, however, that the defining aspect of habits isn't frequency, or repetition, or the familiarity of the cues for a particular behavior. These factors do matter; but in the end, I concluded that the real key to habits is *decision making*—or, more accurately, the *lack of decision making*. A habit requires no decision from me, because I've already decided. Am I going to brush my teeth when I wake up? Am I going to take this pill? I decide, then I don't decide; mindfully, then mindlessly. I shouldn't worry about making healthy choices. I should make one healthy choice, and then stop choosing. This freedom from decision making is crucial, because when I have to decide—which often involves resisting temptation or postponing gratification—I tax my self-control.

I'd asked myself, "Why do habits make it possible for people to change?" and now I knew the answer. *Habits make change possible by freeing us from decision making and from using self-control.*

One day, after checking the time difference to make sure that it wasn't too early in Los Angeles, I called my sister Elizabeth to talk to her about my research. She's five years younger than I am, but I call her "my sister the sage," because she always has tremendous insight into whatever I'm pondering at the moment.

After we talked about my nephew Jack's most recent antics, and the latest news about the TV show that Elizabeth writes for, I told her how preoccupied I'd become with the subject of habits.

"I think I've figured out why habits are so important," I told her. As I explained my conclusions, I could picture her sitting at her crowded desk, dressed in her unvarying outfit of running shoes, jeans, and hoodie. "With habits, we don't make decisions, we don't use self-control, we just do the thing we want ourselves to do—or that we don't want to do. Does that sound right to you?"

"That sounds about right," said Elizabeth agreeably. She's used to hearing me talk about my obsessions.

"But here's another question. How do people compare to each other? Some people love habits, and some people hate them. For some people, habits come fairly easily, other people struggle much more. Why?"

"You should start by figuring that out about yourself—you love habits more than anyone I know."

When I hung up the phone, I realized that as usual, Elizabeth had supplied me with a key insight. I hadn't quite understood this truth about myself before she pointed it out: I'm a wholehearted habits embracer. I love to cultivate habits, and the more I learn about them, the more I've come to recognize their many benefits.

When possible, the brain makes a behavior into a habit, which saves effort and therefore gives us more capacity to deal with complex, novel, or urgent matters. Habits mean we don't strain ourselves to make decisions, weigh choices, dole out rewards, or prod ourselves to begin. Life becomes simpler, and many daily hassles vanish. Because I don't have to think about the multistep process of putting in my contact lenses, I can think about the logistical problems posed by the radiator leak in my home office.

Also, when we're worried or overtaxed, a habit comforts us. Research suggests that people feel more in control and less anxious when engaged in habit behavior. I have a long blue jacket that I wore for two years straight whenever I gave speeches, and now it's quite tired-looking—yet if I feel particularly anxious about some presentation, I still turn to that well-worn jacket. Surprisingly, stress doesn't necessarily make us likely to indulge in bad habits; when we're anxious or tired, we fall back on our habits, whether bad or good. In one study, students in the habit of eating a healthy breakfast were more likely to eat healthfully during exams, while students in the habit of eating an unhealthy breakfast were more likely to eat unhealthfully. For this reason, it's all the more important to try to shape habits mindfully, so that when we fall back on them at times of stress, we're following activities that make our situation better, not worse.

But habits, even good habits, have drawbacks as well as benefits. Habits speed time, because when every day is the same, experience shortens and blurs; by contrast, time slows down when habits are interrupted, when the brain must process new information. That's why the first *month* at a new job seems to last longer than the fifth *year* at that job. And, as it speeds time, habit also deadens. An early-morning cup of coffee was delightful the first few times, until it gradually became part of the background of my day; now I don't really taste it, but I'm frantic if I don't get it. Habit makes it dangerously easy to become numb to our own existence.

For good and bad, habits are the invisible architecture of daily life. Research suggests that about 40 percent of our behavior is repeated almost daily, and mostly in the same context. I bet my own percentage is higher: I wake up at the same time every day; I give my husband, Jamie, a good-morning kiss at the same time; I wear the same outfit of running shoes, yoga pants, and white T-shirt; I work at my laptop in the same places every day; I walk the same routes around my New York City neighborhood; I work on my email at the same time; I put my daughters, thirteen-year-old Eliza and seven-year-old

Eleanor, to bed in the same unchanging sequence. When I ask myself, "Why is my life the way it is today?" I see that it has been shaped, to a great degree, by my habits. As architect Christopher Alexander described it:

> If I consider my life honestly, I see that it is governed by a certain very small number of patterns of events which I take part in over and over again.
>
> Being in bed, having a shower, having breakfast in the kitchen, sitting in my study writing, walking in the garden, cooking and eating our common lunch at my office with my friends, going to the movies, taking my family to eat at a restaurant, having a drink at a friend's house, driving on the freeway, going to bed again. There are a few more.
>
> There are surprisingly few of these patterns of events in any one person's way of life, perhaps no more than a dozen. Look at your own life and you will find the same. It is shocking at first, to see that there are so few patterns of events open to me.
>
> Not that I want more of them. But when I see how very few of them there are, I begin to understand what a huge effect these few patterns have on my life, on my capacity to live. If these few patterns are good for me, I can live well. If they are bad for me, I can't.

In the area of health alone, our unthinking actions may have a profound effect. Poor diet, inactivity, smoking, and drinking are among the leading causes of illness and death in the United States—and these are health habits within our control. In many ways, our habits are our destiny.

And changing our habits allows us to alter that destiny. Generally, I've observed, we seek changes that fall into the "Essential Seven." People—including me—most want to foster the habits that will allow them to:

1. Eat and drink more healthfully (give up sugar, eat more vegetables, drink less alcohol)
2. Exercise regularly
3. Save, spend, and earn wisely (save regularly, pay down debt, donate to worthy causes, stick to a budget)
4. Rest, relax, and enjoy (stop watching TV in bed, turn off a cell phone, spend time in nature, cultivate silence, get enough sleep, spend less time in the car)
5. Accomplish more, stop procrastinating (practice an instrument, work without interruption, learn a language, maintain a blog)
6. Simplify, clear, clean, and organize (make the bed, file regularly, put keys away in the same place, recycle)
7. Engage more deeply in relationships—with other people, with God, with the world (call friends, volunteer, have more sex, spend more time with family, attend religious services)

The same habit can satisfy different needs. A morning walk in the park might be a form of exercise (#2); a way to rest and enjoy (#4); or, in the company of a friend, a way to engage more deeply in a relationship (#7). And people value different habits. For one person, organized files are a crucial tool for creativity; another finds inspiration in unexpected juxtapositions.

The Essential Seven reflect the fact that we often feel both tired and wired. We feel exhausted, but also feel jacked up on adrenaline, caffeine, and sugar. We feel frantically busy, but also feel that we're not spending enough time on the things that really matter. I wasn't going to bed on time, but I wasn't staying up late talking to friends, either; I was watching a midnight episode of *The Office* that I know by heart. I wasn't typing up my work notes or reading a novel, but mindlessly scrolling through the addictive "People You May Know" section on LinkedIn.

Slowly, as my research proceeded, my ideas about habits began to take a more coherent shape. Habits make change possible, I'd concluded, by freeing us from decision making and from using self-control. That notion led to another key issue: *If habits make it possible for us to change, how* exactly, *then, do we shape our habits?* That enormous question became my subject.

First, I settled on some basic definitions and questions. In my study, I would embrace a generous conception of the term "habit," to reflect how people use the term in everyday life: "I'm in the habit of going to the gym" or "I want to improve my eating habits." A "routine" is a string of habits, and a "ritual" is a habit charged with transcendent meaning. I wouldn't attempt to tackle addictions, compulsions, disorders, or nervous habits, or to explain the neuroscience of habits (I was only mildly interested in understanding how my brain lights up when I see a cinnamon-raisin bagel). And while some might argue that it's unhelpful to label habits as "good" or "bad," I decided to use the colloquial term "good habit" for any habit I want to cultivate, and "bad habit" for one I want to squelch.

My main focus would be the *methods* of habit change. From my giant trove of notes about habits—detailing the research I'd examined, the examples I'd witnessed, and the advice I'd read—I'd discern all the various "strategies" that we can use to change a habit. It's odd, most discussions of habit change champion a single approach, as if one approach could work for everyone. Hard experience proves that this assumption isn't true. If only there were one simple, cookie-cutter answer! But I knew that different people need different solutions, so I aimed to identify every possible option.

Because self-knowledge is indispensable to successful habit formation, the first section of the book, "Self-Knowledge," would explore the two strategies that help us to understand ourselves: Four Tendencies and Distinctions. Next would come "Pillars of Habits," the section that would examine the well-known, essential Strategies of Monitoring, Foundation, Scheduling, and Accountability. The section "The Best Time to Begin" would consider the particular importance of the time of *beginning* when forming a habit, as explored in the Strategies of First Steps, Clean Slate, and Lightning Bolt. Next, the section "Desire, Ease, and Excuses" would take into account our desires to avoid effort and experience pleasure—which play a role in the Strategies of Abstaining, Convenience, Inconvenience, Safeguards, Loophole-Spotting, Distraction, Reward, Treats, and Pairing. (Loophole-Spotting is the *funniest* strategy.) Finally, the section "Unique, Just Like Everyone Else" would investigate the strategies that arise from our drive to understand and define ourselves in the context of other people, in the Strategies of Clarity, Identity, and Other People.

Once I'd identified these strategies, I wanted to experiment with them. The twin riddles of how to change ourselves and how to change our habits have vexed mankind throughout the ages. If I was going to try to figure out the answers, I'd have to fortify my analysis with my own experience as guinea pig. Only by putting my theories to the test would I understand what works.

But when I told a friend that I was studying habits, and planned to try out several new habits, he protested, "You should fight habits, not encourage them."

"Are you kidding? I *love* my habits," I said. "No willpower. No agonizing. Like brushing my teeth."

"Not me," my friend said. "Habits make me feel trapped."

I remained firmly pro-habits, but this conversation was an important reminder: Habit is a good servant but a bad master. Although I wanted the benefits that habits offer, I didn't want to become a bureaucrat of my own life, trapped in paperwork of my own making.

As I worked on my habits, I should pursue only those habits that would make me feel freer and stronger. I should keep asking myself, "*To what end* do I pursue this habit?" It was essential that my habits suit *me*, because I can build a happy life only on the foundation of my own nature. And if I wanted to try to help other people shape their habits—a notion that, I had to admit, appealed to me—their habits would have to suit *them*.

One night, as we were getting ready for bed, I was recounting highlights from my day's habit research to Jamie. He'd had a tough day at work and looked weary and preoccupied, but suddenly he started laughing.

"What?" I asked.

"With your books about happiness, you were trying to answer the question 'How do I become happier?' And this habits book is 'No, *seriously*, how do I become happier?'"

"You're right!" I replied. It was really true. "So many people tell me, 'I know what would make me happier, but I can't make myself do what it takes.' Habits are the solution."

When we change our habits, we change our lives. We can use *decision making* to choose the habits we want to form, we can use *willpower* to get the habit started; then—and this is the best part—we can allow the extraordinary power of habit to take over. We take our hands off the wheel of decision, our foot off the gas of willpower, and rely on the cruise control of habits.

That's the promise of habit.

For a happy life, it's important to cultivate an atmosphere of growth—the sense that we're learning new things, getting stronger, forging new relationships, making things better, helping other people. Habits have a tremendous role to play in creating an atmosphere of growth, because they help us make consistent, reliable progress.

Perfection may be an impossible goal, but habits help us to do better. Making headway toward a good habit, doing *better than before*, saves us from facing the end of another year with the mournful wish, once again, that we'd done things differently.

Habit is notorious—and rightly so—for its ability to control our actions, even against our will. By mindfully choosing our habits, we harness the power of mindlessness as a sweeping force for serenity, energy, and growth.

Better than before! It's what we all want.

SELF-KNOWLEDGE

To shape our habits successfully, we must know ourselves. We can't presume that if a habit-formation strategy works for one person, it will work just as well for anyone else, because *people are very different from each other*. This section covers two strategies that allow us to identify important aspects of our habit nature: the Four Tendencies and Distinctions. These observational strategies don't require that we change what we're doing, only that we learn to see ourselves accurately.

THE FATEFUL TENDENCIES WE
BRING INTO THE WORLD

The Four Tendencies

*It is only when you meet someone of a different culture from
yourself that you begin to realise what your own beliefs really are.*

—GEORGE ORWELL, *The Road to Wigan Pier*

I knew exactly where my extended investigation of habits would
begin.

For years, I've kept a list of my "Secrets of Adulthood," which
are the lessons I've learned with time and experience. Some are serious, such as "Just because something is fun for someone else doesn't
mean it's fun for me," and some are goofy, such as "Food tastes better
when I eat with my hands." One of my most important Secrets of
Adulthood, however, is: "I'm more like other people, and less like
other people, than I suppose." While I'm not much different from
other people, those differences are *very important*.

For this reason, the same habit strategies don't work for everyone.
If we know ourselves, we're able to manage ourselves better, and if
we're trying to work with others, it helps to understand *them*.

So I would start with self-knowledge, by identifying how my nature affects my habits. Figuring that out, however, isn't easy. As novelist John Updike observed, "Surprisingly few clues are ever offered
us as to what kind of people we are."

In my research, I'd looked for a good framework to explain differences in how people respond to habits, but to my surprise, none

existed. Was I the only one who wondered why some people adopt habits much more, or less, readily than other people? Or why some people dread habits? Or why some people are able to keep certain habits, in certain situations, but not others?

I couldn't figure out the pattern—then one afternoon, *eureka*. The answer didn't emerge from my library research, but from my preoccupation with the question my friend had asked me. I'd been pondering, yet again, her simple observation: she'd never missed practice for her high school track team, but she can't make herself go running now. Why?

As my idea hit, I felt the same excitement that Archimedes must have felt when he stepped into his bath. Suddenly I grasped it. The first and most important habits question is: *"How does a person respond to an expectation?"* When we try to form a new habit, we set an expectation for ourselves. Therefore, *it's crucial to understand how we respond to expectations.*

We face two kinds of expectations: *outer expectations* (meet work deadlines, observe traffic regulations) and *inner expectations* (stop napping, keep a New Year's resolution). From my observation, just about everyone falls into one of four distinct groups:

Upholders respond readily to both outer expectations and inner expectations.

Questioners question all expectations, and will meet an expectation only if they believe it's justified.

Obligers respond readily to outer expectations but struggle to meet inner expectations (my friend on the track team).

Rebels resist all expectations, outer and inner alike.

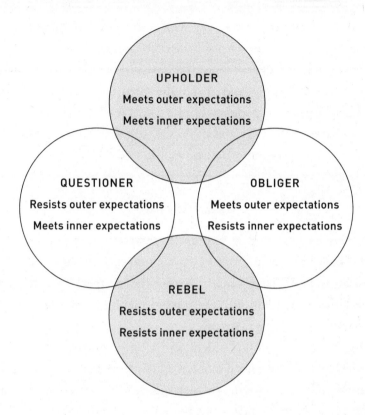

As I struggled to find a name for this framework, one of my favorite passages, from Sigmund Freud's "The Theme of the Three Caskets," floated into my head. Freud explains that the names of the three goddesses of fate mean "the accidental within the decrees of destiny," "the inevitable," and "the fateful tendencies each one of us brings into the world." *The fateful tendencies each one of us brings into the world.*

I decided to name my framework the "Four Tendencies." (The "Four Fateful Tendencies," though accurate, sounded a little melodramatic.)

As I developed the framework of the Four Tendencies, I truly felt as though I were discovering the Periodic Table of the Elements—the elements of character. I wasn't making up a system; I was uncovering a law of nature. Or perhaps I'd created a habits Sorting Hat.

Our Tendency colors the way we see the world and therefore has enormous consequences for our habits. Of course, these are *tendencies*, but I've found, to a degree that surprises me, that most people do fall squarely into one camp, and once I identified the Tendencies, I got a kick from hearing the people within a given Tendency make the same kinds of comments, over and over. Questioners, for example, often remark on how much they hate to wait in line.

UPHOLDERS

Upholders respond readily to outer expectations and inner expectations. They wake up and think: "What's on the schedule and the to-do list for today?" They want to know what's expected of them, and to meet those expectations. They avoid making mistakes or letting people down—*including themselves.*

Others can rely on Upholders, and Upholders can rely on themselves. They're self-directed and have little trouble meeting commitments, keeping resolutions, or meeting deadlines (they often finish early). They want to understand the rules, and often they search for the rules beyond the rules—as in the case of art or ethics.

One friend with an Upholder wife told me, "If something is on the schedule, my wife is going to do it. When we were in Thailand, we'd planned to visit a certain temple, and we went—even though she got food poisoning the night before and was throwing up on our way there."

Because Upholders feel a real obligation to meet their expectations for themselves, they have a strong instinct for self-preservation, and this helps protect them from their tendency to meet others' expectations. "I need a lot of time for myself," an Upholder friend told me, "to exercise, to kick around new ideas for work, to listen to music. If people ask me to do things that interfere, it's easy for me to tell them 'no.'"

However, Upholders may struggle in situations where expectations aren't clear or the rules aren't established. They may feel compelled to meet expectations, even ones that seem pointless. They may feel uneasy when they know they're breaking the rules, even unnecessary rules, unless they work out a powerful justification to do so.

This is my Tendency. I'm an Upholder.

My Upholder Tendency sometimes makes me overly concerned with following the rules. Years ago, when I pulled out my laptop to work in a coffee shop, the barista told me, "You can't use a laptop in here." Now *every time* I go to a new coffee shop, I worry about whether I can use my laptop.

There's a relentless quality to Upholders, too. I'm sure it's tiresome for Jamie—sometimes, it's even tiresome for me—to hear my alarm go off *every* morning at 6:00. I have an Upholder friend who estimates that she skips going to the gym only about six times a year.

"How does your family feel about that?" I asked.

"Well, my husband used to complain. Now he's used to it."

Although I love being an Upholder, I see its dark side, too—the gold-star seeking, the hoop jumping, the sometimes mindless rule following.

When I figured out that I was an Upholder, I understood why I'd been drawn to the study of habits. We Upholders find it relatively easy to cultivate habits—it's not *easy*, but it's easier than for many other people—and we embrace them because we find them gratifying. But the fact that even habit-loving Upholders must struggle to foster good habits shows how challenging it is to form habits.

QUESTIONERS

Questioners question all expectations, and they respond to an expectation only if they conclude that it makes sense. They're motivated by reason, logic, and fairness. They wake up and think, "What needs to get done today, and why?" They decide for themselves whether a course of action is a good idea, and they resist doing anything that seems to lack sound purpose. Essentially, they turn all expectations into inner expectations. As one Questioner wrote on my blog: "I refuse to follow arbitrary rules (I jaywalk, as long as there are no cars coming, and I'll go through a red light if it's the middle of the night, and there's no other traffic in sight) but rules that I find based in morality/ethics/reason are *very* compelling."

A friend said, "Why don't I take my vitamins? My doctor tells me I should, but usually I don't."

She's a Questioner, so I asked, "Do you believe that you need to take vitamins?"

"Well, no," she answered, after a pause, "as a matter of fact, I don't."

"I bet you'd take them if you thought they mattered."

Questioners resist rules for rules' sake. A reader posted on my blog: "My son's school principal said that kids were expected to tuck in their shirts. When I expressed surprise at this seemingly arbitrary rule, the principal said that the school had many rules just for the sake of teaching children to follow rules. That's a dumb reason to ask anyone, including children, to follow a rule. If we know of such rules we should seek and destroy them, to make the world a better place."

Because Questioners like to make well-considered decisions and come to their own conclusions, they're very intellectually engaged, and they're often willing to do exhaustive research. If they decide there's sufficient basis for an expectation, they'll follow it; if not, they won't. Another Questioner said, "My wife is annoyed with me, because she really wants us both to track our spending. But we're not in debt, we spend within our means, so I don't think that getting that information is worth the hassle. So I won't do it."

Questioners resist anything that seems arbitrary; for instance, Questioners often remark, "I can keep a resolution if I think it's important, but I wouldn't make a New Year's resolution, because January first is a meaningless date."

At times, the Questioner's appetite for information and justification can become overwhelming. "My mother makes me insane," one reader reported, "because she expects me to need tons of information the way she does. She constantly asks questions that I didn't ask, wouldn't ask, and generally don't think I need to know the answers to." Questioners themselves sometimes wish they could accept expectations without probing them so relentlessly. A Questioner told me ruefully, "I suffer from analysis paralysis. I always want to have one more piece of information."

Questioners are motivated by sound reasons—or at least what *they believe* to be sound reasons. In fact, Questioners can sometimes seem like crackpots, because they may reject expert opinion in favor of their own conclusions. They ignore those who say, "Why do you think you know more about cancer than your doctor?" or "Everyone prepares the report one way, why do you insist on your own crazy format?"

Questioners come in two flavors: some Questioners have an inclination to Uphold, and others have an inclination to Rebel (like being "Virgo with Scorpio rising"). My husband, Jamie, questions everything, but it's not too hard to persuade him to uphold. As an Upholder, I doubt I could be married happily to someone who wasn't an Upholder or a Questioner/Upholder. Which is a sobering thought.

If Questioners believe that a particular habit is worthwhile, they'll stick to it—but only if they're satisfied about the habit's usefulness.

OBLIGERS

Obligers meet outer expectations, but struggle to meet inner expectations. They're motivated by *external accountability*; they wake up and think, "What *must* I do today?" Because Obligers excel at meeting external demands and deadlines, and go to great lengths to meet their responsibilities, they make terrific colleagues, family members, and friends—which I know firsthand, because my mother and my sister are both Obligers.

Because Obligers resist inner expectations, it's difficult for them to self-motivate—to work on a PhD thesis, to attend networking events, to get their car serviced. Obligers depend on external accountability, with consequences such as deadlines, late fees, or the fear of letting other people down. One Obliger wrote on my blog, "I don't feel a sense of accountability to my calendar, just to the people associated with the appointments. If the entry is just 'go for a jog' I'm not likely to do it." Another Obliger summarized: "Promises made to yourself can be broken. It's the promises made to others that should never be broken." Obligers need external accountability even for activities that they want to do. An Obliger told me, "I never made time to read, so I joined a book group where you're really expected to read the book."

Behavior that Obligers sometimes attribute to *self-sacrifice*—"Why do I always make time for other people's priorities at the expense of my own priorities?"—is often better explained as *need for accountability*.

Obligers find ingenious ways to create external accountability. One Obliger explained, "I wanted to go to basketball games, but I never went. I bought season tickets with my brother, and now I go, because he's annoyed if I don't show." Another said, "If I want to clean out my closet this weekend, I call a charity now, to come and pick up my donations on Monday." Another Obliger said, with regret, "I signed up for a photography course, because I knew I needed assignments and deadlines. I took several classes, then thought, 'I love it, so I don't need to take a class.' Guess how many photos I've taken since? One." Next semester, he's taking a class.

The need to be a role model often prompts Obligers to keep good habits. One Obliger friend eats vegetables only when his children can see him, and another told me, "I knew I'd never practice piano, so I waited until my kids could take lessons—and now we do it together, and I have to practice, because if I don't, they won't." Obligers can sometimes do things for the sake of others that they couldn't do for themselves. Several Obligers told me, practically in the same words,

"If it weren't for the children, I'd still be stuck in a bad marriage. I had to get the divorce for my kids."

The weight of outer expectations can make Obligers susceptible to burnout, because they have trouble telling people "no." An Obliger explained, "I drop everything to proofread my colleagues' reports, but I'm terrible about making time to finish my own reports."

Obligers may find it difficult to form a habit, because often we undertake habits for our own benefit, and Obligers do things more easily for others than for themselves. For them, the key is external accountability.

REBELS

Rebels resist all expectations, outer and inner alike. They choose to act from a sense of choice, of freedom. Rebels wake up and think, "What do I want to do today?" They resist control, even self-control, and enjoy flouting rules and expectations.

Rebels work toward their own goals, in their own way, and while they refuse to do what they're "supposed" to do, they can accomplish their own aims. One Rebel told me, "My master's thesis was ten pages shorter than recommended, and I convinced the department to add an unconventional adviser to my panel. So I got it done and did well on it—but on my terms."

Rebels place a high value on authenticity and self-determination, and bring an unshackled spirit to what they do. A Rebel commented, "I do the assignment I want to complete rather than the one assigned. The problem comes when there's something I'm expected to do regularly (like running weekly quality checks), and therefore I just can't." At times, the Rebel resistance to authority is enormously valuable to society. As one Questioner pointed out, "The Rebels' best asset is their voice of dissent. We shouldn't try to school it out of them, or corporate-culture it out, or shame it out. It's there to protect us all."

But Rebels often frustrate others because they can't be asked or told to do anything. They don't care if "people are counting on you," "you said you'd do it," "your parents will be upset," "it's against the rules," "this is the deadline," or "it's rude." In fact, asking or telling Rebels to do something often makes them do just the *opposite*. A Rebel wrote: "Being told or expected to do something creates a 'stop' sensation that I have to actively overcome. If I'm asked to empty the dishwasher, my brain says, 'Well, I was going to, but now you went and asked, so I can't. So no.'"

The people around Rebels must guard against accidentally igniting their spirit of opposition—particularly challenging for the parents of Rebel children. One parent explained, "The best way to wrangle the Rebel child is to give the kid the information to make a decision, present the issue as a question that he alone can answer, and let him make a decision and act without telling you. Let him make a decision without an audience. Audiences = expectations. If he thinks you're not watching, he won't need to rebel against your expectations." Another parent: "My Rebel son got expelled and didn't want to work toward a career, though he's very smart. When he turned eighteen, we gave him an around-the-world plane ticket and said, 'Over to you!' He traveled for three years, and now he's in grad school, and doing very well."

Rebels sometimes frustrate even themselves, because they can't tell *themselves* what to do. Writer John Gardner observed, "My compulsion not to do what people tell me . . . makes me change places of living or change my life in one way or another, which often make me very unhappy. I wish I could just settle down." On the other hand, Rebels can be skillful at channeling their Rebel energy in constructive ways. A Rebel who wants to stick to a budget might say, "I won't be manipulated by marketers trying to sell me junk," or a Rebel who wants to succeed in school might say, "No one thinks I can get into a good college, but I'll show them."

Rebels often gravitate toward work with a Wild West element—

such as my Rebel friend who works in disruptive technology (not just any technology, he's careful to emphasize, but *disruptive* technology). Rebels resist hierarchies and rules, and they often work better with others when they're in charge. However, the opposite of a profound truth is also true, and surprisingly, some Rebels gravitate to institutions with many rules. As one commenter noted, "Letting others have control can bring freedom as well. You'd probably find more Rebels in the military than you'd suspect." Another Rebel noted: "Perhaps Rebels need a boundary to bend, flex, and break. Left to my own devices, I become restless and unproductive because there are no rules to break or no to-do list, which at the end of the day I look at, and think, 'Hooray, I didn't do any of those things.'"

Anytime I speak about the Tendencies, I ask people to raise their hands to indicate their category. I was surprised when a group of Christian ministers had an unusually high percentage of Rebels. A Rebel clergy member explained: "Clergy think of themselves as called and therefore different. They have the blessing of their colleagues, congregation, and God, which sets them above many things in life, including rules."

No surprise—Rebels resist habits. I met a woman who was, I immediately realized, a Rebel. I asked, "Don't you find it exhausting to make choices every single day?"

"No," she answered. "Making choices makes me feel free."

"I give myself limits to give myself freedom," I told her.

She shook her head. "Freedom means no limits. To me, a life controlled by habits sounds dead."

Rebels resist habits, but they can embrace habit-like behaviors by tying their actions to their choices. A Rebel explained, "If I have to do something 'every day,' it guarantees I won't do it. But if I take it one day at a time, and decide I'll do it *this time*, then more often than not I end up with a streak."

Most people, by a huge margin, are Questioners or Obligers. Very few are Rebels, and, to my astonishment, I discovered that the Upholder category is also tiny. (In fact, because Upholders and Rebels are such small categories, people who try to shape people's habits on a large scale—employers, device manufacturers, insurance companies, instructors—do better to focus on solutions that help Questioners, by providing sound reasons, and Obligers, by providing accountability.)

We often learn most about ourselves by learning about other people, and when I began my habits research, I assumed that I was pretty average—I *feel* pretty average—so it was a shock to realize that as an Upholder, I'm actually an extreme and rare type of personality.

I mentioned my surprise to my husband, Jamie, who said, "Of course you have an extreme personality. I could have told you that."

"*Really?*" I said. "How did you know?"

"I've been married to you for eighteen years."

Novelist Jean Rhys observed, "One is born either to go with or to go against." From what I've observed, our Tendencies are hardwired, and while they can be offset to some degree, they can't be changed. While it's often difficult to identify a child's Tendency (I still can't figure out the Tendencies of my two daughters), by adulthood, most people fall into a Tendency that shapes their perception and behavior in a fundamental way.

Yet whatever our Tendency, with greater experience and wisdom, we can learn to counterbalance its negative aspects. As an Upholder, for instance, I've learned to resist my inclination to meet an expectation unthinkingly, and to ask, "Why am I meeting this expectation, anyway?"

Being married to a Questioner has helped me to learn to question more myself—or I rely on Jamie to question for me. One night we were at the theater, and at intermission I told him, "So far, I really do *not* like this play." Jamie replied, "I don't, either. Let's go home." I thought—what, can we just *go*? And we did. My first instinct is to do what's expected of me, but when Jamie scoffs, "Nah, you don't have to do that," it's easier for me to decide, "That's right, I don't have to do that."

For his part, I think Jamie has become more of an Upholder over the years, at least at home. Although he's inclined to meet my requests with questions—"Why do I have to do that?" "What's the point?" "Can't I do that later?"—he's learned that I always have a reason for a request, and it bugs me to have to spell it out. He's improved (somewhat) at accepting my expectations without prolonged debate.

Knowing our Tendency can help us frame habits in a compelling way. I exercise regularly because it's on my to-do list; a Questioner rattles off the health benefits of exercise; an Obliger takes a weekly bike ride with a partner; and when my Rebel friend Leslie Fandrich wrote about how she started running, she emphasized Rebel values of freedom and desire: "Running seems like the most efficient and independent way to get myself back into shape . . . I can go when it suits my schedule without having to pay for a gym membership. I also love getting outside for some fresh air and it's a great way to listen to new music."

The Four Tendencies can provide valuable guidance to anyone trying to help others change: a boss trying to help employees to be more productive; or a health-care provider trying to prod people to take their medication; or a consultant, coach, trainer, or therapist trying to help people achieve their aims. If we're trying to persuade people to adopt a habit, we have more success if we consider their Tendency. For example, a Questioner may present an Obliger with sound reasons for taking an action, but those logical arguments don't matter nearly as much to an Obliger as external accountability. An Upholder can lecture a Questioner on obligation—and make a Questioner *less* likely to meet an expectation, because Questioners question all obligations. A friend told me her strategy when her Rebel father's doctor prescribed a medication. "The doctor went on about how important it was to take the medicine. I know better than to tell my father what to do, so afterward, when he said, 'What do you think, should I take it?' I said, 'Oh, I wouldn't worry about it.' He said, 'What, you want me to die?' and he takes it."

For the most part, although they may regret the downsides, Upholders, Questioners, and Rebels tend to embrace their category. I love being an Upholder, even though I recognize its pitfalls. My Upholderness allowed me to take the steps that led to a clerkship with Supreme Court Justice Sandra Day O'Connor, and when I decided to become a writer, it enabled me to make an enormous career switch. (Of course, my Upholderness also meant that I spent a lot of time worrying about things like whether a comma should be italicized in a footnote reference to a law journal. For real.) Questioners sometimes feel exhausted by their questioning, but they do think everyone should be Questioners, because that approach is most rational. Rebels sometimes say they wish they could follow the rules, but they wouldn't want to stop being Rebels.

Obligers, however, often dislike their Tendency. They're vexed by the fact that they can meet others' expectations, but not their expectations for themselves. With the other three Tendencies, much of the frustration they create falls on others. Other people may get annoyed by stickler Upholders, or interrogator Questioners, or maverick Rebels, but it's "people pleaser" Obligers themselves who bear the brunt of the downsides of that Tendency.

Obligers, in fact, may reach a point of Obliger rebellion, a striking pattern in which they abruptly refuse to meet an expectation. As one Obliger explained, "Sometimes I 'snap' because I get tired of people making assumptions that I'll always do things as expected. It's sort of a rebellious way of asserting myself." Another added, "I work very hard to keep my commitments to other people, but I'll be darned if I can keep a promise to myself . . . Though every once in a while I will absolutely refuse to please." They may rebel in symbolic ways, with their hair, clothes, car, and the like.

This contrarian streak among Obligers explains another pattern I've noticed: almost always, if a Rebel is in a long-term relationship, that Rebel is paired with an Obliger. Unlike Upholders and Questioners, who are distressed by the Rebel's expectation-rejecting behavior, the Obliger enjoys the Rebel's refusal to truckle to outward expectations. One Rebel explained the dynamics of this combination: "My husband is a big part of how I'm able to look like I function well in the normal adult world. He mails the rent check, which is nice because I always resent it being due on the same day every month. He deals with trash day, and moving the car for snowplows, and he makes sure the peskily regular bills are paid on time. (I really hate punctuality.) While when we talk through big decisions, I'm usually the final word."

But whatever our Tendency, we all share a desire for autonomy. If our feeling of being controlled by others becomes too strong, it can trigger the phenomenon of "reactance," a resistance to something that's experienced as a threat to our freedom or our ability to choose. If we're ordered to do something, we may resist it—even if it's something that we might otherwise want to do. I've watched this happen with my daughter Eliza. If I say, "Why don't you finish your homework, get it out of the way?" she says, "I need a break, I've got to stop." If I say, "You've been working so hard, why don't you take a break?" she says, "I want to finish." It's easy to see why this impulse creates problems—for health-care professionals, for parents, for teachers, for office managers. The more we push, the more a person may resist.

After I gave a talk about the Four Tendencies, a man asked me, "Which Tendency makes people the happiest?" I was startled, because that obvious question had never crossed my mind. "Also," he continued, with an equally obvious follow-up question, "which Tendency is the most successful?"

I didn't have a good response, because I'd been so focused on understanding the Tendencies that I'd never considered them in comparison to each other. After much reflection, however, I realized that the answer—as it usually is, which I sometimes find annoying—is "*It depends*." It depends on how a particular person deals with the upside and downside of a Tendency. The happiest and most successful people are those who have figured out ways to exploit their Tendency to their benefit and, just as important, found ways to counterbalance its limitations.

In an interview in the *Paris Review*, novelist and Rebel John Gardner made an observation that I've never forgotten: "Every time you break the law you pay, and every time you obey the law you pay." Every action, every habit, has its consequences. Upholders, Questioners, Obligers, and Rebels, all must grapple with the consequences of fitting in that Tendency. I get up at 6:00 every morning, and I pay for that; I get more work done, but I also have to go to sleep early.

We all must pay, but we can *choose* that for which we pay.

DIFFERENT SOLUTIONS FOR DIFFERENT PEOPLE

Distinctions

Of course, like all over-simple classifications of this type, the dichotomy becomes, if pressed, artificial, scholastic and ultimately absurd. But . . . like all distinctions which embody any degree of truth, it offers a point of view from which to look and compare, a starting-point for genuine investigation.

—ISAIAH BERLIN, *The Hedgehog and the Fox*

The Four Tendencies framework had given me a crucial insight into human nature, but there was much that it didn't illuminate. I couldn't yet turn to the more concrete, action-oriented strategies that I was eager to investigate because I hadn't yet exhausted the possibilities of self-knowledge.

As one of the exercises for the happiness project I undertook a few years ago, I'd identified my twelve "Personal Commandments," which are the overarching principles by which I want to live my life. My first commandment is to "Be Gretchen"—yet it's very hard to know myself. I get so distracted by the way I wish I were, or the way I assume I am, that I lose sight of what's actually true.

I was slow to understand some of the most basic things about myself. I don't love music. I'm not a big fan of travel. I don't like games, I don't like to shop, I'm not very interested in animals, I like plain food. Why didn't I recognize these aspects of my nature? Partly because I never thought much about it—doesn't everyone love music?—and partly because I expected, based on nothing, that one day I'd out-grow my limitations. I'd learn to love travel, or to appreciate exotic cuisines.

Also, I'd assumed that I was pretty much like everyone else, and that everyone else was pretty much like me. That's true, but our differences are *very important*. And they have a big influence on habit formation. For instance, I kept reading the advice that because our minds are clearest in the morning, we should do our most demanding intellectual work then. I thought I "should" follow this habit, until finally I realized that my own habit—starting my day with an hour of email grunt work—suits me. I need to clear the decks before I can settle down to serious work, and I suspect that if I'd tried to change my habit, I would've failed.

I should tailor my habits to the fundamental aspects of my nature that aren't going to change. It was no use saying "I'll write more every day if I team up with another writer, and we race to see who can finish writing a book faster," because *I don't like competition*.

To avoid wasting my precious habit-formation energy on dead ends, I need to shape my habits to suit me. For this reason, I developed a list of questions to highlight aspects of my nature that are relevant to habit formation.

They say the world is made up of two types of people: those who divide the world into two types of people, and those who don't. I'm clearly in the former category.

AM I A LARK OR AN OWL?

Research shows that morning people, or "Larks," really do differ from night people, or "Owls." Most people fit somewhere in between, but the extremes—the two chronotypes as measured by their sleep midpoint—do exist. The two types are more productive and energetic at different points in the day.

I'm a Lark: I go to sleep and wake on the early side. Owls do just the opposite. I used to believe that Owls could become Larks if they made an effort to go to sleep earlier, but research suggests that this attribute is hardwired. Genes play a big role, as does age: young children tend to be Larkish; adolescents tend to be Owls (with a peak at age 19.5 for women and age 21 for men); older adults tend to be Larks.

Interestingly, research suggests that Larks are likely to be happier, healthier, and more satisfied with life than Owls—in part, because the world favors Larks. Owls fall asleep later than Larks do, and because work, school, and young children start early, Owls get less sleep, which makes their lives harder.

Larks, Owls, and everyone in between should consider that aspect of their nature when trying to shape a habit. An Owl shouldn't bother trying to form the habit of getting up early to study, and a Lark shouldn't try to fit in two hours of writing after dinner.

Sometimes we may not recognize our own type. A friend told me, "I went on a meditation retreat, where we woke up at four. It was like a switch flipped for me, and my life became so much better. Now I go to bed around 9:00 or 9:30, and I wake up at 4:00. I love it."

AM I A MARATHONER, A SPRINTER, OR A PROCRASTINATOR?

Especially for workplace habits, it's key to distinguish the pace at which people prefer to work. I'm a Marathoner. I like to work at a slow and steady clip, and I dislike deadlines—in fact, I often finish work early. In law school, I had two massive writing requirements to complete by graduation, and I wrote them both by the end of my first year. (Side note: perhaps my eagerness to write big papers was a sign that I wanted to be a writer instead of a lawyer, but that's another issue.) Working on projects steadily, over long periods of time, ignites my creativity.

By contrast, Sprinters prefer to work in quick bursts of intense effort, and they deliberately wait for the pressure of a deadline to sharpen their thinking. A Sprinter told me, "I never prepare a speech until the people are in their seats, and I'm heading to the podium. It drives my staff crazy, but that's when I get my ideas." Another Sprinter observed: "I prefer to be completely immersed in a project for a short period of time. The work flows better, I can hold my concentration. Spread things out, and the total hours go way up."

Sprinters and Marathoners usually feel good about their work style, but Procrastinators don't. Procrastinators may resemble Sprinters, because they too tend to finish only when they're against a deadline, but the two types are quite different. Sprinters *choose* to work at the last minute because the pressure of a deadline clarifies their thoughts; Procrastinators hate last-minute pressure and wish they could force themselves to work before the deadline looms. Unlike Sprinters, Procrastinators often agonize about the work they're not doing, which makes it hard for them to do anything fun or meaningful with their time. They may rush around doing busywork as a way to avoid doing what they know they have to do. (It's a Secret of Adulthood: Working is one of the most dangerous forms of procrastination.)

Sprinters call Marathoners "plodding," and Marathoners call Sprinters "irresponsible," but there's no right way. Procrastinators, however, are happier when they change their work habits to work more steadily.

AM I AN UNDERBUYER OR AN OVERBUYER?

Underbuyers hate to shop and buy; overbuyers love to shop and buy. As a confirmed underbuyer, I delay making purchases or buy as little as possible. I scramble to buy items like a winter coat or a bathing suit after the point when I need them. I'm suspicious of buying things with very specific uses—suit bags, hand cream, hair conditioner, rain boots, Kleenex. I often consider buying an item, then decide, "I'll get it some other time" or "Maybe I don't really need it." Because we underbuyers dislike buying, we often resist buying equipment or services that would help us keep our good habits.

Overbuyers, by contrast, find excuses to buy. They accumulate large quantities of office supplies or kitchen gadgets or travel paraphernalia with the thought "This will probably come in handy someday." When trying to shape a habit, overbuyers tend to load up on equipment or services that they imagine will help them keep their good habits.

The underbuyer thinks, "I don't need to buy *running* shoes. These old tennis shoes will be fine." The overbuyer thinks, "I need running shoes, and a spare pair, and a reflector vest, and a pedometer, and a book about avoiding injury." Knowing our inclination to under- or overbuy can help us identify opportunities to buy, or not buy, to foster our healthy habits. Underbuyers should remember that spending money to support a good habit is worthwhile; overbuyers should remember that mere acquisition isn't enough to establish a good habit.

AM I A SIMPLICITY LOVER OR AN ABUNDANCE LOVER?

As an ardent fan of children's literature, I've started three children's literature reading groups. Yes, *three*. (When I started the first group, I truly believed that I was the only adult in New York City who loved children's and YA literature.) At one of our meetings, a friend remarked, "I always want to feel empty," and another responded, "I always want to feel full." This was one of the most interesting brief exchanges I'd ever heard. I didn't understand exactly what these two people meant, but it got me thinking about those who love simplicity, and those who love abundance.

Simplicity lovers are attracted by the idea of "less," of emptiness, bare surfaces and shelves, few choices, a roomy closet. I'm in this camp; I get more pleasure out of shedding things than from acquiring things. I easily feel overwhelmed when there's too much noise, too much stuff, or too much happening at once.

Abundance lovers are attracted by the idea of "more," of overflow, of addition, of ampleness, of a full pantry. They always want to have more than enough. They like a bit of bustle, and they enjoy collecting things and having a wide array of choices.

Simplicity lovers and abundance lovers thrive in different environments. For instance, a simplicity lover is likely to work better in an office that's quiet, with minimal decoration; the abundance lover in an office that's lively and crammed with visual details. I visited a tech company that had just held a "decorate your team's cubicle pod" contest, and stuff was *everywhere*, even hanging from the ceiling. I'm sure the contest was fun, but I thought to myself, "I could never work here."

When changing habits, a simplicity lover may be attracted to elimination and simplification—to saving money by cutting off cable TV or quitting online shopping. An abundance lover may be attracted to addition and variety—to making money by starting a freelance career or learning how to invest.

AM I A FINISHER OR AN OPENER?

Some people love finishing, and some people love opening—both literally and figuratively. Finishers love the feeling of bringing a project to completion, and they're determined to use the last drop in the shampoo bottle; Openers thrill to the excitement of launching a new project, and find pleasure in opening a fresh tube of toothpaste.

I'm a Finisher; Jamie is an Opener. The other day, I looked inside a kitchen cabinet and saw four bags of granola, all open. When I pointed this out to Jamie and demanded that he not open another bag until those were finished, he just laughed, and for the next few weeks, he amused himself by pretending to open more bags in front of me. As a Finisher, I get a sense of accomplishment when I use the last egg in a carton, and I feel a weird satisfaction when something breaks or wears out. I wondered why I liked to see the stuffing peek out of our sofa, or the hole in an old pair of socks, until I realized that it's my Finisher nature, delighting in the finish.

By contrast, an Opener law professor told me, "I'm constantly starting new articles or writing proposals for new courses. I have a stack of drafts that I've never bothered to polish into finished pieces. Plus I always have several open jars of mustard in the fridge."

If we know whether we're a Finisher or an Opener, we can shape our habits to suit that preference. For instance, when I was trying to form the habit of blogging regularly, I created one blog, where I post six days a week; when I've posted for the day, I'm finished. An Opener acquaintance has bought more than three hundred URLs, maintains twelve sites, and is always considering launching a new site. That suits his desire for opening. I like my strength-training gym; I lift weights for twenty minutes, then I'm finished; there's not one more thing I can do. Openers might prefer a gym that allows them to rotate through many types of exercise.

Because Finishers focus on their ability to complete, they may be overly cautious about trying to form new habits; Openers may be overly optimistic about their ability to take on additional habits.

AM I A FAMILIARITY LOVER OR A NOVELTY LOVER?

Some people love familiarity; some love novelty. I'm definitely in the familiarity camp. I love to reread my favorite books and to watch movies over and over. I eat the same foods, more or less, every day. I like returning to places I've visited before. Other people thrive on doing new things.

For familiarity lovers, a habit becomes easier as it becomes familiar. When I felt intimidated by the library when I started law school, I made myself walk through it a few times each day until I felt comfortable enough to work there. When I started blogging, my unfamiliarity with the mechanics of posting made me dread it. But I forced myself to post every day so that the foreign became familiar, and the difficult became automatic.

Novelty lovers may embrace habits more readily when they seem less . . . habit-like. A guy told me, "I feel stale when I go to work every day and see the same faces all the time, so once a week I work in a different satellite office, to shake thing up."

In fact, novelty lovers may do better with a series of short-term activities—thirty-day challenges, for instances—instead of trying to create an enduring, automatic habit. One reader commented, "I love planning routines and planning to create habits as if it's going to work, but the follow-through is rarely there, almost as if I have some inner repulsion to doing the same things in the same way. On the other hand, the buzz I get from trying new things is brilliant."

AM I PROMOTION-FOCUSED OR PREVENTION-FOCUSED?

In their thought-provoking book *Focus*, researchers Tory Higgins and Heidi Grant Halvorson argue that people lean toward being "promotion-focused" or "prevention-focused" in their aims.

Promotion-focused people concentrate on achievement and advancement, on making gains, on getting more love, praise, pleasure. They eagerly and optimistically pursue their goals. By contrast, prevention-focused people concentrate on fulfilling their duties, on avoiding losses, and on minimizing danger, pain, or censure. They're vigilant against possible drawbacks or problems.

A good habit and a bad habit are the mirror images of each other; a person might want to "quit eating junk food" or "eat better," or to "get more sleep" or "stop staying up too late."

A promotion-focused person recycles in order to make the environment cleaner; a prevention-focused person recycles in order to avoid getting a fine. Different arguments resonate with different people, and it's helpful to frame a habit in the way that suits each individual.

DO I LIKE TO TAKE SMALL STEPS OR BIG STEPS?

Many people have better success adopting a habit when they start with modest, manageable steps. A series of minor but real accomplishments gives people the confidence to continue. In what influential behavior researcher B. J. Fogg calls "tiny habits," a person may begin a habit by doing a single sit-up or reading one page, and by taking these tiny steps start on a path toward keeping that habit. The slow accumulation of small triumphs is encouraging—and very sustainable. Keeping changes modest can make it easier to stick to a new habit and to avoid the burnout that can hit when we try to make big changes all at once.

Also, by taking little steps, we gradually become accustomed to including a new habit in the pattern of our days. The habit of the habit is even more valuable than the habit itself; for instance, the habit of tracking expenses each day is more valuable than any one particular calculation. Keeping a habit, in the smallest way, protects and strengthens it. I write every day, even just a sentence, to keep my habit of daily writing strong. In high school, when I was trying to acquire the habit of running, I ran down the block until I'd passed three houses, then I turned back. After a few runs like that, I ran past four houses. Over time, I worked up to a few miles. By taking small, manageable steps, I managed to stick with running long enough to turn it into a habit.

Nevertheless, it's also true that some people do better when they're very ambitious. Sometimes, counterintuitively, it's easier to make a major change than a minor change. If a habit changes very gradually, we may lose interest, give way under stress, or dismiss the change as insignificant.

A big transformation generates an energy and excitement that helps to foster habits. As Steve Jobs reflected, "I have a great respect for incremental improvement, and I've done that sort of thing in my life, but I've always been attracted to the more revolutionary changes. I don't know why." Along the same lines, my college roommate's motto was "Do everything all at once."

A reader quoted a phrase from James Collins and Jerry Porras's book *Built to Last*: "BHAG—Big Hairy Audacious Goals, all the way. I resisted this for years, thinking that to shoot too high only meant I would fail. What I didn't realize was that shooting high motivated me much more."

Sometimes a single unexpected question can illuminate a hidden aspect of my life. A question like "Do you tend to blame other people, or do you blame yourself?" can give me a fresh perspective on myself. So, in addition to identifying big personality distinctions, I came up with a list of short, straightforward questions to help me know myself better, so I could better tailor my habits to my nature.

How I Like to Spend My Time

At what time of day do I feel energized? When do I drag?

Do I like racing from one activity to another, or do I prefer unhurried transitions?

What activities take up my time but aren't particularly useful or stimulating?

Would I like to spend more time with friends, or by myself?

Do I have several things on my calendar that I anticipate with pleasure?

What can I do for hours without feeling bored?

What daily or weekly activity did I do for fun when I was ten years old?

What I Value

What's most satisfying to me: saving time, or money, or effort?

Does it bother me to act differently from other people, or do I get a charge out of it?

Do I spend a lot of time on something that's important to someone else, but not to me?

If I had $500 that I had to spend on fun, how would I spend it?

Do I like to listen to experts, or do I prefer to figure things out for myself?

Does spending money on an activity make me feel more committed to it, or less committed?

Would I be happy to see my children have the life I've had?

My Current Habits

Am I more likely to indulge in a bad habit in a group, or when I'm alone?

If I could magically, effortlessly change one habit in my life, what would it be?

If the people around me could change one of my habits, what would they choose?

Of my existing habits, which would I like to see my children adopt? Or not?

It wasn't until I asked myself, "Do I have several things on my calendar that I anticipate with pleasure?" that I realized my book groups played a crucial role in helping me to keep fun habits. In one book group, we read adult fiction, and in the other three, we read children's or young-adult books, and my belonging to these groups helps me enforce several valuable habits. It boosts my habit of reading (Essential Seven #4, rest, relax, and enjoy); it helps me to read new books instead of rereading old favorites, which is often my inclination (Essential Seven #5, accomplish more); and it means I meet new people and make regular plans with friends (Essential Seven #7, engage more deeply in relationships).

People often ask, "What are the *best* habits to follow?" as though there's one path that everyone should follow. Debate rages about which habits are most likely to foster creativity and productivity, yet the book *Daily Rituals*—Mason Currey's exhaustive examination of the work habits of 161 writers, composers, artists, scientists, and philosophers—makes one thing clear: while these brilliant people vary tremendously in the specific habits they follow, they all know very well what habits work for them, and they make a great effort to maintain those habits.

Some have the habit of getting an early start (like Haruki Murakami) or working late into the night (like Tom Stoppard); of living a life of quiet predictability (like Charles Darwin) or of boozy revelry (like Toulouse-Lautrec); of procrastinating endlessly (like William James) or working regular hours (like Anthony Trollope); of working in silence (like Gustav Mahler) or of working amid a bustle of activity (like Jane Austen); of drinking a lot of alcohol (like Friedrich Schiller) or drinking a lot of coffee (like Kierkegaard); of producing work for many hours a day (like H. L. Mencken) or for just thirty minutes a day (like Gertrude Stein).

There's no magic formula—not for ourselves, and not for the people around us. We won't make ourselves more creative and productive by copying other people's habits, even the habits of geniuses; we must know our own nature, and what habits serve us best.

PILLARS OF
HABITS

Many strategies help us change our habits, and four strategies tower above the others: Monitoring, Foundation, Scheduling, and Accountability. They're so ubiquitous and familiar that it's easy to take them for granted—but they're invaluable. To make the most of the indispensable Pillars of Habits, we must take into account what we've learned about ourselves from the exercises in self-knowledge. For instance, the Strategy of Scheduling works for most people—but not for Rebels. The Strategy of Accountability works for most people—and it's essential for Obligers. The Strategies build on each other.

WE MANAGE WHAT
WE MONITOR

Monitoring

*All our life, so far as it has definite form, is but a mass of habits—
practical, emotional, and intellectual,—systematically organized
for our weal or woe, and bearing us irresistibly toward our destiny.*

—WILLIAM JAMES, *Talks to Teachers and Students*

The Strategy of Monitoring has an uncanny power. It doesn't require change, but it often leads to change. To paraphrase a business school truism, "We manage what we monitor," and keeping close track of our actions means we do better in categories such as eating, drinking, exercising, working, TV and Internet use, spending—and just about anything else. Self-measurement brings self-awareness, and self-awareness strengthens our self-control. Something as simple as a roadside speed display to show motorists how fast they're going helps them to slow down.

A key step for the Strategy of Monitoring is to identify precisely what action is monitored. Specific habits such as "Read the news every morning" or "Call one client each day" are easy to monitor, while vague resolutions such as "Be more informed" or "Cultivate better client relationships" are hard to monitor. I was reminded of Lord Kelvin's observation, overbroad but nevertheless thought-provoking: "When you cannot express it in number, your knowledge is of a meager and unsatisfactory kind." If we want something to count in our lives, we should figure out a way to count it.

Actual measurement is crucial, because when we guess what we're doing, we're often wildly inaccurate. Unsurprisingly, we tend to underestimate how much we eat and overestimate how much we exercise. In one study, people estimated that in the course of daily activities (excluding exercise regimens) they walked about four miles; in fact, most walked less than two miles.

Accurate monitoring helps determine whether a habit is worth the time, money, or energy it consumes. A friend tracked his TV watching because he wanted to know if TV was eating up too much of his day (it was). I read about a woman who quit drinking because she figured that in six years she and her husband had spent almost $30,000 on alcohol—money they would've preferred to spend on something else. Aaron Beck, founder of cognitive behavioral therapy, maintains that people find it easy to notice what their partners do wrong, but not what they do right, so he suggests keeping "marriage diaries" to track partners' considerate behavior; one study showed that 70 percent of couples who did this tracking reported an improved relationship.

People who love to self-monitor can join the Quantified Self movement, a community of those who use technology to track every aspect of their daily life and performance—but most of us aren't ready to make quite such a commitment to the process. Monitoring is valuable, but it's also time-consuming and a bit tiresome, so I monitor only the aspects of my life that really matter.

I decided I needed to have a long talk with my sister Elizabeth about the Strategy of Monitoring. To my continual regret, Elizabeth lives far away; Los Angeles is a long flight from New York City, which means we don't often see each other, and there's a big time difference, which makes it hard to talk by phone. But one day I was determined to track her down, because I knew she'd have interesting insights about monitoring.

Elizabeth has type 1 diabetes, which means that her pancreas doesn't produce enough insulin. (In type 2 diabetes, which is far more common, the body produces insulin but doesn't react properly to it.) Without insulin, blood sugar can spike to dangerous, even life-threatening levels, so Elizabeth must give herself multiple daily insulin injections, and to inject herself correctly, she must know her blood sugar level. For years, she'd tested her blood sugar by pricking her finger to check her blood, but she'd recently gotten a device inserted under her skin to monitor her blood sugar continuously. I wanted to know if she found the monitor effective.

"Monitoring is *key*," she said. "For years, I hated the idea of having a device attached to my stomach, but with diabetes, accurate tracking is so important that I finally caved. Now I can't imagine not having the monitor."

When she told me she was getting the device, I'd imagined that it might administer insulin directly, or tell her what she needed. Nope. The monitor merely provides a continuous record of her blood sugar levels—but that information makes a big difference.

"Without a monitor, I might test my blood sugar ten times a day, but the monitor checks it constantly," she explained. "I know where my blood sugar is and where it's heading. Also, I know the effect of what I'm doing, so I can't kid myself. Like I was eating this frozen yogurt that claimed to be low-carb, but from the readings I got on my monitor, I know that can't be true."

"Even though the monitor doesn't actually *do* anything, seeing the numbers makes you behave differently?"

"For sure. Without a monitor, if I ate something questionable, I might unconsciously wait a few hours to test, so I'd get a better number, but that doesn't work with a monitor. I can't fool myself."

That's why the Strategy of Monitoring works so well: no more fooling ourselves. I decided to exploit it for my own habits. If I had a better handle on what I was doing, I could focus my habit-formation energy in the right place. I suspected that in certain areas, I was giving myself more credit for good habits than I deserved.

———

First up: eating and exercise.

I care a lot about eating and exercise, partly for health, partly out of vanity. It's funny; I've noticed that many people focus mostly on one aspect of their appearance—a bald spot, wrinkles, a paunch, a "bad hair day"—and don't worry much about anything else. That's certainly true for me. I've always been focused on my weight.

I'm not alone in this concern about weight, of course. "Eat and drink more healthfully" is one of the Essential Seven, and while there are many good reasons to eat and drink more healthfully, weight loss is one of most important. As of 2010, 70 percent of Americans were overweight or obese, which increases risk of coronary heart disease, high blood pressure, stroke, type 2 diabetes, cancer, and sleep apnea, among other things. And it's not just about physical health. I felt sad when I overheard a woman at a conference say, "I was asked to give a TED talk, but I thought, 'I can't do it, I'm not at a good weight right now.'"

Until well after college, I'd considered myself overweight—not so overweight that it affected my health, but enough that it affected my self-image—and my weight really bothered me. Finally I managed to get to a number where I felt more at ease, and it's been a huge relief to feel comfortable with my size. This measure of ease still seems new, however, and my desire not to gain weight shapes many of my habits. I try very hard to make healthy food choices, and I exercise fairly regularly (though not very vigorously). Still, I could be doing better, and like just about most people, I loved the idea of painlessly dropping a few pounds. I wondered if monitoring would help.

For people who want to eat and drink more healthfully, keeping a food journal can be extremely effective. For instance, one study showed that dieters who kept a food journal six or seven days a week lost twice as much weight as people who did so once a week or not at all. Although keeping a food journal sounds straightforward, I braced myself for a challenge when I decided to try it. No one ever mentions how hard it is to keep a food journal, but I'd already tried and failed three times.

Along the same lines, I'd tried before to use a pedometer to count my steps. According to a 2003 study, Americans, on average, walked 5,117 steps each day, half of what's recommended. Research shows that wearing a pedometer and trying to hit a goal does make people more physically active, and when I'd worn a pedometer in the past, I'd definitely walked more. I'm the type who really relishes getting "credit" for every step I take. I'd eventually stopped wearing my pedometer, though, because it often fell off (once, into the toilet), and it looked ugly.

As I was considering various methods to track my eating and exercise, I read a *New York Times* article about the Jawbone UP band, and I decided to try it. I'd wear a wristband to track my steps and my sleep, and sync the band to my phone through the headphone jack. I'd use my phone to read my results and to record the food that I ate.

But when the package arrived in the mail, my enthusiasm waned. As I lifted the small black and silver band out of its plastic case, I realized that I'd acquired yet another gadget to learn to use, to keep updated and charged. And more cords. "I'd better be more careful with this cap," I thought, as I dropped the little piece of plastic onto the floor.

However, although I'd expected to find it onerous to sync the wristband to my phone twice a day, by the second day, I was syncing away, because I loved watching my activity numbers rise. Walking a mile requires about 2,000 steps, and I aimed to walk 10,000 steps each day. While research suggests that taking 10,000 steps does reduce obesity and heart disease, there's no particular evidence for 10,000 as opposed to 8,000 or 12,000. But 10,000 was a satisfying number, so I stuck with it.

The UP band also helped me do a much better job of food tracking than I'd ever done with my little notebook. In a surprisingly short period, I started to feel uneasy until I'd recorded food in my log. I'd think, "It's too much trouble to go get my phone now, I'll add this yogurt later," but before long, I was hunting for my phone whenever I ate something.

As I tracked, I noticed several aspects of eating that make monitoring difficult. For one thing, it's often surprisingly hard to gauge "servings." We're poor judges of how much we're eating, and studies suggest that we can eat servings that are about 20 percent bigger or smaller than a "serving size" without realizing it. Also, in what's called "unit bias," we tend to finish a serving if it seems like a natural portion of "one," and we tend to take one serving, no matter what the size. In a study where people could help themselves to big pretzels, people took one; when people were instead offered big pretzels cut in half, they took one half-pretzel. Also, eating directly from the container makes it impossible to monitor how much we're eating. Whether the product is candy or shampoo or cat food, the bigger the package, the more people use. (In what seems like an aspect of the same principle, I've noticed that I finish books faster when I have a bigger stack from the library.)

Taking bites while cooking, eating off plates, sharing food, or eating food served in multiple bite-sized servings—dim sum, tapas, hors d'oeuvres, petits fours, appetizers ordered for the table—also makes it hard to track consumption accurately (which is likely part of their appeal). One way to monitor is to save the evidence left behind—the pile of bones, the peanut shells, the candy wrappers, the day's coffee cups or soda cans or beer bottles.

Context matters, too. One study of package design showed that people avoid the smallest and largest beverage sizes; therefore, if the smallest drink size is dropped, or a larger drink size is added (such as the Starbucks Trenta), people adjust their choices upward.

As the weeks wore on, along with keeping a food journal, I added a new monitoring habit: *No seconds.* When people preplate their food and eat just one helping, they eat about 14 percent less than when they take smaller servings and return for more helpings. I'd often pulled this trick myself: I'd give myself a small serving, then go back for more. The need to monitor exactly what I'd eaten, in order to record it, forced me to stop this little game.

As part of the Strategy of Monitoring, I decided to buy a digital scale to weigh myself. Although some experts advise people to weigh themselves just once a week to avoid becoming discouraged by natural fluctuations, current research suggests that weighing each day—which may strike some people as excessive—is associated with losing weight and keeping it off. Until now, I'd only weighed myself when I went to my cardio gym, but now I wanted to get serious about monitoring. (Side note: people weigh their highest on Sunday; their lowest, on Friday morning.)

I'd wanted to buy a scale for more than a year, but I put it off because of my daughter Eliza. Eliza is very easygoing, and although she spends a lot of time choosing her outfits, changing the color of her nail polish, and trying to grow her long brown hair still longer, she isn't preoccupied with her weight or any particular body part. Nevertheless, plunking down a scale in the bathroom that she shares with Jamie and me seemed like exactly the wrong message to send to a thirteen-year-old girl.

One of my Personal Commandments is to "Identify the problem." What was the problem? "I want a digital scale, but I don't want Eliza to see it." Solution: I bought the scale and put it in a little-used closet where she'd probably never find it.

People find other ways to monitor their bodies. A friend has a pair of jeans that she never wears except to pull them on to see whether they're tighter or looser than before. For myself, I'm much happier relying on my digital scale than on form-fitting clothes. Most days, I wear yoga pants and a hoodie—the point of which is that they're delightfully stretchy and nonconfining.

———

When I first started to use the UP band, I ignored its mood-monitoring and sleep-monitoring functions. Perhaps surprisingly for someone who's preoccupied with happiness, I had no interest in tracking my moods. As for sleep—I was a sleep *zealot*, so I didn't think I needed to monitor it. Sleep, as I remind anyone who gives me the opportunity, is crucial for good mental and physical health and a critical time for bodily repair and regulation. Lack of sleep negatively affects mood, memory, immune function, and pain sensitivity; it makes people more likely to fight with their partners; it contributes to weight gain.

Lack of sleep also leads to dithering. Procrastination expert Piers Steel reports that being "too tired" is the most common reason people give for procrastination. One study estimated that for every hour of interrupted sleep during the previous night, people wasted 8.4 minutes in online puttering—checking email, Internet surfing, and the like. And while many people claim, "I've trained myself to get by with five hours" and say they don't feel particularly sleepy, research shows that the chronically sleep-deprived are quite impaired. Yet many adults routinely sleep less than seven hours.

On a flight to San Francisco, I saw with my own eyes the evidence of people's sleep deprivation. At midday, many passengers were fast asleep. Not dozing; completely zonked out.

I mentioned this to a friend, and he bragged, "Oh, I always sleep on planes. I can fall asleep anywhere, anytime."

"Maybe you're chronically underslept," I suggested. It took all my strength not to launch into a lecture on the importance of sleep.

"No, I'm not," he said. "I've learned to adjust to very little sleep."

"If you sit still for ten minutes in a quiet room," I asked, "can you fall asleep?"

"Yes."

"Are you dragged out of a sound sleep by the alarm every morning?"

"Is there any other way to wake up?"

"Do you depend on caffeine and sugar to give you energy spikes?"

"Sure."

"Do you feel too tired at night to do anything but watch TV or surf the Internet?"

"What else would I do?"

"Do you binge-sleep on the weekends by sleeping in very late or taking lots of naps?"

"Of course."

Hmmmm.

He didn't mind being sleep-deprived, but I needed my seven hours, and I fought to protect my sleep time against any encroachment. Or so I thought, until I decided to use the UP band's sleep-tracking function. (Or try to use it—some nights I forgot to press the button to start the sleep tracker. Finally, instead of trying to "remember," I piggybacked this new habit onto my old habit of setting my alarm.)

To my dismay, the UP band revealed that even an avowed sleep nut like me often stayed up too late. I'd fallen into a classic failure-to-monitor trap: because I felt smug about my good sleep habits, I remembered the nights when I went to bed at 9:45, but overlooked the nights when I stayed up until 11:30 or later.

Once monitoring showed that I wasn't getting enough sleep, I decided to give myself a specific bedtime. Every night, if I was home, I'd aim to be in bed by 10:30.

Now, every night at 10:30, I tell myself, "It's my bedtime," and if I'm still up at 11:00, I say, "It's thirty minutes past my bedtime." Using a clear rule, instead of "feeling sleepy," helps because too often I get into that restless, wired-but-tired state that tricks me into thinking that I'm not ready for bed, when I'm actually exhausted.

In addition to tracking these health habits, I wanted to deploy the Strategy of Monitoring in the important area of *time*. I know that if I don't measure certain values in my life, I neglect them. I decided to track how much time I spent reading; reading is both my cubicle and my playground, and it's my favorite thing to do—if I'm honest with myself, it's practically the only pastime I really enjoy. I'm not a very well-rounded person.

For the last few years, however, it seemed as though I never did any reading. Objectively this couldn't be true. I checked books out of the library and returned them after I'd finished them. I bought books and put them on the shelf, read. I took notes on my reading. Yet I had no idea when I found time to read. *When did I read?*

My friend Laura Vanderkam, a time-management expert, emphasizes the power of tracking time use, so I decided to try that. I made a daily time log—a simple grid with the days of the week mapped against the hours of the day in thirty-minute increments. The log could be used to track any activity, but I planned to record my reading time.

Or maybe not. After a few days, I admitted defeat. Many people find the time log to be an invaluable tool, but I just *could not* use it. The paper was never in the right place, or I kept forgetting to enter my reading time.

I disliked the idea of getting more dependent on my phone—after all, I still rely on my ancient Filofax—but I was already using my phone to monitor, so I decided to use it to monitor my reading, too. After some cursory research into time-tracking apps (Secret of Adulthood: Most decisions don't require extensive research), I downloaded the TimeJot app. I couldn't get myself to use it. Next, HoursTracker. No luck. I just couldn't get in the habit of recording my reading time, and the more I tried, the more annoyed I got. This attempted habit wasn't doing any good, so I junked it.

However, even this failed attempt to monitor made me more aware of my desire to read. So, although I can't point to a time log to prove that I'm reading more, I'm pretty sure that I am.

I considered monitoring spending, as well. People aren't very good at tracking their expenditures; in one study, when thirty people were asked to estimate the amount on their credit card bill, every person underestimated that number, by an average of almost 30 percent. For many people, credit cards are themselves an obstacle to accurate monitoring of spending, because while handing over a wad of cash makes spending seem vividly real, using a charge card makes parting with money easier. The same principle of disguised expenditure explains why casinos require that gamblers play with chips, not bills, and why it's easy to overspend in a foreign country, where money looks as if it came from a board game.

For some people, however, plastic works better than cash. A reader noted, "When I get cash, it always seems to disappear quickly, and I have little idea how it was spent. I buy almost everything with one credit card. I log in to my account online regularly, and I can see what I've bought and how much I've spent."

In the end, however, I decided not to monitor my spending. Monitoring is a powerful tool, and it would probably give me valuable insights into how Jamie and I spend money. But my spending was well under control—in fact, as an underbuyer, I often need to prod myself to *buy*. (For instance, my family is perpetually short of mittens and gloves.) Since monitoring takes time and energy, I decided that monitoring expenditures would only sap the energy I needed for monitoring the aspects of my life that I truly want to track.

As I talked to people about how they monitor themselves, the potentially dangerous concept of *moderation* kept cropping up. Framing a level of activity or consumption as moderate can be misleading, because while the word "moderation" implies reasonableness and restraint, it's actually a relative term. Moderate in comparison to what? Two hundred years ago, Americans ate less than a fifth of the sugar that we eat today. So a "moderate" amount of sugar by today's standards could be considered excessive by historical standards. Monitoring requires us to make an actual reckoning, which defeats the comfortable fuzziness of "moderation."

———

As I'd hoped, Monitoring was having a good effect on my habits. Even before applying more active habits strategies, I'd noticed myself making small shifts, as the data provided by tracking helped nudge me to do *better than before*.

Also, I enjoyed monitoring. As an Upholder, I like watching my progress and getting credit for my accomplishments, and in some situations, I didn't mind the grunt work of tracking. Monitoring tends to appeal to Questioners, too, because they love getting information and using it to shape their habits. From what I've observed, however, Obligers may struggle to monitor unless someone is checking on them. Just wearing a UP band might not supply enough external accountability for some Obligers—but activating the "team" feature, to allow other people to check their stats, might help. Rebels? It depends on whether Rebels *want* to monitor.

My biggest monitoring challenge was my urge to monitor myself selectively, because it's tempting to record only my virtuous moments. On the other hand, when I feel as though I haven't made much progress, monitoring is a reminder of what I *have* accomplished. Progress, not perfection, is the goal. I'm a gold-star junkie, and I love scrolling back on my UP report to see that I exceeded my 10,000-step goal, but I also know that 5,000 steps are better than 1,000. A Secret of Adulthood (cribbed from Voltaire) is "Don't let the perfect be the enemy of the good." Monitoring makes it possible to remember everything I've accomplished.

At times, I did find that my monitoring distracted me from my own experience, and perhaps kept me from encountering it as deeply as I might have done if I hadn't been monitoring. If I'm fussing with the sleep function on my UP band, I may not notice how good it feels to stretch out in bed. Nonetheless, monitoring is invaluable, because it helps ensure that I *get to bed*. How will I get a good night's sleep if I stay glued to my computer until midnight? By monitoring the activities that I want to foster, I get an accurate picture of what I'm doing, which helps me see what I want to do differently.

My sister Elizabeth had decided that knowing her blood sugar level was so important that she had to monitor it as closely as possible; I wasn't monitoring anything nearly as vital, of course, but the same principle applied: I should monitor whatever is essential to me. In that way, I ensure that my life reflects my values.

FIRST THINGS FIRST

Foundation

Habits gradually change the face of one's life as time changes one's physical face; & one does not know it.

—Virginia Woolf, diary, April 13, 1929

The observational Strategies of Four Tendencies, Distinctions, and Monitoring take their power from self-awareness. Because I tend to gravitate toward the concrete, I was eager to get out of my own head to start acting on what I'd learned. I'd begin by working on the Strategy of Foundation, because I'd have an easier time fostering good habits if my Foundation was strong.

While some experts advise focusing on one habit project at a time to avoid draining willpower, others note that people who work on one positive habit often find it easier to improve in other areas; for instance, people who stick to a program of exercise also show better health- and work-related behaviors. Maybe that's one reason so many major religions have periods of ritualized self-denial, like Lent, Ramadan, and Yom Kippur. Self-command breeds self-command, and change fosters change. The reverse is true, too: undesirable habits often cluster together and reinforce each other.

If we want to improve our habits, where should we begin? I often remind myself, "First things first." That is, begin by addressing big, obvious problems.

Surprisingly often, when people want to improve their habits, they begin with a habit that won't deliver much payoff in return for the habit-formation energy required. I knew a guy who was chronically sleep-deprived, never exercised, could never find his keys or his wallet, was constantly late for work, never had time to play the tennis that he loved, and who chewed gum constantly, and he told me, "I've *got* to make some changes. I'm going to give up gum."

I didn't tell him, but his decision reminded me of an old joke. Late one night, a policeman sees a man weaving around under a streetlight.

"Sir, what are you doing?" the policeman asks.

"I'm looking for my car keys," answers the man, obviously drunk.

"Is this where you lost them?"

"No, I lost them back there," the man replies, as he points over his shoulder to a dark area of the sidewalk, "but the light is better here."

I've noticed that when many people decide to improve their habits, they don't begin by looking where their keys are; they begin by looking in an easy spot. But then they don't find their keys.

So where *should* we start? It's helpful to begin with habits that most directly strengthen self-control; these habits serve as the Foundation for forming other good habits. They protect us from getting so physically taxed or mentally frazzled that we can't manage ourselves.

From my observation, habits in four areas do most to boost feelings of self-control, and in this way strengthen the Foundation of all our habits. We do well to begin by tackling the habits that help us to:

1. sleep
2. move
3. eat and drink right
4. unclutter

Foundation habits tend to reinforce each other—for instance, exercise helps people sleep, and sleep helps people do everything better—so they're a good place to start for any kind of habit change. Furthermore, somewhat mysteriously, Foundation habits sometimes make profound change possible. A friend once told me, "I cleaned out my fridge, and now I feel like I can switch careers." I knew *exactly* what she meant.

For this reason, Foundation habits deserve special priority. It was no coincidence, I realized, that for my monitoring experiment, I'd chosen to monitor habits that fall into three of the four areas of Foundation. Even before I'd pinpointed the idea of the "Foundation," I'd intuited the significance of these particular areas.

Although my habits are pretty good, the Strategy of Monitoring had shown me that I could do a lot to improve my own Foundation.

First: sleep. My bedtime was 10:30, but I felt a persistent tug to stay up later. Finally, I realized that although I'd always assumed that feeling tired pushed me toward sleep, feeling exhausted often made me stay up *later*. Going to bed demands a real burst of psychic and physical energy. When I'm too tired to switch gears, and I can't face the thought of washing my face, I delay going to bed.

I started to prepare for sleep earlier. Now I wash my face, brush my teeth, swap my contact lenses for glasses, and put on my pajamas well before 10:30. Clearing away these minor tasks makes it easier to go to bed when it's time.

I discovered an unexpected bonus to sticking to my bedtime. The last thirty minutes before bed is a danger zone; my self-control is depleted, so I struggle with my good habits. I often head to the kitchen for a last snack. (Being mildly but chronically short of sleep makes people more susceptible to hunger and temptation—perhaps one reason that obesity is more common among those who get less than six hours of sleep.) I'm cranky, so I sometimes pick a fight with Jamie by wildly overreacting to his failure to change a lightbulb or answer an email. Going to sleep on time means that I spend less time awake in that depleted state.

As I talked to other people about their sleep habits, however, something puzzled me. Repeatedly, people told me that they were painfully, chronically exhausted—yet when I made the unoriginal suggestion that they go to bed earlier, they became upset and resentful. Why?

I began to understand. These folks schedule very little time for themselves, they race around without a break, and their only leisure time comes at night. Some use that time to catch up on work—to knock off some emails or to read a report. Others use the time for fun. Their kids are asleep, the trash is out, office emails have stopped, and they can finally spend the time with their spouse, or enjoy some solitude, or goof off.

A law school friend told me, with surprising vehemence, "I work at a shitty job at a law firm from morning to night. Without that time at the end of the day, to read, to relax, I have nothing for myself."

"You might feel better if you got more sleep," I pointed out.

"If I went to sleep earlier, that would mean the firm is getting *all* of me." He shook his head. "No way."

People don't want to lose that precious open slot of time, even to sleep. It feels like a deprivation—and people *hate* to feel deprived. This it's-my-only-time-to-myself phenomenon is a big habits challenge. "Rest, relax, and enjoy" is #4 of the Essential Seven, and many people complain of constant exhaustion yet cling to that last outpost of open time. But the fact is, we need sleep.

Second: move. Physical activity is the magical elixir of practically everything. Exercise relieves anxiety, boosts energy and mood, improves memory, sharpens executive function, and contributes to weight maintenance. It both energizes us and calms us. Among its most helpful benefits, it can help us stick to our other good habits by strengthening our self-command. Also, it certainly makes everyday life easier. At Parents' Night at my daughters' school, I see many parents wait in a long line to take the elevator rather than face three flights of stairs.

Some people assume that "exercise" requires a long visit to the gym, complete with shower, but just moving around gives benefits. The people who get the biggest boost in health are those who go from being completely sedentary to being slightly less sedentary, with the main drop in mortality rates coming from people doing their first twenty minutes of exercise (about 40 percent of Americans report that they get *no* exercise).

However, of people who start an exercise program, about half have dropped out by the six-month point. The reason, I suspect, is that people often choose a form of exercise based on misleading factors, such as how they want to change their appearance; what's in fashion (as with clothes and hairstyles, different forms of exercise go in and out of vogue); or what someone else suggests. These considerations can be helpful, but in the end, we're far more likely to stick with an exercise routine that suits our temperament and schedule. For instance, a night person shouldn't expect to get up early to exercise; it's just not going to happen.

Many factors contribute to whether an exercise regimen is likely to suit a particular individual. It's important to consider:

Are you a morning person or a night person (Lark or Owl)?

Do you enjoy spending time outdoors, or do you prefer not to deal with weather?

Are you motivated by competition?

Do you enjoy exercising to strong music and a driving beat, or do you prefer a quiet background?

Do you respond well to some form of external accountability (a trainer, a running group), or is internal accountability sufficient?

Do you like to challenge yourself with exercise (learning a new skill, pushing yourself physically), or do you prefer familiar activities?

Do you like sports and games?

Is it inconvenient for you to take a shower afterward?

As I considered my own answers—Lark, both, no, quiet, internal, familiar, no, sometimes—I realized why my exercise routine works well for me. I don't like to push myself very hard at all, or try new things, and I don't. Each week, indoors, I take one relaxed yoga class and make one or two trips to a cardio gym for forty undemanding minutes split between the StairMaster and the stationary bike. Once a week, I do push myself hard, in my work-to-failure strength-training session; it's extremely challenging, but it lasts only twenty minutes, so I can stand it.

Other people, of course, have a completely different set of preferences. Someone told me: "I finally realized that I'm motivated by competition. Since I realized that, I've been having weekly 'events' with my friends. For the longest time I've wanted to be this excited about working out."

In tackling this area of my Foundation, I didn't want to add more official periods of "exercise" to my week, but I did want to move around more. As a writer, I sit for many hours to work, and I spend most of my free time sitting as well, so I looked for a few habits to help pull me onto my feet.

One of my twelve Personal Commandments is to "Act the way I want to feel." It's easy to assume that we *act* because of the way we *feel*, but to a very great degree, we *feel* because of the way we *act*. If I act with more energy, I'll feel more energetic.

I decided to set myself the habit of going for a walk once each weekend. Each time I set off, it was an effort to get myself out the door, but I did return each time with more energy.

While physical activity is a key aspect of the Foundation and has many emotional and physical benefits, people often assume that its most important benefit is something that, ironically, it doesn't provide: *exercise doesn't promote weight loss*. It seems to help people maintain their weight—active people are less likely to gain or regain weight than inactive people—but it's *not* associated with weight loss. There are many compelling reasons to exercise, but study after study shows that weight loss isn't one of them. The way to lose weight is to change eating habits.

Third: eat and drink right. Few aspects of everyday life are more foundational than eating, but many people feel out of control with food. There's a paradox: because the brain needs food to manage impulses, one of the best ways to avoid impulsive overeating is to eat.

For my Foundation, I decided to make it a habit to eat only when I was hungry, and stop as soon as I was full. This is harder than it sounds, however, because so many cues overwhelm our sense of physical hunger. Often we eat not from hunger, but because of routine, social influences, the sight or smell of food, and other external triggers. (Unfortunately, being "on a diet" seems to make people more sensitive to outside cues.) Also, although the average meal is eaten in about twelve minutes, it takes twenty minutes for the body to register a feeling of fullness. In practice, I discovered, "eat only when I'm hungry" and "no seconds" turned out to be among the habits that I break most often. The logistics of life, and the temptations of food, make them hard to follow.

But while I still sometimes eat when I'm not hungry, I *always* eat when I'm hungry. I hate being hungry and was astonished when a friend told me, "My favorite thing is to wake up hungry in the middle of the night." When I'm hungry, I get "hangry," with a quick temper, and I can't work or think.

To that end, I always eat breakfast.

There's some controversy about breakfast. Many people point to studies showing that breakfast eaters tend to be thinner, but this is an observation about correlation, not causation; a study of existing research concluded that the habit of skipping breakfast showed little or no effect on weight gain. Nevertheless, although I'm not convinced there's any special magic to breakfast, I always do eat breakfast. Not letting myself get too hungry is part of my Foundation.

Research suggests that skipping meals is a bad idea, perhaps because being hungry makes it harder to control impulses to overeat. In one study of dieting women, the women who didn't skip meals lost almost eight more pounds than those who sometimes did skip. Also, for many people, skipping breakfast leads to a whole day of bargaining and bad choices. As a friend and I waited to collect our daughters from a birthday party, she picked up a cupcake and explained, "I didn't eat breakfast this morning, so this is okay."

Paired with eating is—drinking. Alcohol can interfere with the Foundation in many ways: it lowers our inhibitions (that's why it's fun) so we're more likely to overeat and drink more, disrupts sleep, makes people less likely to exercise, and undercuts efforts at self-control.

In my case, alcohol wasn't an issue for Foundation. I'd given it up years ago, more or less, because alcohol makes me belligerent, indiscreet, and sleepy. Not drinking wasn't hard for me because I've never enjoyed alcohol much; also, Jamie has hepatitis C, which means he can't drink at all, so I feel less inclined to drink, out of team spirit.

Alcohol isn't the only drinking issue that gets attention, however. Some people worry about drinking enough water. Waiting in a drugstore line, I overheard a woman say to her friend, "I'm making a big effort to drink more water. I buy a big bottle every day, and I drink from it constantly."

I wished that I could tell her not to bother, that water drinking is credited with vastly greater health benefits than it actually provides. Contrary to popular belief, we're not likely to mistake thirst for hunger, and we don't have to try to drink water, because if we're dehydrated, we'll feel uncomfortably thirsty. And we don't have to drink eight glasses of water a day; a person who doesn't feel thirsty and produces a good amount of slightly yellow urine is probably getting enough water.

Of course, for people who love to drink water, or believe that it makes them feel good, great. And it's better to drink water than sweet tea. But I regret the waste of precious habit-formation effort when I see people wearily force themselves to chug from their water bottles, or when I see "Drink more water" at the top of the lists of desired habits.

Fostering good habits takes energy, and that energy is in short supply; we're better off exploiting that energy to create the habits that will do the most good. First things first.

Fourth: unclutter. I'm constantly surprised by the degree to which, for most people, outer order contributes to inner calm. Order contributes to the Foundation more, really, than it should. A crowded coat closet or an overflowing in-box seems like a trivial thing—and it *is* trivial—yet an orderly environment makes me feel more in control of myself. If this is an illusion, it's a helpful illusion.

Outer disorder may act as a *broken window*. The "broken windows" theory of crime prevention was introduced in the 1980s by social scientists who observed that when a community tolerates disorder and petty crime, such as breaking of windows, graffiti, turnstile jumping, or drinking in public, people are more likely to commit more serious crimes. As a law enforcement theory, it's controversial; but whether or not it's true on a community-wide level, it's true on a personal level.

For many people—like me—a clean, well-maintained environment helps to foster a sense of self-command, which in turn makes it easier to maintain good habits.

In law school, I happened to visit the group houses of two friends in one day, and I remember being struck by the difference in their kitchens. At the first stop, the kitchen was orderly. My friend pulled a box of crackers out of the cabinet and some cheese from the fridge, and both packages were closed and neatly stowed away. When I visited the second friend, she said, "Help yourself to anything." Several open bags lay scattered on the counter—pretzels, chips, and Entenmann's mini-chocolate-chip cookies—and as we sat talking at the kitchen table, other people wandered through, and everyone grabbed a few handfuls. "If I lived here, I could eat an entire box of cookies in a day," I thought, "and not even notice." We were all young and single, and no one wanted to eat junk food, but the habits of that house made it much harder to resist.

People get a real lift when they put things in their place, tackle nagging tasks, clear surfaces, and get rid of things that don't work or aren't used. This surge of energy makes it easier to ask more of ourselves, to use our self-control, and to stick to a challenging habit. Also, accomplishing small tasks boosts our sense of "self-efficacy." The more we trust ourselves to follow through on our own commitments, the more likely we are to believe that we can keep an important habit.

Of course, it's also true that some people thrive in an atmosphere of disarray. For them, an uncluttered environment doesn't help—or may even stifle—their productivity, their creativity, and their peace of mind.

But for me, messy surroundings are a broken window that makes me feel less productive and creative, not more. When my office is crammed with open books, scribbled notes, half-empty coffee cups, and uncapped pens, I feel overwhelmed. Clearing my space clears my mind.

Each person has different broken windows. An unmade bed is a common broken window, which is why "Make the bed" is one of the most popular happiness-project resolutions, and in fact, as Charles Duhigg points out in his fascinating book *The Power of Habit*, the habit of bed making is correlated with a sense of greater well-being and higher productivity. Other common broken windows include having a messy car; accumulating piles of laundry or trash; not being able to find important items, like a passport or a phone charger; hanging on to stacks of newspapers, magazines, and catalogs; wearing pajamas or sweats all day; or not shaving or showering.

For Jamie, as he often emphatically reminds me, dirty dishes left overnight are broken windows; for me, if the dishes make it into the sink, life feels under control. One of my broken windows? Falling asleep in front of the TV.

When I started my inquiry into habit formation, my sister Elizabeth agreed to be my habits "recruit," to allow me to test some of my theories on her. In one of my first attempts to tinker with her habits, I tried to persuade her to change her sleep habits—but it wasn't something she wanted to work on.

"Sometimes when I'm watching TV at the end of the day, I'll take a nap on the sofa," she told me. "That's when I get the best, deepest sleep."

"You're not taking a *nap*," I protested, "you're passing out in front of the TV! For me, that's a broken window. It seems so sad."

"To me, going to bed before midnight seems depressing. I'm losing one of the good parts of my day."

Elizabeth, I realized, is one of the people who feels cheated if she doesn't have that end-of-the-day time to herself, even at the expense of getting enough quality sleep. So I dropped the subject.

I decided to repair some of my own broken windows. I began with my bad habit of leaving piles of my clothes around the bedroom—for days. Especially when I feel rushed, I tell myself, "A pile of clothes won't make any difference." But maintaining order makes me feel calmer and more in control; letting my environment get messy makes me feel worse. Once I started the habit, I realized, too, that putting away my clothes nightly meant that the task stayed small. Secret of Adulthood: Keeping up is easier than catching up.

Next, I turned to the nagging task of phone messages. I dislike the beep that tells me that we have messages—and our phone is always beeping, because I hate to pick up messages. Instead, I declared a new habit. Every time I hear the beep, I *must* pick up the messages.

But before long, I admitted defeat. I just couldn't make myself do it. I switched to a new habit: handing pen, paper, and phone to Jamie when he comes home from work, and making *him* get the messages. He doesn't seem to mind.

I also considered my office habits. Each morning, I sit down at my desk, with a cup of coffee on one side and a diet soda on the other, and connect to the world through email and social media. As I start clicking around, I feel reassuringly in command—like an airplane pilot running a system check in a cockpit, or a surgeon reaching for an instrument.

I wanted the end of my workday to be as satisfying as the beginning. My habit had been to walk away from a messy desk, but now, for my last ten minutes of work, I file papers, blast through some emails, fill out forms, put my pens in the pen cup, check the next day's calendar, and gather items that need to go somewhere else in the apartment.

I soon discovered that this habit also makes it much easier to walk into my office the next morning; I hadn't realized how discouraging it was to sift through the papers and coffee mugs to get started afresh.

The Foundation Four made a big difference to my own habits—but did they matter as much to everyone? To experiment with my theory about the importance of the Foundation, I asked my friend Marshall if he'd let me make him a habits recruit to help him clear his clutter.

I knew Marshall through one of my children's literature reading groups. He's a newspaper columnist with enormous creativity, but as he told me one day, "I don't have any trouble finishing my assignments, but I put off doing my own work."

"What work?" I asked.

"Work on my spec script, my idea for a novel, or the collaboration I might do with my brother." (He's an Obliger.)

Because I'd been to his apartment, I knew it was fairly messy, and I was eager to test my theory that clearing clutter—and in this way, strengthening his Foundation—would help him with his writing habits. As I explained to him, "My theory is that Foundation habits make it easier to form other good habits, so creating more order might help you with writing. Over and over, people tell me that getting control of their *stuff* makes them feel more in control of their *lives*. Also, there was a Princeton study that found that visual clutter reduces your ability to focus and process information." (I love to throw in research—it's more convincing to people if I cite a study.)

"Okay," he answered, with cautious enthusiasm.

I arrived at his place, a classic one-bedroom New York City apartment in Greenwich Village, armed with a snack and my little notebook; I was ready to take notes if some habit-formation truth revealed itself. I couldn't wait to begin—but Marshall looked as though he might be having second thoughts.

Since he'd met my sister when he was living in Los Angeles, I invoked her now. "Remember, I helped Elizabeth clear her clutter. People often feel bad about their clutter, but *no one* is messier than Elizabeth. Though it's true, she has gotten a lot better," I added, to be fair. "Nothing will shock me. Okay?"

"Okay."

As we worked, I mentioned some favorite clutter-clearing habits, in case any happened to appeal to Marshall. "Follow the one-minute rule: if you can do a task in less than a minute, do it." "Never keep newspapers overnight." "Use counters for activities, not for storage." I told little inspirational clutter-clearing teaching stories. "I met this guy who has a complete set of the *Believer* magazine," I said, "and somehow the fact that he has a set makes him think they're valuable." I shook my head. "It's easy to get in the habit of collecting things that aren't actually meaningful or useful, and then you have to organize them and store them. Like shopping bags. I want to save them. But who can use fifty shopping bags?"

He responded by handing me a yellowing stack of newspapers. "Would you add these to the pile inside that cabinet?"

I looked inside. "Why are you keeping all these?"

"They're the newspaper sections with my column." He looked at the pile. "Maybe I could hire someone to clip the pieces. And put them in a book. Or *scan* them. Then I could put the pieces online."

"Do you have a site?"

"No, but maybe I should have a site."

Marshall's suggestions gave me pause: was he "raising the bar"? People *raise the bar* when they consider starting a new habit, and then, from an impulse that's either enthusiasm or unconscious self-sabotage, they suggest refinements that make the habit prohibitively challenging. A person decides to start exercising, and instead of aiming to walk for twenty minutes a day, he decides to start a routine that rotates between cardio, weights, and balance, four times a week for an hour. The bar is so high that it's impossible to clear.

Marshall might be raising the bar. He'd moved from keeping old newspapers stuffed in a cabinet to hiring someone to clip, scan, and upload them to an as-yet-to-be-created website. On the other hand, journalism was his livelihood.

Well, at least the papers were stacked neatly out of sight for now.

Marshall was sorting through a giant box of old papers, and in a surprisingly short time, he'd emptied it out.

"Wow, that was fast!" I said. "You only started forty minutes ago."

"No," he shook his head. "It took me *seven years* to clean out that box. There was mail in there from 2006." We both took a moment to ponder that.

After a few hours, Marshall got the stunned look that I often see when I'm helping people clear clutter. I, on the other hand, felt more exhilarated the longer we cleared. By this point, his apartment was crammed with bags and piles. "I know it looks overwhelming," I admitted. "A Secret of Adulthood is that things look messier before they look tidier. This is the messy stage."

"That's okay," he said.

I started laughing.

"What?" he asked.

"I realize that although you'll be glad we did this, it's a huge pain for you. I get a big kick out of it, and thanks for being so game. I know I can be kind of relentless."

"No, it's good to clear out all this junk."

I remembered a conversation I'd had with Elizabeth a few years before. She was moving, and I'd gone to L.A. to help her box up her possessions. We cleared and packed without a break for two days. A typical moment: just when we thought we'd finished the kitchen, Elizabeth opened the oven and discovered that it was jammed with long-forgotten items. I love this kind of challenge, and I worked until the minute I had to leave for the airport. Elizabeth had collapsed on the couch with a pair of scissors in one limp hand and a roll of packing tape in the other. "Would you mind taking a taxi?" she asked. "I think I'm too tired to drive you."

"Sure," I said. I gave her a hard look. "Admit it. You'll be glad to see me go."

She couldn't even deny it! "But later I'll be *so glad* you came," she said earnestly.

I knew Marshall was feeling the same way. He seemed glad to be rid of some clutter, and his apartment looked better than before, but I suspected that I got more of a lift out of this improvement than he did. I'd offered to help Marshall work on the "unclutter" aspect of the Foundation because I'd assumed the change would make a difference for his writing—but the clutter in his apartment didn't bother him the way it would have bothered me. And because it didn't really matter to him, probably it hadn't been interfering much with his productivity. Even among the Foundation Four, we all must make choices that reflect our values.

The deeper I went into my investigation of habits, the more I appreciated the importance of understanding each person's values and temperament. It was so easy to assume that the steps that work for me would work for others—but habits don't operate that way. Individual differences mattered even more than I'd believed when I started.

First things first—but we must all decide what comes first, for us.

IF IT'S ON THE CALENDAR, IT HAPPENS

Scheduling

I'm a full-time believer in writing habits . . . You may be able to do without them if you have genius but most of us only have talent and this is simply something that has to be assisted all the time by physical and mental habits or it dries up and blows away. . . . Of course you have to make your habits in this conform to what you can do. I write only about two hours every day because that's all the energy I have, but I don't let anything interfere with those two hours, at the same time and the same place.

—FLANNERY O'CONNOR, letter, September 22, 1957

The Strategy of Scheduling, of setting a specific, regular time for an activity to recur, is one of the most familiar and powerful strategies of habit formation—and it's one of my favorites. Scheduling makes us far more likely to convert an activity into a habit (well, except for Rebels), so for that reason, I schedule even some slightly ridiculous habits, such as "Kiss Jamie every morning and every night."

Habits grow strongest and fastest when they're repeated in predictable ways, and for most of us, putting an activity on the schedule tends to lock us into doing it. In college and law school, I never asked myself, "Should I go to class?" or "Do I need to do this reading tonight?" If class was scheduled, I went. If reading was on the syllabus, I read it.

A friend with a daily schedule gets up at 4:30 a.m., meditates for twenty minutes, grabs a flashlight for a forty-minute walk, eats breakfast with her two sons, showers, dresses, and is on the train to work at 7:30. (She's a Lark, clearly.) For someone else, any of these activities might be a challenge, but not for her; she's already decided what to do.

Scheduling also forces us to confront the natural limits of the day. It's tempting to pretend that I can do everything if only I get the "balance" right, but scheduling requires choices. Scheduling one activity makes that time unavailable for anything else. Which is *good*—especially for people who have trouble saying no. Every week, Eliza and I go on a "Wednesday afternoon adventure" (though we're not particularly adventurous, and usually end up at a museum). Especially now that Eliza is in the tricky teenage years, I want to make sure we have some pleasant time together each week. So I put our adventure on the schedule, and if I'm asked to do anything that would interfere, I say automatically, "I'm not available at that time." Scheduling makes activities automatic, which builds habits.

Scheduling appeals to many people, but Upholders are particularly attracted to the predictability of schedules and the satisfaction of crossing items off to-do lists. Questioners see the sound reason behind adding an item to the calendar, and for some Obligers, merely seeing an item pop up on the schedule creates a helpful sense of accountability. However, because Rebels want to *choose* to do an activity, putting an activity on their schedule may dramatically diminish their inclination to do it.

I decided to use Scheduling to start an ambitious new habit: meditation. Meditation is the practice of focusing attention on the present moment—on our breath, or an image, or nothing—in a non-analytical and nonjudgmental way. Though it's particularly associated with Buddhism, meditation has existed in various forms in many traditions. Because of the evidence of its mental and physical benefits, increasing numbers of people practice a secular form of mindfulness meditation; according to a 2007 survey, almost one in ten Americans had meditated in the previous year.

I'd resisted meditation for years; it never appealed to me. My most important Personal Commandment is to "Be Gretchen." "Be Gretchen," I thought, "and skip meditation." I became intrigued, however, when in the space of a month, three people told me how much they'd benefited from it. Their firsthand accounts carried more weight with me than everything I'd read in the literature.

Maybe I *should* try it, I thought. After all, was I going to let my sense of identity, my sense of Gretchen, congeal in ways that kept me from trying new things? Happiness expert Daniel Gilbert suggests that a useful way to predict whether an experience will make us happy is to ask other people currently undergoing the experience we're contemplating how *they* feel. He argues that we tend to overestimate the degree to which we're different from other people, and generally, an activity that one person finds satisfying is likely to satisfy someone else. I half agree with Professor Gilbert. As my oft-invoked Secret of Adulthood holds, we're both more alike than we think, and less alike. What finally made me decide to try meditation was someone telling me, "I know people who tried meditation who haven't stuck with it. But I don't know anyone who thought it was a waste of time."

To learn to meditate, I did what I always do, and headed to the library. After reading books such as Thich Nhat Hanh's *The Miracle of Mindfulness* and Sharon Salzberg's *Real Happiness*, I came up with my plan. Though Salzberg suggests starting with twenty minutes of meditation three days a week, twenty minutes sounded like a *long* time, so I decided to make meditation a daily five-minute habit.

When scheduling a new habit, it helps to tie it to an existing habit, such as "after breakfast," or to an external cue, such as "when my alarm rings," because without such a trigger, it's easy to forget to do the new action. An existing habit or cue works better than using a particular start time, because it's so easy to lose track of the hour. In-stead of "meditating at 6:15 a.m.," therefore, I inserted "meditate" into my schedule right after waking up and getting dressed.

When I woke up that first morning, I felt unusually tired, even though my handy sleep monitor reported that I'd slept for six hours and fifty-two minutes. "Maybe I should wait to start meditating when I'm more energetic," a devious part of my brain suggested. "It will be tough today, when I'm sleepy." Hah! I knew better than to be-lieve *that*. The desire to start something at the "right" time is usually just a justification for delay. In almost every case, the best time to start is *now*.

So right after getting dressed—I was already wearing yoga pants, because I wear yoga pants every single day—I set my phone alarm for five minutes (the alarm sound of "crickets" seemed suitable), pulled a pillow off the sofa, and put it down on the floor.

I settled myself in the lotus position with my hands palms up, right hand cupped inside left, and the tips of my thumbs forming a triangle (very specific, but that's what the book said to do). I checked my posture, then remembered that my knees should be lower than my hips, so I hopped up to get another pillow.

After a few minutes of squirming to get my balance, I sat up straight, lowered my shoulders, relaxed my jaw, deliberately com-posed my mind, and began to focus on my breath flowing in and out, smoothly and deeply.

After about ten seconds, my mind wandered. I tried to notice this shift without judgment and returned to the focus on my breath. Thinking about breathing reminded me of that scene from the Woody Allen movie *Husbands and Wives* where the character Sally lies in bed next to a man, and while he's kissing her, she thinks about the fact that he's a "hedgehog," and she starts sorting her friends into hedgehogs or foxes. That got me thinking about the Archilochus fragment "The fox knows many things, but the hedgehog knows one big thing," and that got me thinking about the Isaiah Berlin essay "The Hedgehog and the Fox," and that got me thinking about my mixed feelings about Tolstoy . . . *now back to my breath*. I thought about breath for a few seconds, then thought about the fact that I'd have to remember to write about having been distracted from my breath by a scene from a Woody Allen movie.

I observed myself thinking. I observed myself thinking about the fact that I was thinking. I observed myself thinking about the fact that I was thinking about the fact that I was thinking. All this metacognition was dizzying.

Breath.

I wondered how much time had gone by.

Breath.

I sure wouldn't want to do this for twenty minutes. Or even ten minutes.

Breath.

I tried to observe these distractions without frustration or judgment. They were just floating by. At last! I heard the sound of crickets.

Over the next few days of meditation, I noticed a few things. First, as soon as I started to focus on breathing, my breath felt constricted and artificial. *I thought I'd mastered breathing by now.*

Also, I kept teetering off my pillows. Thoreau warned, "Beware of all enterprises that require new clothes," and I wanted to beware of all meditation practices that required new stuff; on the other hand, if I was going to meditate every day, a better sitting pillow seemed like a worthwhile investment (even for an underbuyer like me). I looked online and was amazed by the assortment of meditation paraphernalia on offer. I'd never heard of a "zabuton zafu set," but when I saw a picture, it looked like exactly what I needed. I hit "Buy now."

To apply the Strategy of Scheduling, we must decide when, and how often, a habit should occur. Generally, advice about habit formation focuses on *fixed habits*—that is, habits that always happen in the same way, without conscious thought. Every day I'm up and brushing my teeth before I know it; I put on my seat belt; I meditate after I get dressed.

However, I've noticed that I have both *fixed habits* and *unfixed habits*. An *unfixed habit* requires more decision making and adjustment: I'm in the habit of going to the gym on Mondays, and I write every day, but every Monday I must decide when to go to the gym, and I must decide when and where I'll do my daily writing. I try to make my good habits as fixed as possible, because the more consistently I perform an action, the more automatic it becomes, and the fewer decisions it requires; but given the complexities of life, many habits can't be made completely automatic.

I'd given up the idea that I can create a habit simply by scheduling an action a certain number of times. Although many people believe that habits form in twenty-one days, when researchers at University College London examined how long people took to adopt a daily habit, such as drinking water or doing sit-ups, they found that, on average, a habit took sixty-six days to form. An average number isn't very useful, however, because—as we all know from experience—some people adopt habits more easily than others (say, habit-embracing Upholders vs. habit-resisting Rebels), and some habits form more quickly than others. Bad habits can be easy to create, though they make life harder, while good habits can be hard to create, though they make life easier.

We may not be able to form a habit in twenty-one days, but in many situations, we do benefit from scheduling a habit *every day*. The things we do every day take on a certain beauty, and funnily enough, two very unconventional geniuses wrote about the power of daily repetition. Andy Warhol said, "Either *once only, or every day*. If you do something once it's exciting, and if you do it every day it's exciting. But if you do it, say, twice or just almost every day, it's not good any more." Gertrude Stein made a related point: "Anything one does every day is important and imposing."

One of my most helpful Secrets of Adulthood is "What I do *every day* matters more than what I do *once in a while*." Perhaps surprisingly, I've found that it's actually easier to do something *every* day than *some* days. For me, the more regular and frequent the work, the more creative and productive I am—and the more I enjoy it—so I write every single day, including weekends, holidays, and vacations. Similarly, it's easier for me to post to my blog six days a week, instead of four days a week, because if I do it four days a week, I spend a lot of time arguing with myself about whether today is the day. Did the week start on Sunday or Monday? Do I deserve a break? Did yesterday "count"? When I post six days a week, I don't have to make any decisions.

Along with meditation, I identified two new habits to follow every day. First, I wanted to email more often with my sister. I don't get to spend nearly enough time with Elizabeth, and it's hard even to find time to talk by phone. I could at least schedule a daily email— even if I only wrote a few words in the subject line.

Also, I decided to take a daily photo of something beautiful or interesting. I hoped this exercise would sharpen my sensibilities by requiring that I watch, throughout the day, for a subject worthy of photographing.

Doing a habit *every day* is helpful; does *time of day* matter?

For most people, whenever possible, important habits should be scheduled for the morning. Mornings tend to unfold in a predictable way, and as the day goes on, more complications arise—whether real or invented—which is one reason why I'd scheduled my new meditation habit in the morning. Also, self-control is strongest then; I heard about one corporate dining room that encourages healthier eating habits by requiring people to place their lunch orders by 9:30 a.m., no changes permitted. By contrast, self-control wanes as the day wears on, which helps explain why sexual indiscretions, excessive gambling, overconsumption of alcohol, and impulsive crimes usually happen at night.

To clear time to schedule a new morning habit, many people try waking up a bit earlier, but this can be tough. One trick? Use the autumn end to daylight saving time as a painless way to add an hour to the morning. Most people relish the extra hour of sleep when time "falls back" (fewer car accidents occur on the Monday after the time change, because people are better rested). The time change, however, offers an easy opportunity to change daily habits. We can start waking up an hour early, and we can do a lot with that hour.

The early-morning approach won't work for Owls of course—children and work usually force them to wake up too early already. They may do better if they schedule habits later in the day. However, even Larks sometimes overlook the possibilities of early morning. I sent a friend an email:

> From: Gretchen
>
> I'm thinking about something you said. You said you were a real morning person—as a child, you volunteered to be an altar boy for the early morning Mass, because you liked to be up early.
>
> Now you wake up at 8:30.
>
> In my gentle habits bully way, I would propose that you try getting up earlier, to take advantage of morning time—to go to the gym, read, write your books, walk in the park with your dogs, whatever. As a morning person I think you would love it.
>
> I recognize that this is unsolicited meddling of course!

He responded:

> From: Michael
>
> So I'm 9 days or so into my getting-up-earlier habit. Picking something pleasurable is transformative. I've been reading for pleasure (also sometimes taking early am walks and cooking breakfast, and using my light therapy device). I never realized before how my prior efforts to wake up early were all basically variations on the "get cracking at work" theme.

> It's all about the motivation to get up. I realize that often I
> woke up early, but would go back to bed because I didn't feel like
> working. Now sometimes I just get up.

I'd been meditating faithfully, when one morning, while on a business trip, I woke up in the dark, quiet hotel room—at 4:20 a.m., because of the time change—and thought, "I'm traveling. Maybe I should skip meditating."

Then I realized how ludicrous this excuse was. I was alone, and I needed only five minutes, yet my mind had seized on "I'm traveling" as an excuse to skip my habit. "I always meditate as soon as I get up, no excuses," I told myself. "I'm sticking to my meditation practice." (Everything sounds more high-minded when described as a "practice": the practice of meditation, the practice of writing, the practice of gardening.)

Consistency, repetition, *no decision*—this was the way to develop the ease of a true habit. In fact, I knew, the habit of the habit is more important than the habit itself. On any particular morning, it was more important to try to meditate than actually to meditate.

At the same time, I realized that for some habits, *mostly* was good enough. I enjoyed my new habit of taking a daily photo, and I loved being in closer contact with my sister, but after a reasonable trial period, I decided that I didn't need to push myself to keep those habits every single day. *Mostly* was good enough to keep those habits strong, and to accomplish the aim of the habit.

While Scheduling helps prod me to do things that I'm reluctant to do, it also helps me to do things I *do* want to do. Counterintuitively, I often find it harder to make myself do something that I *enjoy* than something that I *don't enjoy*. And I'm not alone. A reader posted: "My 'thing' is song-writing on the piano. But a lot of days, I will do everything else before I sit down to compose." A friend told me, "It may seem weird to schedule sex, but that's what works for me and my husband." For some of us, it takes discipline to take pleasure.

One day Eleanor showed me a copy of her daily school schedule. She's an imaginative and orderly child, with a desk loaded with journals, eyeglasses cases, and office supplies ranging from a quill pen to a defunct wireless phone, and she loves her schedule. Her second-grade schedule included many elements that I want for my own day: snack, physical education, DEAR ("Drop Everything and Read"), and my favorite entry, Choice Time. Seeing "Choice Time" was a reminder that for people like me, leisure must be entered on the schedule as its own activity; it's not something I get only when I have nothing else to do. Because I *always* have something else to do.

Having fun is important, if only because it's easier to demand more of ourselves when we're giving more to ourselves. According to procrastination expert Neil Fiore, people who schedule playtime are more likely to tackle unappealing projects than people who never let themselves enjoy guilt-free fun until after their work is finished. Scheduling can solve this problem. For instance, in *The Artist's Way*, her influential book about cultivating creativity, Julia Cameron suggests scheduling an "artist's date," that is, taking a few hours each week to "nurture your creative consciousness," with activities such as visiting an art gallery, checking out a junk store, exploring a new neighborhood, or going for a walk.

Inspired by Choice Time to set aside time for leisure, I decided that each day I would observe "Quitting Time." Now, after Quitting Time, I don't check my email, read or write anything on social media, or do original writing. It's nice to push back from my computer or hang up the phone, and think, "It's Quitting Time. Time to goof off." Every day is different, however, so I don't set a standard quitting time; it's an unfixed habit that varies from day to day. I decide "when," but not "whether."

I wanted some habits, like meditation, to happen daily, but for other habits, once a week was enough. For fun, I'd proposed family

"Game Time," when on weekend afternoons we'd all play a game and drink hot cocoa. But after a few weeks of Game Time, I remembered something important about myself: *I don't like games.*

"What would everyone think of alternating weeks of Game Time with Reading Time?" I asked.

"Would we still drink hot cocoa?" asked Eleanor. Eleanor loves hot cocoa.

"Of course!"

"Okay," she answered, and everyone agreed.

I remind myself: Just because something is fun for *other people* doesn't mean it's fun for *me*—and it's a lot easier to stick to a habit that I honestly enjoy.

I also wanted to use weekly Scheduling to tackle the long list of small, mildly unpleasant tasks that I kept putting off. These tasks weren't urgent (which was the reason they didn't get done), but because they weighed on my mind, they sapped my energy. I decided that once a week, for one hour, I'd work on these chores. While we often over-estimate what we can accomplish in the short term (in one afternoon, in one week), we often underestimate what we can accomplish over the long term if we work consistently. A friend wrote a well-regarded novel by sticking to a habit of writing for just four hours a week—every Sat-urday, he and his wife gave each other a half day free—over the course of several years. As novelist Anthony Trollope observed, "A small daily task, if it be really daily, will beat the labours of a spasmodic Hercules."

I enjoy inventing labels and new vocabulary, and I considered call-ing this my "To-Do List Time." Then I remembered that because of the "fluency heuristic," an idea seems more valuable if it's easier to say or think. An idea expressed in rhyme seems more convincing than the same idea paraphrased in a non-rhyme, which is why "Haste makes waste" is more compelling than "Haste fosters error." I decided to name my new habit "Power Hour."

First, I made a running list of the tasks I wanted to complete. That was almost fun; I get a weird satisfaction from adding items to my to-do list. I didn't add any task with a deadline, such as planning my talk for a conference or buying plane tickets (for some reason, I loathe buying plane tickets), because I knew these tasks would get done anyway. And I didn't allow myself to use Power Hour for recurring tasks, like paying bills or answering emails. Power Hour was only for those one-time tasks that I kept postponing. Something that can be done at *any time* is often done at *no time*. I wrote:

Replace my broken office chair
Make a photo album of our vacation
Use up store credits
Donate books to Housing Works
Round up and recycle batteries and devices

For my first Power Hour, I tackled our long-neglected shredder. We'd never had a shredder, then finally I bought one, which broke right away, so I bought a replacement—and it had been sitting in a corner for months. I hadn't been able to face reading the directions or figuring out how to plug it into the inaccessible wall socket, and in the meantime, I'd accumulated a gigantic pile of mail to be shredded. The unused shredder bugged me, the pile of shred-worthy mail bugged me, and the trivial matter of shredding was taking up way too much room in my head.

"Power Hour!" I thought grimly, that first Saturday afternoon. I sat down with the shredder, figured out how to plug it in, and voilà—it was working. Not so bad.

"Hey, Eliza, want to do some shredding?" I yelled over my shoulder.

"Yes!" She came running. "I love shredding!"

Scheduling can also be used to *restrict* the time spent on an activity. A friend with a packed calendar uses the restriction angle of Scheduling to manage her workweek. "I tell my assistant to try to limit calls, meetings, and lunches to Tuesday, Wednesday, and Thursday. I need Monday to gear up for my week, and Friday to process it." A friend from college allowed herself to daydream about her latest crush for only fifteen minutes a night. I know someone who eats fast food twice a week, which means he's not eating fast food five times a week.

When I saw a photograph of Johnny Cash's to-do list in the newspaper, I saw that he'd used the Strategy of Scheduling, too. On a sheet printed with the words "Things To Do Today!" he wrote:

Not smoke
Kiss June
Not kiss anyone else
Cough
Pee
Eat
Not eat too much
Worry
Go see Mama
Practice piano

Johnny Cash used Scheduling to "Worry." Although scheduling time to worry sounds odd, it's a proven strategy for reducing anxiety. Instead of worrying continually, a person saves the worry until the appointed time, and then worries until the time is up. When I wanted to try to write a magazine piece around the publication of *Happier at Home,* I was worrying well before it was time to write it. I decided, "Don't worry about writing it until the last day of the month"—and I didn't.

The Strategy of Scheduling is a powerful weapon against procrastination. Because of *tomorrow logic,* we tend to feel confident that we'll be productive and virtuous—*tomorrow*. (The word "procrastinate" comes from *cras*, the Latin word for "tomorrow.") In one study, when subjects made a shopping list for what they'd eat in a week, more chose a healthy snack instead of an unhealthy snack; when asked what they'd choose now, more people chose the unhealthy over the healthy snack. As St. Augustine famously prayed, "Grant me chastity and continency, only not yet." *Tomorrow.*

Around this time, Elizabeth and I managed to get our two families to Kansas City for a brief visit with our parents. I'd been thinking about how Scheduling could help procrastinators, and I realized I had another potential subject for my experiments. When I'd started my research, I'd convinced Elizabeth to be one of my habits recruits; now I turned my sights on her husband, Adam. Like my sister, Adam is a brilliant TV writer, and like many writers, he sometimes battles with procrastination. Procrastinators can't make themselves work—often, ironically, because they're so anxious about work that they have to distract themselves from it—but they can't enjoy free time, either, because they know they *should* be working. A regular work schedule can help procrastinators because progress and engagement relieve their anxiety.

"Adam, how would you like for me to suggest some habits for you?" I proposed. "Like I'm doing for Elizabeth. You can follow them or not."

"Sure," said Adam, sounding game. I worried that I was taking advantage of his easygoing nature. Elizabeth knew what she was getting herself into, but Adam might not. He grew up outside Los Angeles and has the relaxed outlook associated with California—combined with a very dry sense of humor. I remember one night when he and Elizabeth came to visit Kansas City just after they'd got engaged, and we were all going to dinner with some family friends. Jamie asked my mother, "What should Adam and I wear tonight?"

"It's very casual," she said. "Khakis and loafers would be fine."

"I'm from California," Adam remarked to me. "Wearing khakis and loafers is like wearing an ascot."

I, on the other hand, have a tendency to be a little . . . *tightly wound*. I vowed not to drive Adam nuts, and I showed great restraint—at least in my own mind—by not immediately launching into a long disquisition about habits. But I did give him a short pep talk about the Strategy of Scheduling.

"Scheduling reduces pressure," I told him. "If you write every day, no one day's work is particularly important. And when you're working, you're working, and when you're not working, you're off duty. Without scheduling, it's easy to spend the whole day worrying about working, so you're not working but not relaxing either."

"I know the feeling," he said.

I suggested that he write from 11:00 to 1:00 every weekday. During that time, he was to write or *do nothing*. No email; no calls; no research; no clearing off a desk; no hanging out with Jack, my adorable, three-year-old, train-obsessed nephew. Write, or stare out the window.

"Remember," I added, "working is one of the most dangerous forms of procrastination. You want to use your writing time for writing only. *Nothing else*, including no other kinds of work."

I'd grasped this principle by accident. In my home office, I do work such as responding to comments on my blog, posting to Twitter or LinkedIn, checking Facebook, or answering emails. But when I want to do original writing—my most intellectually demanding work—I go to the library or to a coffee shop, where I don't connect to the Internet. This habit protects me from the pull of email, the web, and household tasks and forces me to do nothing but write. I decide, "I'll stay in the library for two hours," and then I'm stuck. I end up writing just to pass the time.

A professor friend told me, "One of the faculty who recruited me told me that if I accepted the offer, he'd reveal the secret to how to be a productive academic. On days set aside for research and writing, he disciplines himself not to answer any phone calls or check any email until 4:00 p.m., at which point he spends one or two hours only doing that. Also, once he started it, colleagues learned not to bother him before 4:00, so it's self-reinforcing."

After some time had gone by, I sent Adam an email to ask whether Scheduling was working. He answered:

From: Adam
  Scheduling is the answer for me. This week, I had lots of meetings, but if I'm missing my usual time, I'm making it up later in the day. I used to spend the day gearing up to work, and not always getting it done. Now it's like having an appointment. I feel very drawn to working during that period now in general. I'm not sure yet if it's the formation of a habit, my commitment to keeping the schedule, or a combination of both.

When I had lunch with two writer friends, one of whom had just quit her day job to work on her book full-time for a year, I couldn't resist delivering a short lecture on scheduling.

She talked about what her schedule might be, and our other friend added, "When she's making her schedule, shouldn't she decide what things she won't have much time for?"

"Like what?" I asked.

"Like not dating as much, or not making as many plans with friends."

"Well, does she need to do that?" I didn't want to contradict her, but I disagreed. "If she makes a schedule, she can set aside time for all her priorities."

"I'm pretty social," the first friend added. "I'm concerned about spending so much time alone, writing."

"So make sure you schedule enough social time."

The goal is to develop habits that allow us to have time for everything we value—work, fun, exercise, friends, errands, study—in a way that's sustainable, *forever*. Favoring work at the expense of everything else makes work itself less pleasant, diminishes quality of life, and creates a constant feeling of "emergency." Also, what happens if a person sacrifices a social life to write a book, the book is published, and it fails? The price would be too high. Even if the book were a *success*, the price would be too high.

Scheduling is an invaluable tool for habit formation: it helps to eliminate decision making; it helps us make the most of our limited self-command; it helps us fight procrastination. Most important, perhaps, the Strategy of Scheduling helps us make time for the things that are most important to us. How we schedule our days is how we spend our lives.

SOMEONE'S WATCHING

Accountability

Tell me with whom you consort and I will tell you who you are;
if I know how you spend your time, then I know what might
become of you.

—GOETHE, *Maxims and Reflections*

To be effective, the Strategy of Scheduling often must be paired with the essential Strategy of Accountability. It's not enough to schedule a habit; we must actually *follow* that habit. Accountability means that we face consequences for what we're doing—even if that consequence is merely the fact that someone else is monitoring us.

Accountability is a powerful factor in habit formation, and a ubiquitous feature in our lives. If we believe that someone's watching, we behave differently. Deadlines help us keep the habit of working. Late fees help us pay our bills on time. Grades help us study. Attendance records help us get our children to school on time. When we believe that we may be held accountable for our actions—even when we're accountable only to *ourselves*—we show more self-command.

This tendency is very marked. In one study, where people were asked to pay voluntarily for the beverages they took from an office kitchen, people paid more honestly when the price list was accompanied by an image of two eyes than when it was accompanied by a flower image; in Boston, when a life-sized cutout of a policeman was placed at a train station's bicycle cage, bike thefts dropped 67 percent. The mere presence of a mirror—which allows people literally to watch over themselves—makes people more likely to resist bullying, to argue their own opinions, to work harder at tasks, and to resist temptation.

On the flip side, when we don't feel accountable, we behave worse. The anonymity of hotels and travel makes it easier for people to break a healthy habit or moral code; using a pseudonym makes people more likely to act badly; even the slight disguise of sunglasses makes people feel freer to break their usual standards of conduct.

For this reason, it's often worthwhile to invest in systems of accountability. A chief benefit of fitness trainers, financial planners, life coaches, executive coaches, personal organizers, and nutritionists, in addition to their expertise, is the accountability they provide. For Obligers, most of all, this kind of external accountability is absolutely essential.

Another way to create accountability is to go public. In his memoir *The Writing of One Novel*, novelist Irving Wallace explained, "When you are a free and independent writer, without employer, without hours or deadlines, you have to play little games to force yourself into the actual writing. For me, one game is to announce . . . that I have finally decided on my next book, that I am ready to write it . . . to put my pride on the line."

Someone wrote on my blog: "I publicly announce that I'm going to do something, because I know the downside of people giving me crap for not doing it will motivate me to do it, even more so than any intrinsic motivation I may attach to the task itself." Another reader agreed: "When I tell people my goals, I feel 'uber' committed to them. I'm very careful about any commitment I make out loud, because it's almost as if I feel there's no way out of the commitment after I own it."

My sister Elizabeth used public accountability to deter herself from eating junk food, which is bad for anyone's health but especially for hers, because of her diabetes. When she started her new job, she made a point of telling her coworkers that she was committed to eating healthfully. Eating right was a particular challenge, because TV-writer custom dictates that the office kitchen is jammed with goodies—countless varieties of muffins, cookies, candy, cereal, chips, and any other food that writers add to the grocery store list—all free, which makes the array even more enticing. (Workplaces in general seem increasingly filled with food temptations. Many more employers now offer free food, not to mention the birthday cakes, treats served at going-away parties and office showers, Girl Scout cookies, pizza runs, leftover holiday goodies, vending machines, and so on.)

I asked her if she thought that telling her colleagues had helped her keep better eating habits. "Yes, because for me," she said, "declarations are important. I have to say, 'I don't eat cupcakes' to make myself go through with it."

"Because then you'd be embarrassed for other people to see you eat junk? Or because declaring the habit somehow makes it more real?"

"Partly I don't want to disappoint myself by not following through. Also, at this point, if I ate a cupcake at work, it would be a huge office-wide story. I am *so* on the record about not wanting to eat that stuff."

"So that makes it easier?"

"Yes. Plus no one even offers it to me anymore."

"Do you ever resent that? That they don't even ask you if you want it?"

"No! That's what I tried to *encourage*. We get the most unbelievable food at work—like we were sent these super-gourmet cupcakes from the best bakery in L.A. The first time I didn't eat a cupcake, I almost felt like crying. But now it doesn't seem like a big deal."

Elizabeth is a public resolver, but for some people, public declarations actually *undermine* their ability to stick to a new habit. A private resolver wrote: "I have to keep my goals private or they lose their magic." Another private resolver added, "The more I talk to other people about what I'm thinking about doing, the less likely I am to do it! The more I work on a goal in secret, the more likely I am to accomplish it."

The key, as always, is to use self-knowledge and to consider our own nature—to know whether we're public resolvers or private resolvers. For an Upholder like me, the public announcement of a habit doesn't make much of a difference. It's more helpful to have systems of *self*-accountability. For instance, I have my "Resolutions Charts," the charts where I track whether I've kept or broken the many resolutions I've made as part of my happiness projects. (It took me years to grasp that my desire to follow these *resolutions* could also be understood as a desire to shape my good *habits*.) In the same way, my UP band keeps a record of my actions, and even though no one sees it but me, that information allows me to hold myself accountable.

Another way to use Accountability, and an approach that Obligers find invaluable, is to team up with an accountability partner. They appear in many forms: a language tutor who charges for a no-show, or a friend who gets angry if he has to work out alone, or an instructor who insists on perfect attendance, or a coach who checks in with daily emails. Such partners can help protect a good habit. In one intervention, people who enrolled in a weight-loss program with an accountability partner maintained their weight loss more successfully than people who joined alone.

A psychiatrist friend made an interesting point about the difference between accountability partners and psychotherapists. "In the kind of therapy that I do, I don't hold you accountable," she explained. "I try to help you learn to hold yourself accountable to yourself. A coach holds you accountable."

"Then I wonder if some people need a coach more than a therapist," I said, thinking of Obligers. "Accountability to someone else is what they're really looking for."

For instance, my friend Adam Gilbert founded My Body Tutor, a program that provides this kind of accountability. Daily interaction with a "tutor" helps people monitor and change their diet and exercise habits. "People want to do it alone," he said, "but why? I tell them, 'You get help in other areas of your life. Why not with this?'"

An accountability partner doesn't even need to be human. For years, I felt accountable to our family schnauzer, Paddywhack. In high school, when I was trying to stick to the habit of regular running, I always took Paddywhack with me. She leaped with joy every time I put on my running shoes, and her eagerness made it harder for me to skip a day, and strengthened my exercise habit. In fact, one study—admittedly, by a pet-health-care company—showed that dog owners get more exercise, and enjoy it more, than people who go to the gym; older people walk more regularly with a dog than when they walk with another person.

Even imaginary accountability can be helpful. I'm a devout fan of the gym InForm Fitness and its "Super Slow" strength-training method, and I've persuaded so many friends and family members to go that I'm their number-one referrer. One day my trainer told me, "A lot of your friends think you're keeping tabs on them."

"Really?" I was somehow flattered to hear this. "Why? I don't know what they do."

"They think you know whether they're showing up."

I thought this over as I suffered through the leg press machine. "Do you think it helps them to keep coming regularly?"

"I think it does."

I'd become an accountability partner without even knowing it.

But acting as an accountability partner can be tricky. I don't want people to dread contact with me because I make them feel guilty about some broken habit. Also, it's a lot of work to be a reliable accountability partner. Accountability partners often work better if the people aren't particularly close, or if the accountability is mutual, or if a person is paid to hold someone accountable. Adam Gilbert calls this the "peer or pro" issue, and he's very pro-pro. "People don't take peers seriously," he told me. "They do better with a pro."

"Because they're paying?" I asked.

"Maybe people value it more if they pay for it. But I don't think it's really about money. A peer isn't going to tell you the hard truths. You need a pro."

Sometimes we expect someone to act as an accountability partner—but that person doesn't accept that responsibility. A writer friend is an Obliger, and she asked her editor to give her accountability.

"When I signed the contract to write this memoir," she said, "I told my editor, 'I can only write when I have to turn something in, and I don't want to wait until the last minute to work on this book. Please, give me some fake deadlines along the way.' But he said, 'Don't worry, the book will be great, you'll get it done, blah, blah.' He just kept being so generous and understanding."

"What happened?"

"I wrote the whole thing the three weeks before it was due. It could have been so much better if I'd started work earlier."

Out of misguided consideration, the editor had refused to provide accountability. If he'd understood that my friend was an Obliger, he could've taken a different approach.

While individuals can be accountability partners, it can also be useful to join an accountability group. As Alcoholics Anonymous, Weight Watchers, and Happiness Project groups demonstrate, we give and get accountability, as well as energy and ideas, when we meet with like-minded people. For several years, some friends were in a thesis-writing group. They met regularly at a bar to report on their progress—and to hold each other accountable. "The accountability to the group really helped me get work done," one friend told me. "And it was a lot of fun."

A *Better Than Before* habits group would be a terrific way for people to hold each other accountable for whatever habits they're trying to form. A group might be made up of friends, family members, co-workers, or strangers brought together by a common desire to work on their habits. Members of the group need not even share the same aims; it's enough that they're all determined to change their habits.

Nothing can replace face-to-face interactions, but when that's not practical, accountability groups and accountability partners can use technology to help them connect. Virtual accountability is less intense, but more convenient.

Another way to harness the Strategy of Accountability is to use a "commitment device"—that is, some mechanism that bolsters our habits by locking us into a decision. We can't change our minds, or if we do, we're heavily penalized. The lowly china piggy bank is a child's commitment device, and adults may open a Christmas account, which levies charges against account holders who withdraw savings before the holiday. According to legend, novelist Victor Hugo's eccentric commitment device was to order his servant to take away his clothing for the day. Left naked in his study, with only paper and pen, Hugo had nothing to do but write.

Many people will pay extra for a commitment device. Half of a popular snack item's loyal buyers said they'd pay 15 percent more if the snack came in a package that helped them control their consumption. As an example of this attitude, I saw a neighborhood gourmet grocery store cleverly exploit people's desire to eat less Halloween candy: when the chain store across the street was selling big bags of mini candy bars for $2.99, the gourmet store offered its own smaller, homemade bags of the identical candy for $4.99. A customer paid more to get less candy.

Cost can be an effective commitment device in other ways, too. A friend who goes to my gym got special permission to buy a package of fifty sessions, instead of the usual twenty-four maximum, as a way to deepen her commitment to exercise; she knew she'd never allow herself to waste that money.

One flashy kind of commitment device is the "nuclear option." A friend who enjoys experimenting with strategies of personal productivity used this approach to quit drinking for sixty days. He gave his assistant a stamped, addressed envelope with a check he'd written to an "anti-charity," an organization whose policies he passionately opposes, with the instruction to mail the check if he had a drink before the time was up.

"Did it work?" I asked.

"Absolutely. I'd raised the stakes, plus I'd tied drinking to my core values. There's no way I'd send a check to that hateful group. It worked so well," he added, "that my mother did it too. If she had a drink before her time was up, she had to give money to her grandsons to buy video games. She considers that a terrible waste of money."

"Did she stick to it?"

"Yes, and it was funny to hear my nephews beg her, 'Come on, Grandma! Have a glass of wine. You deserve it!'"

This kind of commitment device is probably more useful for hitting a limited goal, such as giving up drinking for sixty days or finishing a big report, rather than for tackling a habit change that's intended to last indefinitely. However, used wisely, it might help to jump-start a long-term habit.

All Four Tendencies (even, under certain circumstances, Rebels) find Accountability to be useful for developing habits. Obligers, however, *require* structures of external accountability to meet expectations. Therefore, when trying to form a habit, they benefit enormously from oversight, deadlines, and consequences, and from the involvement of accountability partners, such as coaches, trainers, personal health navigators, financial planners, personal organizers, friends—or, often, their own children. Many Obligers feel a powerful sense of obligation to be good role models.

From the vantage point of our own Tendency, it can be hard to remember how different the world looks to people in the other categories, and how important the Strategy of Accountability can be. While

I was waiting to speak at a conference, I fell into conversation with a computer science professor. A thirty-second conversation established that he was, beyond any doubt, a fellow Upholder.

"I've been thinking about how to help my grad students be more productive," he told me. "During our weekly meetings about their papers, they often don't have much progress to show me. It's a waste of everyone's time. So I'm thinking they might do better if I get rid of the weekly meetings and just meet with them when they have progress to report."

"No, no, *no!*" I said, before I stopped myself and tried to make my tone more reasonable. "I'm not sure that would be helpful." I gave him a quick overview of my taxonomy and suggested, "Getting rid of that meeting is something that would appeal to Upholders like us, because we don't need much supervision and don't struggle with deadlines. But very few people are Upholders, and many of your struggling students are probably Obligers, which means they need *more* accountability, not less. Or else they're Questioners, who may be thinking, 'Why do I have to work on this now? Why not next week? My paper isn't due for such a long time.' Don't worry about the Rebels. They'll do the work in their own time, in their own way."

"So what could I do?"

"Provide external accountability. Tell them you expect to see substantial new progress each week. Give them milestones to hit and hold them to it. The more accountable they feel, and the more they believe you expect to see consistent progress, the better they'll do."

"Then there's the problem of deadlines," he added. "One of my most brilliant students does great work, but his grade drops because he's always late."

"Well, that may be something different. Failing to hit a deadline may be plain old procrastination—'a due date is a suggestion, not a deadline'—or it may be self-sabotage. Instead of doing his best work and being judged, he does it at the last minute. That way, if he does well, he can say, 'I'm so brilliant that I do well even when I throw something together,' and if he does poorly, he can say, 'What do you expect? I did that work in two days.'"

It was time for me to give my presentation, but as we said good-bye, I couldn't help adding one last word. "Remember, Upholders like you and me don't need a lot of external accountability because we're accountable to ourselves, but other people don't see the world the way we do." I was reminding myself of this truth as much as I was reminding him.

THE BEST TIME
TO BEGIN

Any beginning presents an important opportunity for habit formation, because a beginning allows two powerful elements to combine: *novelty* and *habit*. The novelty of a new start wipes out our previous habits, and that absence allows new habits to crowd in. With a little effort, we can take advantage of this window of possibility to shape the habits we want. This section explores three strategies that take their power from new endeavors, new circumstances, and new ideas: First Steps, Clean Slate, and Lightning Bolt.

IT'S ENOUGH TO BEGIN

First Steps

What saves a man is to take a step. Then another step. It is always the same step, but you have to take it.

—ANTOINE DE SAINT-EXUPÉRY, *Wind, Sand and Stars*

Some habit-formation strategies are familiar and obvious—like Monitoring or Scheduling—but others took me more time to understand. As I studied habits, I slowly began to recognize the tremendous importance of the time of beginning.

The most important step is the *first step*. All those old sayings are really true. Well begun is half done. Don't get it perfect, get it going. A journey of a thousand miles begins with a single step. Nothing is more exhausting than the task that's never started, and strangely, *starting* is often far harder than *continuing*.

That first step is tough. Every action has an ignition cost: getting myself to the gym and changed into my gym clothes can be more challenging than actually working out. That's why good habits are a tremendous help: they make the starting process automatic.

Without yet having a name for it, in fact, I'd invoked the power of the Strategy of First Steps as I was starting to write this book. I'd spent months reading and taking copious notes, and I had a giant document with a jumble of material about habits. This initial period of research for a book is always exhilarating, but eventually I have to begin the painstaking labor of actual analysis and writing.

What was the most auspicious date to start? I asked myself. The first day of the week, or the month, or the year? Or my birthday? Or the start of the school year? Then I realized that I was beginning to invoke tomorrow logic.

Nope. *Begin now.* I was ready. Take the first step. It's enough to begin.

Now is an unpopular time to take a first step. Won't things be easier—for some not-quite-specified reason—in the future? I have a fantasy of what I'll be like tomorrow: Future-Gretchen will spontaneously start a good new habit, with no planning and no effort necessary; it's quite pleasant to think about how virtuous I'll be, *tomorrow.* But there is no Future-Gretchen, only Now-Gretchen.

A friend told me about how she used tomorrow logic: "I use a kind of magical thinking to procrastinate. I make up questionable rules like 'I can't start working at 10:10, I need to start on the hour' or 'It's already 4:00, it's too late to start working.' But the truth is that I should just *start.*" It's common to hear people say, "I'll start my new habit after the holidays are over/I've settled into my new job/my kids are a little older." Or worse, the double-remove: "I'll start my new habit once I'm back in shape."

Tomorrow logic wastes time, and also it may allow us to deny that our current actions clash with our intentions. In an argument worthy of the White Queen, we tell ourselves, absolutely, I'm committed to reading aloud to my children, and I will read to them tomorrow, and tomorrow, and tomorrow—just not today.

The same tendency can lead us to overcommit to responsibilities that take place in the comfortably distant future—but eventually the future arrives, and then we're stuck. My father-in-law has a mental habit to correct for that kind of tomorrow logic. He told me, "If I'm asked to do something—give a speech, attend an event—I always imagine that it's happening next week. It's too easy to agree to do something that's six months off, then the time comes, and I'm sorry I agreed to do it."

When taking the first step toward a new habit, a key question from the Strategy of Distinctions is "Do I prefer to take small steps or big steps?"

Many people succeed best when they keep their starting steps as small and manageable as possible; by doing so, they gain the habit of the habit, and the feeling of mastery. They begin their new yoga routine by doing three poses, or start work on a big writing project by drafting a single sentence in a writing session.

As an exercise zealot, I was pleased when my mother told me that she was trying to make a habit of going for a daily walk.

"But I'm having trouble sticking to it," she told me.

"How far are you going?"

"Twice around Loose Park," she told me, "which is about two miles."

"Try going just *once* around the park," I suggested. That worked. When she started smaller, she was able to form the habit.

Small steps can be particularly helpful when we're trying to do something that seems overwhelming. If I can get myself to take that first small step, I usually find that I can keep going. I invoked this principle when I was prodding myself to master Scrivener, a writers' software program. Scrivener would help me organize my enormous trove of notes, but I dreaded starting: installing the software; synchronizing between my laptop and desktop computers; and most difficult, figuring out how to use it.

Each day gave me a new opportunity to push the task off until tomorrow. Tomorrow, I'd feel like dealing with it. "Start *now*," I finally thought. "Just take the first step." I started with the smallest possible step, which was to find the website where I could buy the software. Okay, I thought. I can do that. And then I did. I had a lot of hard work ahead of me—it's a Secret of Adulthood: things often get harder before they get easier—but I'd started. The next day, with a feeling of much greater confidence and calm, I watched the tutorial video. Then I created my document. And then—I started my book.

However, some people do better when they push themselves more boldly; a big challenge holds their interest and helps them persist. A friend was determined to learn French, so he moved to France for six months.

Along those lines, the *Blast Start* can be a helpful way to take a first step. The Blast Start is the opposite of taking the smallest possible first step because it requires a period of high commitment. It's demanding, but its intensity can energize a habit. For instance, after reading Chris Baty's book *No Plot? No Problem!*—which explains how to write a novel in a month—I wrote a novel in thirty days, as a way to spark my creativity. This kind of shock treatment can't be maintained forever, but it's fun and gives momentum to the habit. A twenty-one-day project, a detox, a cleanse, an ambitious goal, a boot camp—by tackling *more* instead of *less* for a certain period, I get a surge of energy and focus. (Not to mention bragging rights.) In particular, I love the retreat model. Three times, I've set aside a few days to work on a book during every waking hour, with breaks only for meals and for exercise. These periods of intensity help fuel my daily writing habit.

However, a Blast Start is, by definition, unsustainable over the long term. It's very important to plan specifically how to shift from the intensity of the Blast Start into the habit that will continue indefinitely.

There's no right way or wrong way, just whatever works.

I'd noticed something perverse in myself. If I feel anxious about the fact that I haven't started, I become even more reluctant to start, which just makes me more anxious. When I fretted about the fact that I hadn't sent out Eleanor's birthday party invitations, I felt an almost irresistible urge to put off dealing with them. When I took too long to reply to an irksome email, I kept putting it off for another day.

That's the trap of procrastination, and taking the first step is a way to escape. If I dread starting a task, just making a plan for beginning—

jotting down a to-do list, finding the right link (as I did for the Scrivener website), locating the instructions—helps me start. This first step almost feels like cheating, because I'm not actually doing the task I'm avoiding. But taking this first step makes taking the second and third steps much easier, because I've already started.

For me, it's hard to make phone calls. Except to speak to family members, I put off making phone calls, which makes daily life more difficult.

So I decided to make a new habit: make the call today. I have to call eventually, and postponement just makes it worse. I note any calls that I need to make, and as soon as possible, I follow through. The call to the eye doctor about Eliza's dry eyes. The call to my accountant. The call about the leaky pipe in my home office.

"Make the call today" helped me start a new habit of donating regularly to a thrift shop. I want to keep our apartment clutter-free, and I'd accumulated a cabinet full of things we no longer wanted. I live in a neighborhood with several thrift stores, and since we moved here *eleven years ago* I'd been meaning to stop in to ask the store's policies on donations.

Because I didn't know exactly what to do, the discard pile kept growing. Somehow—even though I knew it was ridiculous—I worried that the shops would scoff at my donations, or tell me I was doing something wrong (Upholder concerns). But I knew that if I found a place where I could easily drop things off, I'd get in the habit of doing so.

I'd never been able to get started. Okay, start now, make the call.

I got the number of the closest thrift shop, just three blocks away, and steeled myself to pick up the phone—and I spoke to a very nice man at the Arthritis Foundation. Yes, they accepted VHS tapes and shoes, but not books.

Making this phone call had a surprising effect on me. Suddenly, I could envision myself dropping things off at the thrift store. And what was the worst they could do? Reject my box of VHS tapes? The next Saturday, I walked the three blocks to the store, spotted a "Do-nations" sign at the back, and deposited my box under the sign. Done.

Taking the first step is hard, and every first step requires some kind of transition. Adults help children to manage transition—by giving them bedtime routines, cleanup reminders, and warnings of "Five more minutes!"—but we adults often expect ourselves to career effortlessly from one activity to the next. I'm in the habit of writing a blog post every day, yet every day I have to gear up to start. Running activities too closely together makes me feel harried and irritable, and habits of transition help me to switch gears more calmly.

I love my morning transition from sleep to family time. I wake up early, even on the weekends, because I never want to miss that time to myself.

Other people have their own transition rituals. A friend said, "I drop my son off at school, then I buy myself coffee and read celebrity gossip from 9:15 to 10:00, then I start work." Another friend explained: "When I was working on my daily writing habit, I didn't think about writing, I thought about my prewriting ritual. I sat down at the computer, put on my headphones, and turned on my Writing Music mix. By the second or third song, I wouldn't even hear the music anymore, but it was a clear signal that it was time to write. I've listened to it 267 times." Another friend said, "I can't just show up at the gym and work out. There's a cafe there, so I take my laptop and work on my thesis. After an hour or so, I'm ready to exercise."

Jamie has a transition habit when he comes home from work. He gives everyone a hello kiss, then disappears for twenty minutes or so. He changes out of his suit, sends one last round of emails, glances at a magazine, and then he's ready to join the family. Because I'm always eager to cross things off my to-do list, I often want to hit him with scheduling issues or chore requests as soon as I see him. Thinking about the importance of transitions made me realize that I should respect his habit and save my questions until he'd settled in.

A friend's husband has a more idiosyncratic transition. He sits on a sofa that faces a built-in bookcase, and, one arm flung over the sofa back, looks at the bookcase. "He calls it 'staring at the bookcase,'" she told me. "He's not meditating or anything like that, and I can talk to him, but he wants fifteen minutes to stare at the bookcase when he gets home."

Regular bedtime habits can ease the challenging transition from waking to sleeping, and help us fall sleep faster and sleep more deeply. A friend who works in finance and travels all the time, and who definitely doesn't seem to be the bath type, needs a bath before he can get into bed, no matter how late his day ends.

I wish Jamie had a habit like that, because he really struggles to fall asleep. Habits cheerleader that I am, I kept pointing out good sleep habits, such as "Don't watch TV before bedtime," "Don't check your email before bed, it gets you all riled up," "Don't stare into a glowing screen, the light will make you more alert," and "Let's open a window, because cooling the body down helps to prepare for sleep." He ignored all these suggestions—except for the open window.

Finally, though, I dropped the issue. If Jamie didn't want to change his habits, I couldn't change them for him. I remembered a joke that a psychiatrist friend told me, "How many shrinks does it take to change a lightbulb?" "Only one, but the lightbulb has to want to change." My lightbulb didn't want to change.

I had a problem nighttime habit myself. For me, and for many people, transitions often trigger the urge to snack or drink—and choices are generally not of the celery or chamomile tea variety. I'd fallen into the habit of wandering into the kitchen around 9:00 to forage, because even though I wasn't hungry, I craved a snack. The evening felt incomplete without it. But I didn't like this habit, so I decided to quit eating after dinner.

I'd often heard the advice to brush my teeth after dinner, as a way to quit night snacking. I doubted that this could make a difference, but decided to give it a try. Instead of brushing my teeth right before I went to bed, I started to brush my teeth after I finished tucking in Eleanor, around 8:30.

To my astonishment, this simple habit proved highly effective; my urge to snack drops after I brush my teeth. As I brush, I think, "No more eating for today, that's finished," and that thought, along with the clean feeling in my mouth, helps to end the eating portion of my evening. Also, many years of nightly brushing have made me connect the experience of toothpaste with the transition to bedtime.

By examining these moments of transition, we can make small changes that yield big benefits.

I pay a lot of attention to *starting*—and also to *stopping*. Because taking the first step is so important, and often so difficult, I try not to falter in my steps once I've started. But any change can trigger a stop: bad weather, work travel, vacation, illness, a new boss, a new baby, a change in a child's schedule, a new home, someone else's stopping (a coworker can no longer go for a lunchtime run). If I stop, I have to take that very first step all over again—and I very well may not do it.

Stopping halts momentum, breeds guilt, makes us feel bad about losing ground, and, worst of all, breaks the habit so that the need for decision making returns—which demands energy, and often results in making a bad decision.

Stopping is a particular problem with the habit of exercise, and for this reason, my yoga instructor doesn't let people stop. He gives a lot of private instruction, and many of his clients leave town in the summer. "People tell me, 'I'm stopping for the summer, but I'll call you when I get back in September,'" he told me. "I say, 'No, you're not stopping. I'm canceling these certain appointments, but you're still in my schedule, and I'll see you at the usual time on September 4. If you can't make it that day, we'll reschedule.' "

"That way, they don't feel like they're stopping?"

"Right. If they stop, they might not start, but this way, they never do 'stop.' "

Along the same lines, when Lori, my trainer at the strength-training gym, left the gym, I switched to another trainer without hesitation. However, many of my friends also trained with Lori, and I discovered that for several of them, Lori's departure was a "stopping" point. Again and again, I heard, "I just don't want to train with anyone but Lori." And I noticed that this feeling seemed stronger among people who were more reluctant to visit a gym.

One friend told me, "I don't want to go if Lori is gone. I'd like to do some different kind of exercise anyway, just for a change. I'm going to find something else."

Now, this is a friend I know *very well*—well enough to be very skeptical of this plan. She'll ski, play tennis, hike, and swim, but she hates regular "exercise." Nevertheless, she'd managed to form the habit of strength training.

"You're going to find exercise you like better than this—once a week for twenty minutes, no shower, no music, no mirrors? Like *what*?" I pressed. "It seems like a bad idea to let yourself stop this habit before you're well started on something else."

I saw her several weeks later. "What did you do about strength training?" I asked.

"Oh, you're right," she said with a sigh. "I have to find something new before I quit. Anyway, I worked out with a new trainer, and it was fine."

The fact is, while some habits are almost unbreakable, some habits remain fragile, even after years. We must guard against anything that might weaken a valuable habit. Every added link in the chain strengthens the habit—and any break in the chain marks a potential stopping point.

For many people, don't-break-the-chain is a powerful strategy—
for the same reason that some people want to get the attendance award
in grade school. It's very satisfying to have a perfect record. Comedian Jerry Seinfeld advised aspiring comedian Brad Isaac that, because
daily writing was the key to writing better jokes, Isaac should buy a
calendar with a box for every day of the year, and every day, after
writing, cross off the day with a big red X. "After a few days you'll
have a chain," Seinfeld explained. "You'll like seeing that chain, especially when you get a few weeks under your belt. Your only job next
is to not break the chain."

A friend told me, "I got in a bad habit of blowing off our three-
times-a-week staff meeting. Most of the meeting is irrelevant to me,
but often I did miss a few key points. After one particularly bad situation, I made a rule: I'd never miss a single staff meeting. Now I want
to keep my perfect record."

Upholders find this chain approach very satisfying, because they
love to cross items off a to-do list. Questioners find it useful if they
expect to find it useful; otherwise, they won't bother with it. Rebels
resist the notion of the chain—and just the name "chain" explains
why. They want to choose an action each time and generally won't
bind themselves. For some Obligers, the chain approach is helpful,
if they develop a feeling of accountability to the chain itself. These
Obligers may need a form of external accountability to get the chain
started, but once it's under way, they often can keep it going out of a
sense of obligation.

No matter what our Tendency, when faced with an unavoidable
stopping point—such as a long trip or a summer break—it helps to
commit to a specific day to jump back into the habit, as my yoga instructor requires. Something that can be done at *any* time often happens at *no* time, and waiting vaguely for the right time to start again
is very risky. (Starting *tomorrow* usually sounds like a good plan.) But
the more tomorrows go by, the more intimidating it becomes to take
that first step back.

Another reason to avoid stopping a good habit is that, sadly, starting *again* is often far harder than starting the *first time*. It's natural to think, "Oh, I did this before, it will be easy to do it again," but often it's much harder to start again. True, taking that first step the first time around can be hard, but there's also a special energy and optimism to launching a new habit. When I've tried to summon up the same energy for restarting a lapsed habit, it hasn't worked very well. The novelty has worn off, I've remembered all the reasons I struggle with that habit, and it's discouraging to feel myself backsliding.

A friend told me, "I quit drinking for a month, and I really enjoyed the challenge. When the month was up, I started drinking again, as I'd planned to do. After a while, I thought it would be good to give up alcohol again for another month. I expected it to be easy because it had been easy the first time, but I couldn't do it again. It wasn't the same."

"Indefinitely"—or even worse, "forever"—is where habit change becomes unnerving. Often, with our good habits, *there is no finish line.* We can imagine taking those first steps but become overwhelmed at the prospect of never stopping. Am I going to meditate *forever*?

It's one thing to resist a single major temptation, or to make a brief, heroic effort during a Blast Start, or even to train for a marathon or to give up chocolate for a year, but to trudge along with a good habit, *forever*, can feel too demanding. It requires a surrender—an acceptance of the way we must live to abide by our own values.

Persisting with a habit can be particularly hard when the habit doesn't yield flashy results. While there's the satisfaction of knowing that I'm doing what's good for me and holding myself to my intentions, rarely do I achieve glorious outcomes. I've found, however, that if I can get through this dry period, the habit truly takes over and proves itself by making my life better than before.

I'd been wondering whether I should drop the habit of meditation because it seemed pointless. Then, for the first time, it seemed as though it might be making a difference. Late one night, I was ruminating about various disagreeable moments from my day, and the longer I lay awake, the angrier I got at the thought of how much sleep I was losing. Then I envisioned my most helpful meditation image: snow falling on Bethesda Fountain in Central Park. It sort of worked. So I decided to stick to the meditation habit, at least for now. Or rather, I decided not to make a decision about it.

Habits are the behaviors that I want to follow forever, without decisions, without debate, no stopping, no finish lines. Thinking about *forever* can be intimidating, so the one-day-at-a-time concept helps many people stick to their good habits. A friend told me, "I remind myself, 'What I'm eating now isn't necessarily forever, it's just for right now,' and that helps me stick to it. One day at a time—even though I do plan to eat this way forever."

Again, this is where deciding-not-to-decide comes to the rescue. I don't revisit my habits. I just think, "This is what I'm doing today." Trust the habit. I take that first step, over and over and over.

TEMPORARY BECOMES PERMANENT

Clean Slate

There is no creature whose inward being is so strong that it is not greatly determined by what lies outside it.

—GEORGE ELIOT, *Middlemarch*

Any *beginning* is a time of special power for habit creation, and at certain times we experience a clean slate, in which circumstances change in a way that makes a fresh start possible—if we're alert for the opportunity.

Many people deliberately use the New Year or their birthdays as a clean slate, but it can take many forms. The slate may be wiped clean by a change in personal relationships: marriage, divorce, a new baby, a new puppy, a breakup, a new friend, a death. Or the slate may be wiped clean by a change in surroundings: a new apartment, a new city, even rearranged furniture. Or some major aspect of life may change: a new job, a new school, a new doctor. A lawyer friend told me, "As a single parent, I've always felt a duty to maximize my earnings. Last year, my son graduated, and I realized, 'I've paid my last tuition payment. He's grown up. Now what am I working for?' It was like a whole new world of possibilities opened up." Sometimes a major change leads to a clean slate, but even a minor change can be sufficient—a change as seemingly insignificant as taking a different route to work, or watching TV in a different room.

Even an unhappy change can be a chance for a fresh start. A reader posted on my blog: "My husband died in November. I've always been introverted, and while I love people, I found socializing tiring. But after losing my husband, I was worried about depression and loneliness, so I made a *ton* of social plans. I knew people would understand if I cancelled, and I thought that having lots of people around would be smart. Six months later, I still make plans to do something social almost every day. It's a striking change, and it's really working for me."

Another aspect of the Strategy of the Clean Slate? There's a magic to the beginning of anything. We want to begin right, and a good start feels auspicious. Anytime I'm trying to work on a habit, I make sure to follow it on Monday, because if I start my week feeling in control and virtuous, I'm more likely to maintain that good habit.

We can take steps to heighten the sense of possibility, of newness—the luxury of untracked snow or a new carton of eggs—afforded by the clean slate. One person might begin an important habit in a place that's very beautiful, such as a grand hotel or the beach at sunset; another person might make an extravagant gesture, such as putting a hammer through a TV screen or cutting up credit cards; another person might transform a home or office by painting the walls and buying new furniture. I talked to a woman who marks the clean slate of the new year in a very literal way by tossing out everything in her fridge, right down to the mustard and pickles. As an underbuyer, I was a bit shocked by this, but when I pressed her to explain, all she could say was "I want to start fresh."

The clean slate moment is easy to overlook, however, and too often we don't recognize that some fresh start is triggering a habit change. Because we're creatures of habit, the first marks on that slate often prove indelible. We should start the way we want to continue.

In the first few days after we moved to a new apartment, I started my workday with an hour of email and social media—and bam! this habit locked into my day with iron strength. Whether or not it's the best habit to follow, I wouldn't be able to change it now without terrific effort. In college, where I sat on the first day of class determined where I sat for the rest of the semester. I now pay very close attention to the first few times I do anything because I know those decisions will shape my baseline habits; to deviate from them will feel like a deprivation or an imposition.

The Strategy of the Clean Slate can help us launch a new habit with less effort. During law school, I would have declared it impossible to wake up and go to the gym. But without consciously considering the clean slate, when I started a clerkship, I made the gym part of my daily routine. From my first day on the job, I went to the gym before work. It wasn't easy, even with a clean slate, but if I'd waited a month—or even a week—to start this routine, it would've felt much more burdensome. I would've thought, how can I possibly get up earlier, work out, shower away from home, dress at the gym, and walk ten blocks to my judge's chambers, before 9:00?

A workaholic friend told me that she was starting a new job and wanted to work more reasonable hours than she had at her last job.

"Use the Strategy of the Clean Slate," I suggested. "Decide when you think you should leave the office and start the habit of leaving at that time every night for the first week. That will set your habits going forward."

"Leaving about 6:30 or 7:00 sounds good to me, but I think I'll want to stay later during my first week, to get settled in."

"Don't you think you're likely to continue the way you start?" I pointed out. "Decide what you want your habit to be and discipline yourself to walk out the door at that time, right from the beginning. It's not going to get *easier* to leave, you're not going to have *less* work do after six months than you do on the first day."

I know how tight the grip of habit can be, and my friend was still, mentally, in the habit of leaving at 9:00. But if she didn't use the clean slate to start over, she was unlikely to shake that habit.

It's a Secret of Adulthood: What we assume will be temporary often becomes permanent; what we assume is permanent often proves temporary.

It's a shame not to exploit the power of the Strategy of the Clean Slate when it presents itself. For instance, the time of *moving* introduces so much upheaval into our customary habits that change becomes far easier. In one study of people trying to make a change—such as changes in career or education, relationships, addictive behaviors, or health behaviors including dieting—36 percent of successful changes were associated with a move to a new place. Another study found that if students wanted to watch less TV and exercise more, they changed habits more easily after a switch to a new university. A blog reader commented, "My family is about to purchase a new home. In previous moves, I've made the mistake of thinking that I'd magically change my old cluttering habits just because I'd be living in a new place and making a fresh start. The problem was, I didn't understand exactly what I was doing that allowed the clutter to accumulate, and I didn't have a plan for preventing it. This time we're trying to prepare first by cleaning out and by planning ahead for the new habits, to avoid falling into the same old traps."

Even a temporary move or a trip can act as a clean slate. My father told me, "Quitting smoking was the hardest thing I've ever done. But right after I quit, I went on a business trip to Micronesia for ten weeks, and that made it easier." All his old habits were disrupted, and the flood of new impressions helped to keep the thought of cigarettes at bay.

As I'd told my workaholic friend, the Clean Slate of a new job is a good time to enforce a new habit. One guy told me how he managed to change his email habits: "For years, I'd been drowning in email. I switched jobs, and ever since I got that new email address, I've forced myself to get to inbox-zero every night: I answer, delete, or file *every single* email for the day. I could never have caught up with the emails for my old job," he explained, "but I could start fresh."

Sometimes a clean slate takes us by surprise. For instance, my mother has always had a very strong sweet tooth. A few years ago, she caught a terrible stomach flu, and when she at last recovered, she found that she'd lost her craving for sweets. It would have been easy for her to slip back into her former eating habits, but fortunately, she realized that she had a clean slate, and although her sweet tooth returned, she has avoided eating sweets ever since.

While the clean slate offers tremendous opportunity for forming new habits, it can disrupt a person's existing good habits by eliminating a useful cue or breaking up a positive routine. Routines are chains of habits, and when just one seemingly insignificant link weakens, it can disrupt the entire habit chain. For instance, research shows that people are more likely to alter their buying habits—often without noticing—when they're experiencing a major life change, such as marriage, divorce, career change, or having someone join or leave the household. Eating habits may also shift at times of significant change. Marriage and divorce can affect people's weight, especially after age thirty: for women, the risk of a large weight gain comes after marriage, for men, after divorce. One blog reader wrote: "I've always been a regular exerciser, but once my son started taking the bus to school, I stopped. Why? Because my routine was to drop him off at school, then go right to the gym. It was an ingrained habit. When he stopped taking the bus, the trigger was gone." Someone else wrote: "We're a military family who moves every few years. That means I have to be very careful about sticking to my good habits, even when everything keeps changing around me. It's really hard."

It can be surprisingly hard to recognize when change threatens to wipe the slate clean—another reason why Monitoring is helpful. When we monitor, we notice as soon as a good habit becomes disrupted.

———

Studying the power of the Strategy of the Clean Slate made me want to harness it for my own benefit. But how? No major aspect of my life was likely to change soon—or if something did change, it would likely be for the worse. I didn't anticipate having a clean slate in my family, my work, my apartment, or my neighborhood. I wished I could think of a way to start something new.

Eight years ago, I started my blog, and the clean slate it provided was enormously satisfying. Because I'd decided to post six days a week, the blog had a tremendous effect on my daily habits: I had to master the mechanics of blogging; I had to write and publish a piece every day; I had to adopt the habit of reaching out to other people; and because I post a weekly video, I had to adopt the habit of making videos. I met new people, learned new skills, and increased the amount of writing I did every day.

That clean slate had been terrific. But what could I do now? One idea: get a dog. Jamie and my daughters would love to have a dog, and people get so much happiness from dogs—and they do tend to foster good habits. But I can't even manage to take care of a houseplant. These days, in the rush hour of life, I didn't want the added responsibility and time commitment required by a dog (because I wasn't going to kid myself, all the unpleasant tasks of dog ownership would fall to me). So no. No dog.

Could I join a new group? Joining a group is a clean slate of relationships. It's a way to enter a new social scene and, often, an area of learning. Every time I've joined a group, I've made new friends, gained knowledge, and had fun. Again, however, I felt pressed for time. I'd reached my limit for extracurriculars, if I wanted to have enough time for my family and my work.

My opportunities to use the Strategy of the Clean Slate seemed limited—but maybe I was just falling prey to inertia and lack of imagination. Surely I could find a way to make a new beginning.

In the end, I couldn't think of a dramatic clean slate, so I decided to try something simple—very simple—to invoke its power. I cleared and rearranged Eleanor's room and gave away many toys that she'd outgrown. Though I felt wistful as I packed up her Fisher-Price Farm and My Little Pony Castle (I took photos to help us remember them), I discovered that the big pile of give-away boxes gave me a shot of energy and cheer. If I kept my eyes open, I'd surely find some additional opportunities for a clean slate.

DATA POINT OF ONE

Lightning Bolt

The conduct of our lives is the true reflection of our thoughts.

—MICHEL DE MONTAIGNE, "Of the Education of Children"

A clean slate can prompt us to make sudden and profound changes in our habits, both for good and for ill. But I discovered another, unexpected way to achieve an abrupt change—when, to my astonishment, I experienced this kind of new beginning, myself. But I didn't move to a new city or start a new job or get a puppy. None of my outward circumstances changed. All I did was read a book, and that action unleashed an enormous force: the Strategy of the Lightning Bolt.

Discussions of habit change often emphasize the importance of repeating an action, over and over, until it becomes automatic, and such repetition does indeed help to form habits. However, it's also true that sometimes we're hit by a lightning bolt that transforms our habits, instantly. We encounter some new idea, and suddenly a new habit replaces a long-standing habit—without preparation, without small steps, without wavering—and we pass from *before* to *after* in a moment. The Strategy of the Lightning Bolt takes its power from knowledge, beliefs, and ideas.

The Lightning Bolt is a highly effective strategy, but unfortunately, it's practically impossible to invoke on command. Unlike all the other strategies, it's not a strategy that we can decide to follow; *it's something that happens to us.* In an instant, we quit cursing or become vegetarian or begin a prayer practice or give up alcohol or stop using plastic shopping bags.

A milestone event—a marriage, a diagnosis, a death, an anniversary, hitting bottom, a birthday, an accident, a midlife crisis, a long journey taken alone—often triggers a Lightning Bolt, because we're smacked with some new idea that jolts us into change.

I know a doctor who treats many patients who have problems with drugs, alcohol, nicotine, junk food, and bad relationships. He told me, "There's one thing that sometimes allows people to change their habits overnight. They may have tried for years, but this happens and—bam, they're done, no problem."

"*What?*" I asked.

"Oh, you know it," he teased. "Think about it."

"I have no idea."

"Pregnancy," he said. "Over and over, I've seen a woman find out she's pregnant, and she's able to make a change. Not always, but sometimes. The idea that she's now a mother, and that the health of her baby depends on her actions, makes it possible."

But while sometimes a big event triggers a Lightning Bolt, sometimes it's something small, such as a passage in a book, a scene from a movie, or a casual comment by a stranger. A friend told me that he broke up with his girlfriend, and quit the heroin they'd both been using for years, when someone told him, "You act like she's the smarter one of the two of you, the better-looking one, the cooler one. But she's not, *you* are."

"But how did such a simple observation unleash such a huge change?" I asked, stunned.

"I'm not really sure," he answered. "It's just that I knew that was right. And I knew it was time to change." The Zen saying is eerily true: "When the student is ready, the teacher appears."

A friend who lost thirty-five pounds told me, "My weight has been a constant battle in my life. I was working out with a trainer who pushed me too hard, and I got tears in the meniscus in both knees, and I was in a lot of pain. When I asked the doctor, 'What can I do about this?' he said, 'Well, losing weight would help.' All of a sudden, it hit me. The pain will get worse; it won't get better unless I change."

A new insight can inspire a flash change. A friend was chronically late dropping off her son at sports activities until he said, "You're always late dropping me off because it doesn't affect you, but you're always on time to pick me up because you'd be embarrassed to be the last parent at pickup." She was never late again. Or change may be triggered by some small incident, as in the case of my friend who got in shape after he couldn't play touch football at his twenty-fifth college reunion.

The most surprising kind of Lightning Bolt is the bolt-from-the-blue change, which seems to lack any perceptible cause. A friend who smoked two packs of cigarettes a day for years quit smoking instantly. One night, on her way to meet someone for dinner, she was pulling a cigarette out of the pack when she thought, "Why am I doing this? Time to stop." She threw the pack in the trash and never smoked again. The physical discomfort lasted for three months, but she never wavered. "I just wasn't a smoker anymore," she told me. She hadn't planned ahead, she hadn't consciously been considering quitting, but she was hit by that Lightning Bolt.

A reader posted about a more modest change: "I dreaded my dentist appointment because I knew they'd ask how often I floss. It occurred to me that I could just floss every day, and then that question would never bother me. It puzzles me why the solution suddenly became so obvious and so easy in that moment."

Because the Strategy of the Lightning Bolt violates the assumption that habits are most enduring when they accrue gradually, some people overlook or dismiss it. But if it strikes, the Lightning Bolt can be enormously powerful, so we should watch for it and take advantage of its effortless, instantaneous change whenever we feel it at work in our minds.

―――――

I experienced a Lightning Bolt when a new idea about food over-turned my existing beliefs. I started a radical new habit almost on a whim, and since I started, I've never stopped.

I hadn't expected to make this change. When packing for a family beach vacation, I'd thrown in Gary Taubes's book *Why We Get Fat*. I wasn't interested in reading the book to lose weight myself. While I was careful about what I chose to eat, I was pretty comfortable with my current weight. I was intrigued by the title, however, and when I'd flipped through the book, I'd noticed that it included an extensive discussion of insulin—a subject that has interested me ever since Elizabeth was diagnosed with diabetes.

I read the entire book in two days, and it hit me with the force of the Lightning Bolt. Taubes's book makes a compelling case for "why we get fat," based on widely accepted facts about how the body works, observations of large populations, and a thorough review of the scientific research. It focuses on the effects of insulin, the hormone that's the main regulator of blood sugar and the use and storage of fat. There's no debate about the basic facts: a high insulin level causes the body to move glucose into fat cells to be stored, which means that the body will accumulate fat; a low insulin level causes glucose to be burned as fuel. And what causes a body's insulin level to be high or low? For the most part, diet. The more carbohydrates a person eats, and the easier these carbohydrates are to metabolize, the more insulin in the blood, and the more fat that accumulates.

Therefore, Taubes argues—and this is where controversy sets in—that in order to lower insulin and the body's tendency to accumulate fat, we should avoid eating easily digestible, high-carb food: sugar, bread, cereal, grains, pasta, potatoes, rice, corn, juice, beer, wine, soda. Taubes maintains that the quantity and quality of carbohydrates, not calories or exercise, chiefly accounts for why we get fat.

Taubes's heavily researched and carefully argued conclusions came as a shock to me. Since high school, I'd tried hard to eat healthfully. I ate almost no sugary foods and rarely drank alcohol. Oatmeal was one of my staples, along with thin-sliced whole-wheat bread, fruit, brown rice, and breakfast cereal with skim milk. For years, I'd made a hobby of eating the nonfat version of everything: nonfat yogurt, skim milk, egg whites only, turkey burgers. I almost never ate cheese or red meat.

I hadn't been planning to alter the way that I ate, but reading *Why We Get Fat* triggered a Lightning Bolt change in me. I saw my staple foods in a completely different way. Whole grains are carbohydrates. Meat is fine. Dietary fat, unsaturated or saturated, doesn't cause obesity or heart disease. Practically all processed foods are loaded with carbs. I put down the book, and overnight, I changed my entire approach to food.

Vacation was an excellent place to start. Because we were staying at a hotel, I didn't need to shop or cook different foods; I just ordered differently from the menu. With considerable trepidation, that first morning, instead of getting my usual hotel breakfast of bran cereal, skim milk, and fruit salad, I ate scrambled eggs and *bacon*.

Over the next several weeks, I continued to eat completely different foods from before, and the effect was dramatic. I was eating more calories than I had in years, I was never hungry between meals (which had been a real problem before), and pounds kept dropping off me until I stabilized at an all-time adult low, close to the bottom of my healthy weight range. I was convinced.

The Lightning Bolt gave me the passion of the new believer, and as a low-carb zealot, I became inspired to try to persuade others. My first real convert was my father. Eating healthfully is an important issue for him. He's in his mid-seventies, and he was always trying to lose some weight. He's taken statins and blood pressure medication for years. He's very focused on heart health because his grandfather died at sixty-four, and his father died at fifty-seven, both from heart attacks.

For me, a Lightning Bolt triggered the changes in my eating habits, but when my father changed his eating habits, it was due less to a sudden Lightning Bolt (though I'm sure that he was impressed by the abrupt transformation I underwent) and more to an appeal to his Questioner nature, through his exposure to new arguments and data. I told him to read *Why We Get Fat* and *Good Calories, Bad Calories*, and he became entirely convinced by the research. Instead of making a dramatic, overnight change, as I'd done, he began by making a few simple substitutions—having a side of vegetables instead of potatoes and ordering steak instead of pasta. Getting good results convinced him of the validity of the low-carb approach, and over time he began to follow it more rigorously.

"I'm inching down toward two hundred pounds, and my weight just slowly keeps dropping," he reported several weeks after he'd read the book. "I can eat this way forever."

"But he's still drinking wine," added my mother, who was also on the phone.

"Yes, that'd be the last thing to go," he said cheerfully. "But I'm still seeing a good result."

"Progress, not perfection," I told him. "Even if you make exceptions sometimes, you're eating better than before."

My father had read the book and embraced this approach with gratifying enthusiasm, but most people were skeptical. One friend, in particular, thought I'd lost my mind and quizzed me at length.

"You don't eat *fruit*?" he asked. (I've learned it's the fact that I don't eat fruit that makes many people decide I'm crazy.)

"Sometimes I eat berries," I said. "Look, I know it sounds extreme, but it really doesn't feel that way."

I knew how unlikely that must sound to him, but it was true. I read a book, and suddenly, effortlessly, I ate in a completely different way—it was as if those other foods were no longer edible. But that's the power of the Lightning Bolt. People raise valid environmental and humane concerns about eating meat, but I'm more focused on the aspect of nutrition and health.

Plus, as often happens with habits, the habit became self-reinforcing. Once I stopped eating carbs, I lost my taste for them. Whether or not people actually get "addicted" to sugar, the more I ate foods like bread, cereal, and sweets, the more I wanted them. Now I don't even think about them.

"So when do you go back to eating normally?" my friend asked.

"This *is* eating normally." No finish line.

He shook his head. He had no interest in giving this approach a try.

After I'd adopted my new eating habits, I saw my friend, the hilarious writer A. J. Jacobs, at a reading for his book *Drop Dead Healthy*, at a hip indie bookstore in Brooklyn. Before his talk, I quizzed him about his decision, described in the book, to follow a mostly plant-based diet rather than a low-carb diet.

"But A. J.," I said, "I can't believe you weren't convinced about the low-carb approach."

He laughed. "There are a lot of scientists making arguments on the other side."

"Yes, but I've read all the arguments, and these arguments are better. Plus I've tried eating this way myself, and I'm less hungry and weigh less."

"But Gretchen, you're a data point of one," he pointed out. Meaning the experience of just one person isn't scientifically valid.

"True, but I'm the only data point I care about. That's the *most persuasive data point!*"

The person I really wanted to persuade about eating low-carb was my sister Elizabeth but I wasn't sure how to broach it. Because she's a type 1 diabetic, I believed this way of eating might help her bring her blood sugar level down and decrease her need for insulin. But Elizabeth bristles at requirements, and she dislikes having to give things up, and her diabetes already demanded so much from her. She had to inject herself with insulin five times a day, wear a monitor on her stomach, visit the doctor frequently, and watch what she ate. In general, she kept an eye on insulin-jacking foods such as bread, sugar, and potatoes, but she "cheated" fairly often and dealt with it by increasing her insulin dosage. *Why We Get Fat* would make the case that she should take a far stricter approach to her eating, which I knew she wouldn't like, so I kept delaying the conversation.

Finally, on the phone, she gave me the opening I'd been waiting for.

"What's this new way of eating you have?" she asked. "Mom said you and Dad have lost weight without dieting."

"Yes!" I said with relief. "I read this book about nutrition, and I really think you should read it too." And with that, I told her about the argument that it's the insulin caused by carbohydrate consumption that makes people gain weight.

I couldn't tell from her reaction whether she was interested. A few weeks went by, then I got an email.

From: Liz

I told my doctor this morning that I'm officially starting a new low-carb lifestyle today. It's time. I've only read about 10 pages of the book so far, but I get it. On so many levels, this must be done.

I was thrilled that she was willing to give it a try, and also glad that she'd checked with her doctor. After her email, I periodically called to check in with her, to see how it was going.

A few weeks in she told me, "I'm getting used to it. It's not as bad as I expected."

This wasn't a wildly enthusiastic endorsement, but she seemed game to keep trying.

———

After eating low-carb for about six months, my father got a blood test, and I was anxious to hear the results. It was one thing for me to undertake this low-carb experiment, but how were these new eating habits affecting my father? Sure, I believed in the validity of this new way of eating, but I wasn't a doctor or a scientist.

He called to tell me his results. "I just got my blood work back," he reported, "and my numbers are *extraordinarily* good. Everything has improved."

"Really?" Relief flooded through me. "What do the tests say?"

He started rattling off his numbers. For years, all his numbers—for his weight, LDL, HDL, and other markers—had been inching in the wrong direction, but now they'd suddenly changed course. "I haven't even been perfect," he added. "This period covers Thanksgiving, Christmas, our trip with friends to Phoenix. And the best thing is, I feel I can eat this way *forever*."

After Elizabeth had been eating low-carb for a few months, she went to the doctor for an A1C test, which measures glycated hemoglobin and is used to track average plasma glucose concentration over the past three months. This test, along with her monitor's constant tracking of her blood sugar levels, helps her manage her diabetes.

"I feel very different," she said. "My A1C hasn't dropped as much as I would like—though it's trending in the right direction—but I feel much better. I don't have those crazy spikes and drops anymore. After a meal, I don't fall into a stupor."

Elizabeth had made a good start going down the low-carb path, but soon it would be time for her to leave for Budapest to film the pilot for a TV show.

"I'm worried," she told me. "I'll be there for five weeks, and it's going to be tough to eat healthy there. Foreign country, no kitchen, working around the clock, and a giant amount of stress."

And sure enough, while she was there, she found it impossible to stick to this way of eating—though, as she said, she did better than she'd be doing if she weren't trying. Finally, at the end of her trip, I got this message:

From: Liz

Last night of shooting. I totally broke down the last week. No fries but tons of bread and cookies. I was just so worn down. Middle of the night, snowing, raining, freezing, no normal coffee. I lost it. Back to my low carb life in LA!

But when Elizabeth got back home, she found it very hard to return to the low-carb approach.

"How's it going?" I asked after she'd been back for a few weeks.

"It hasn't been easy. I'm doing better, but I'm not where I was before. I'm at about 85 percent."

"Why do you think it's harder?"

"I'm not sure. It's just not coming easily. Partly because I'd forgotten how much I like certain foods, like Goldfish crackers. But when I started eating them, I remembered. So now it's hard to give them up."

"Like getting an hour of free time back in your schedule if you skip an exercise class," I answered.

"Right."

This was exactly what I had noticed about the "stopping" aspect of First Steps. When we try a new habit for the first time, it feels full of promise, even if it's arduous. But most of that excitement is gone the second time, and the habit's drawbacks are more apparent. Plus, there's the discouraging feeling of having lost ground, of going backwards.

"Hang in there," I said. "It's hard to change your habits."

I'm sure that eating low-carb is easier for me than it is for many people, partly because while I like to eat, I don't *revel* in food. I have an unadventurous palate. I don't love going to restaurants or trying new flavors. I wish I enjoyed the whole world of food, which gives so many people such pleasure, but it's never been particularly interesting to me. But it turns out that this limitation, which has always made me a little sad, has some benefits. Be Gretchen.

Also, I was certain, eating low-carb came easier to me because of my embrace of the next strategy in my framework: the Strategy of Abstaining.

DESIRE, EASE, AND EXCUSES

We want good habits—but we also want to make life easier and more pleasant. Because these aims often clash, this section encompasses many strategies. The Strategies of Abstaining, Convenience, and Inconvenience examine how we can shape our habits by adjusting the amount of effort involved. Safeguards, Loophole-Spotting, and Distraction address the challenges of failure and temptation. Reward, Treats, and Pairing focus on exploiting pleasure to strengthen our good habits. By guarding against excuses and justifications, and by making our habits as enjoyable as possible, we help ourselves succeed.

FREE FROM FRENCH FRIES

Abstaining

It is well to yield up a pleasure, when a pain goes with it.

—Publilius Syrus

Often, we know we'd be better off if we refused a temptation, but it's hard to resist that extra glass of wine, that impulse purchase, that last hour of TV.

When I was in high school, the seniors sold doughnuts every Friday morning to raise money for the prom, and my friends and I took turns making the early-morning pickup. LaMar's Donuts was a modest place, housed in an old gas station, but the doughnuts were legendary throughout Kansas City. Whenever I was on pickup duty, these doughnuts bedeviled me. I'd be sitting with several heavy boxes in my lap as we drove back to school, and first I'd take a bite of one doughnut, then I'd eat a quarter, then half, then . . . why not just finish it? And then another. I ate the doughnuts in pieces, so I never knew how many I'd eaten (the phenomenon of avoiding monitoring). It was always the same—the temptation, the giving in, the promise of moderation, and then the slide into overindulgence.

For dealing with this kind of temptation, we're often told, "Be moderate. Don't indulge every day, but don't deny yourself altogether, because if you do, you'll fall even further off the wagon." For a long time, I kept trying this strategy of moderation—and failing. With LaMar's doughnuts, and so many other things.

Eventually I learned to reject this advice. Somehow, I figured out that it was easier for me to resist certain temptations by never giving in to them. I kept hearing advice from experts that this strategy was bound to backfire, however—so why did it work?

I came across the answer in a casual remark made by one of my favorite writers, the eighteenth-century essayist Samuel Johnson. When a friend urged him "to take a *little* wine," Dr. Johnson explained, "I can't drink a *little*, child; therefore I never touch it. Abstinence is as easy to me, as *temperance* would be difficult."

That's me, I realized, with a sudden thrill of identification. *That's exactly how I am.*

Like Dr. Johnson, I'm an Abstainer: I find it far easier to give up something *altogether* than to indulge *moderately*. And this distinction has profound implications for habits.

Within the study of habits, certain tensions reappear: whether to accept myself or expect more from myself; whether to embrace the present or consider the future; whether to think about myself or forget myself. Because habit formation often requires us to relinquish something we want, a constant challenge is: How can I *deprive myself* of something without feeling *deprived*? When it comes to habits, feeling deprived is a pernicious state. When we feel deprived, we feel entitled to compensate ourselves—often, in ways that undermine our good habits.

I realized that *one way to deprive myself without creating a feeling of deprivation is to deprive myself totally*. Weirdly, when I deprive myself altogether, I feel as though I haven't deprived myself at all. When we Abstainers deprive ourselves totally, we conserve energy and will-power, because there are no decisions to make and no self-control to muster.

"Abstainers" do better when they follow all-or-nothing habits.

"Moderators," by contrast, are people who do better when they indulge moderately.

Abstaining is a counterintuitive and nonuniversal strategy. It absolutely doesn't work for everyone. But for people like me, it's enormously useful.

As an Abstainer, if I try to be moderate, I exhaust myself debating: How much can I have? Does this time "count"? If I had it yesterday, can I have it today? In Oscar Wilde's novel *The Picture of Dorian Gray*, a character remarks, "The only way to get rid of a temptation is to yield to it," and it can be a relief to give in, to end the tiresome mental chatter about whether and why and when to indulge. But, I'd discovered, *abstaining* cures that noise just as effectively. I'm not tempted by things I've decided are off-limits. If I *never* do something, it requires no self-control to maintain that habit. If only I'd known to abstain from LaMar's doughnuts! I'd tried to eat just a few bites, and that was my mistake. It's a Secret of Adulthood: By giving something up, I gain.

I once talked to a guy who explained how he'd used abstaining to change his eating habits. He was young and lean, so I was surprised when he told me that until recently, he'd been very overweight. "Oh yeah, fat camp as a kid, the whole thing," he explained. But by the time I met him he had successfully kept his weight off for years.

"First, I gave up dairy," he explained. "That didn't seem too hard. No milk in my coffee, no ice cream. Then I gave up rice. Then bread. Each time I had to decide that I would give it up *forever*. But it never seemed very hard to stop eating a particular thing, and then I never thought about it again."

A blog reader agreed: "Much easier to say no to something *once* and be done with the whole issue than to go back and forth endlessly. Abstinence takes *zero* mental effort." That was my experience. For instance, in the past, I'd worked hard to keep sweets out of the apartment, so I wouldn't have to resist eating them. Now that I abstain, the presence of sweets doesn't bother me, and my family is happier.

Many people aren't Abstainers, of course. Moderators, for their part, find that occasional indulgence both heightens their pleasure and strengthens their resolve; they get panicky or rebellious at the thought of "never" getting or doing something. They do better when they avoid strict rules. They may even find that keeping treats near at hand makes them less likely to indulge, because when they know they can have something, they don't crave it. One Moderator posted: "By allowing myself an occasional splurge, I don't feel like I'm missing out on something . . . Tell me 'no' and I just want it more." In fact, from what I've seen, Moderators shouldn't try to abstain; if they try to deny themselves, they can become very preoccupied with indulging.

A Moderator friend told me, "When I'm supposed to fast for Yom Kippur, I end up eating a huge amount of food by 9:00 a.m. on that first morning. Every other day, I can go for hours in the morning with no food, without even noticing it, but when I'm supposed to fast—I have to eat." His wife added, "He eats more on Yom Kippur than any other day of the year."

Abstainers and Moderators can be surprisingly judgmental of each other. A Moderator nutritionist once gave me the familiar mainstream advice, "You're making a mistake by denying yourself all the time. Follow the 80/20 rule, and be healthy 80 percent of the time, and indulge within reason 20 percent of the time." When I tried to explain about being an Abstainer, she couldn't believe that a 100 percent rule might be easier for people like me. (Side note: every nutritionist I've ever met is a Moderator.) Moderators often make disapproving comments to me like "It's not healthy to be so rigid" or "It would be better to learn how to manage yourself." Ironically, I feel much less rigid, and far more relaxed, now that I use Abstaining to maintain some habits. On the other hand, my impulse is to say to Moderators, "You can't keep cheating and expect to make progress" or "Why not just go cold turkey?" But there's no one universal answer. It's a matter of what's better for a particular person.

Abstainers and Moderators behave very differently. A Moderator told me, "Every month or so, I buy some bars of really fine chocolate. Every afternoon, I eat one square of chocolate."

"You're never tempted to eat more?"

"No, I just want the one square," he said.

It would be impossible for me to eat one square of chocolate a day. For the rest of the day, I'd be thinking about that bar of chocolate. In fact, I discovered that the question "Could you eat one square of chocolate every day?" is a good way to distinguish Abstainers from Moderators. All Moderators seem to keep a bar of chocolate stashed away to eat one square at a time. (Maybe this explains the mystery of why chocolate bars are divided into squares.)

A conversation with a Moderator friend revealed another telling distinction. "I got a sundae from my favorite ice-cream store," she told me, "and it was delicious. But after a while, I could hardly taste it. I let a friend finish it."

"I've never left ice cream unfinished in my life," I said.

For Moderators, the first bite tastes the best, and then their pleasure gradually drops, and they might even stop eating before they're finished. For Abstainers, however, the desire for each bite is just as strong as for the first bite—or stronger, so they may want seconds, too. In other words, for Abstainers, having something makes them want it *more*; for Moderators, having something makes them want it *less*.

As an Abstainer, I've learned not to succumb to the "one-bite" argument: "What difference does one bite make?" "I just want a taste, that's all." Hah! As La Rochefoucauld wrote, "It is much easier to extinguish a first desire than to satisfy all of those that follow it."

Abstaining can serve well outside the context of eating; it works whenever we feel that moderation is too difficult to manage. For instance, many people use the Strategy of Abstaining to control their use of technology. A friend loves the word game Ruzzle, and she had the habit of playing it on her phone every night before bed.

"I had to quit it," she told me. "Between work and the kids, the only time I have to read is before bed, but I was using that time to play Ruzzle. I was addicted. I adore reading, and I bought four books to read on vacation, and I thought—I'll never read these books unless I stop playing Ruzzle."

"Are you going to start playing again eventually?"

"Nope. I deleted the app from all my devices."

"Couldn't you limit yourself to twenty minutes, or just a few times a week?"

"Absolutely not."

A guy told me ruefully, "I wish I'd tried giving up video games in grad school. I'm a hundred percent confident that my playing made me need an extra year to write my PhD thesis. I was always trying to play for 'just a little while.'"

A blog reader posted: "When my husband and I lived in Rome in student poverty (which is not real poverty), we literally were counting every lira. There's a high-end fashion street near the Spanish Steps, and I never enjoyed window shopping so much—I knew I couldn't afford anything, so I just enjoyed strolling and admiring the beauty. No questions to ask, decisions to make, or even entertain—I was forced to be an Abstainer."

Some Abstainers are like me, and abstain very strictly from whatever we're trying to resist. Other Abstainers aren't quite so punctilious. Like my father. He *mostly* abstains. After he had been on the low-carb diet, mostly, for some months, I asked him, "You have dessert sometimes, and you drink wine and scotch. Do you worry that you'll gradually lose your healthy eating habits?" I knew I wouldn't be able to pull off this approach myself.

"No, really, I know I can eat this way forever," he said, as he'd told me many times before. "I allow myself a few exceptions, and anytime I eat something that isn't low-carb, I just go right back to my usual choices at the next meal. It's not hard." Self-knowledge will enable us to use the approach that works for us—which may also mean ignoring the advice of people who insist that their way is the right way.

In fact, a person might be both an Abstainer and a Moderator, depending on the context. A friend confessed, "Mac and cheese is my Kryptonite. If I have a single bite, I eat it *all*. But with something like potato chips, I don't have trouble stopping after a few handfuls." Another friend said, "I can have no wine, or three glasses of wine. I can't have one or two glasses of wine. But I can eat half a slice of cake, and my wife can never do that."

Abstainers and Moderators alike are sometimes able to invoke "consumption snobbery" to avoid feelings of deprivation. One friend buys only the most expensive wine he can afford. "If it's cheap, I gulp it down," he said. "If it's expensive, I take my time, I enjoy every sip. And I don't open bottle after bottle." Another friend said, "I used to buy a crazy number of books, and my apartment was getting too crowded. But I didn't want to give up book buying, which I love. Now I only buy first editions, so I get the pleasure of buying them, but in much smaller quantities."

Also, it's true that for Abstainers and Moderators alike, there can be a kind of "Lent pleasure" in abstinence, in relinquishment, for a limited time. As Muriel Spark observed, "The sacrifice of pleasures is of course itself a pleasure." We sometimes enjoy choosing to give things up temporarily, for fasts, cleanses, technology breaks, retreats, or religious observances. And when abstaining is tied to a transcendent value, in actions such as observing the Sabbath, keeping kosher, or shopping locally to support independent businesses, it's far more meaningful, and therefore sometimes more enjoyable, or at least more sustainable.

Lent pleasure is a gratifying exercise in self-control; we set an expectation for ourselves, and we meet it. Also, giving up something for a short time reawakens our pleasure in it. A friend who works in fashion did a "color cleanse" and wore only neutrals for a week. Temporarily to give up color, or coffee, or a credit card makes us appreciate it much more. Alternatively, temporarily giving it up may help us to see that we're happier when we permanently drop it from our stock of habits.

After Elizabeth had been trying to follow the low-carb approach for a while, I had the chance to ask her about it in person when I stayed at her house during a work visit to L.A. The first morning, as we poured ourselves more coffee, I asked for the latest report on her eating habits.

She sighed. "It's not going great. You don't mind giving up those carb foods, but I like more variety. I like eating pizza or pasta now and then." Then, to my astonishment, she added, "But you know what I figured out? I'm actually an Abstainer. My weakness is French fries, and now I don't eat them, ever."

"*You're* an *Abstainer*?" I was amazed. When I was first identifying the concepts of Abstainers and Moderators, Elizabeth had been my model Moderator.

"Yes. It turns out that it's easier to give something up altogether. With some things, I can't be moderate. Abstaining's easier."

"But how do you feel about saying no to yourself all the time?" While I find it fairly easy to tell myself "no," "stop," or "never," Elizabeth is a person who resents restrictions and does much better with positive resolutions.

"I can't give myself a negative," she told me. "I have to make this a positive thing. So I tell myself, 'Now I'm free from French fries.'"

" '*Free from French fries!*' Exactly!" I said. "Free from decisions, free from guilt! Free from the breadbasket and the candy bowl."

Since that conversation, I've concluded that many people are Abstainers who don't realize it. Abstaining sounds demanding and inflexible, so people assume that they're Moderators, even if they've never successfully followed that strategy. But counterintuitively, for many people abstaining is *easier*.

Research—and my own experience—suggests that the less we indulge in something, the less we want it. When we believe that a craving will remain unsatisfied, it may diminish; cravings are more provoked by possibility than by denial. William James observed, "It is surprising how soon a desire will die of inanition if it be never fed." One study of flight attendants who were smokers compared their nicotine cravings during short flights (three to five and a half hours) and long flights (eight to thirteen hours). Attendants' cravings increased as the plane was about to land, regardless of whether the flight had been short or long. In other words, the duration of abstinence didn't predict a nicotine craving as well as the knowledge that the flight was ending—and a cigarette was coming within reach.

Certainly for me, the Strategy of Abstaining makes some challenging habits far easier to foster. Abstaining *sounds* so hard, but really, it's easier. And while it isn't a universal tool, no habit-formation strategy is universally useful. Different solutions for different people.

Also, the more I worked on my habits, the more I became convinced that most successful habit changes required the coordination of multiple strategies, all aimed at a single behavior. In my case, the Strategy of the Lightning Bolt had made me want to abstain from carbs in the first place, Abstaining had made it easy to eat low-carb, and Monitoring allowed me to track what I was eating. Changing a habit may be simple, but it's not easy, and the more tools used, the better.

IT'S HARD TO MAKE
THINGS EASIER

Convenience

There is a myth, sometimes widespread, that a person need do only inner work . . . that a man is entirely responsible for his own problems; and that to cure himself, he need only change himself. . . . The fact is, a person is so formed by his surroundings, that his state of harmony depends entirely on his harmony with his surroundings.

—CHRISTOPHER ALEXANDER, *The Timeless Way of Building*

People often ask me, "What surprises you most about habits?" One thing that continually astonishes me is the degree to which we're influenced by sheer *convenience*. The amount of effort, time, or decision making required by an action has a huge influence on habit formation. To a truly remarkable extent, we're more likely to do something if it's convenient, and less likely if it's not.

For this reason, we should pay close attention to the convenience of any activity we want to make into a habit. Putting a wastebasket next to our front door made mail sorting slightly more convenient, and I stopped procrastinating with this chore. Many people report that they do a much better job of staying close to distant family members now that tools like Facebook, Skype, FaceTime, and group chats make it easy to stay in touch.

Elizabeth decided to employ the Strategy of Convenience to deal with her eating habits. Ever since she'd come back from the shoot in

Budapest, her blood sugar had been far too high, the low-carb approach wasn't working for her, and her doctor advised fast action. Like many people struggling with the decisions and effort involved in eating and cooking right, she decided to try a meal plan that provides prepared food.

> From: Liz
>
> Now I'm on Jenny Craig. Adam is doing it too. I feel bad for (temporarily) abandoning the low carb life. I've got to get in better control of my diabetes which just got so off track in Hungary, etc. So I figure I'll do this and then transition back to low carb. Ugh.

I did a little research, and this plan seemed like a good choice for Elizabeth. It definitely wasn't low-carb, but it was probably *lower* carb, especially given the portion control it provided. Also, I'd read a study that found that dieters get the best results when they're in programs that provide meals. Super-convenience was just what Elizabeth needed—not only because she needed to get her blood sugar under control, but also because she was starting work as a show-runner on a new TV show, so she'd be even busier and more stressed than usual.

I called her after her first day of work to see how it went, and she told me, "To celebrate, the studio sent us pizza from the best pizza place in L.A. Plus it was two people's birthdays, so we had cupcakes."

"What did you have?"

"I had *none* of it. I'm really sticking to the plan, especially at the office."

"So it's working. Why, do you think?"

"It's the convenience," she said with conviction.

Elizabeth made a big change in her habits to take advantage of the Strategy of Convenience, but even the tiniest tweaks in convenience affect people's eating. People take less food when using tongs, instead of spoons, to serve themselves. In one cafeteria, when an ice-cream cooler's lid was left open, 30 percent of diners bought ice cream, but when diners had to open the lid, only 14 percent bought ice cream, even though the ice cream was visible in both situations.

Convenience shapes everything we do. When it's convenient to spend, we spend. That's why merchants constantly dream up new ways to make spending more convenient, with impulse items arrayed next to the checkout line, offers of easy credit, and websites that store information to make pushing the "buy" button an easy, one-click habit. Hotels stock handy in-room minibars with overpriced items, and nowadays some hotels even place the items in plain sight, right on the tabletop, to make it even easier to rip open that four-dollar bag of chocolate-covered peanuts.

But we can also exploit the Strategy of Convenience to help us save. A reader (who likes "small steps") wrote: "When I was about fifteen, I started putting my coins into a jar. When the jar was full, I'd roll up the coins and deposit them into my savings account. I've never stopped this habit—and even keep the coins in the same jar I started with fifty years ago. This means $300 to $400 a year for the vacation account."

We can use the Strategy of Convenience to expand and deepen our relationships. We're much more likely to be friends with people whom we see without making an effort—those we run into frequently at work, in class, or around the neighborhood. In what's called the "mere exposure effect," repeated exposure makes people like each other better. Relationship Convenience is why I love to belong to groups. Belonging to a group that meets regularly is a convenient way of making a habit of seeing people. It sounds odd to talk about "convenience" in the context of friendship, but in truth, it's convenient to see people in groups, and as I see people more, I grow closer to them. If I miss one meeting, I'll see everyone at the next meeting. I don't have the headache of trying to make individual plans. Also, I have the chance to spend time with people whom I don't yet know well, which broadens my relationships in a natural way. It's not easy, as an adult, to make a new friend. It can feel very awkward to say, "Would you like to get a cup of coffee sometime?" The convenience of group membership makes it easier to become friends.

This issue of convenience often arises as an obstacle to regular exercise. Common obstacles include:

It's a pain to pack up the gear when I'm leaving the house.
It's a pain to drive and park there.
It takes too much time to work out.
It's a pain to get a place in a popular class or to wait my turn on equipment.
I don't know how to use the equipment or do the exercises.
I always forget something I need.
It's a pain to shower.

If we tell ourselves, "Oh, I can't exercise, it's too inconvenient," we don't see ways to make it more convenient; identifying *exactly* why exercise feels inconvenient helps to reveal possible solutions. Identify the problem.

Of course, to make exercise more convenient, and therefore more likely to become a habit, the solution must solve a person's particular problem. One person might realize that the problem isn't the gym, but getting to the gym; or the problem might not be the exercise itself, but feeling embarrassed in a gym environment. A reader wrote: "My gym has multiple branches, but I found it inconvenient. I finally realized that sometimes I'd go to the gym from home, or from work, or from my girlfriend's apartment, so I never had what I needed. I bought multiple sets of everything—deodorant, shoes, a giant bag of cheap socks—and I keep a set in each place. Now I don't have an excuse to skip." (Not an underbuyer, clearly.)

Buying home exercise equipment is a popular way to make exercise more convenient, so I briefly considered that approach. My sister and my in-laws have a treadmill at home, but with a New York City apartment, we would have no place to put it. Plus Jamie refuses to get one. "It's better to go to a gym and have a real workout," he insists, "than to have equipment at home."

In any event, *acquiring* equipment isn't the same as *using* it. According to *Consumer Reports*, more than 30 percent of people who buy home exercise equipment admit that they use it less than they expected. A reader commented: "I know deep down that if I really wish to start exercising, all I have to do is step outside. But I still manage to convince myself that buying a 'nice' pair of running shoes and a book about exercise will make me *really* do it."

For people who go to a gym, the structure of payment can make exercise feel more or less convenient. When an activity feels free (even if it's not actually free), it seems more convenient. Because 70 percent of people who belong to a gym rarely go, for most people it would be cheaper to pay for the gym on a per-visit basis instead of forking over a monthly fee. But although the monthly system may not make financial sense, it makes psychological sense; paying per visit means that each workout costs extra and feels less convenient, while monthly payments make each visit feel free.

I wanted to find additional ways to exploit the Strategy of Convenience to improve my habit habitat. For instance, I decided to apply Convenience to my email habits. I read that office workers spend a staggering 28 percent of their office time on email, but I bet I spend more time than that. To make my email habit more convenient, I decided to cut out salutations and closings. I'd fallen into the habit of writing an email like an old-fashioned letter, instead of using the casualness and brevity now appropriate to email.

An email that says:

Hi Peter—
Thanks so much for the link. I'm off to read the article right now.
Warmly,
Gretchen

takes a lot more work than an email that says:

Thanks! Off to read the article right now.

The first version is more formal and polite, but the second version conveys the same tone and information, and is *much* quicker to write.

It took a surprising amount of discipline to change my response habits. It can be hard to make things easier. I had to push myself to erase the "Hi" and to hit "send" without typing a closing. But before long, it became automatic.

Not long after I'd instituted my new convenient email habits, however, I responded to a reader with an email that omitted a salutation and closing, and received a pointed email in return: "I find it really interesting that you don't say 'Hi Lisa' or end your email in any kind of salutation, or say 'if I have any more questions to drop you a line.' Please excuse me if this is rude, I am truly just curious. Is this because you are super busy (understandably) or just not your style? I had this preconceived notion after reading your book that your dialogue would be so much more friendly/happy and personal."

Sheesh. This was nicely put, but clearly the message was "You don't sound very friendly." I was taken aback. Should I go back to using more elaborate courtesy? Then I decided—no. I was sorry if I didn't sound friendly to her, but I wanted to be able to answer emails from readers, and to keep up, I needed to make this work as convenient as possible. My habits had to reflect my values. I wrote her back, very nicely, and without a salutation or closing, to explain.

I looked for other areas to make more convenient. Often, a modest purchase can make a habit more convenient, so to control my almond-eating habit, I bought a pack of forty-eight premeasured one-ounce bags of almonds. The additional packaging seemed wasteful, and my mother-in-law laughed at me for not just pouring the almonds into baggies myself, but for me, having a convenient way to control portion size was worth it.

Along the same lines, I needed to improve my cell-phone-charging habit, so to make that task more convenient, I bought an extra charger cord. Now I can charge in two different spots in the apartment, and this small change made a ridiculously large improvement in my daily life. A reader wrote: "It was hard to motivate myself to walk after dark, the only time available to me for exercise. After a few weeks with my dad, who lives in a well-lit subdivision, I was reminded how much I enjoyed walking in the evenings. I decided to 'identify the problem' and I realized that at home, where the streets aren't well lit, I felt invisible and unsafe walking at night. I bought a reflective vest with LED strips, and it has made such a difference."

However, purchasing more convenience can be challenging for an underbuyer like me. I have to remind myself that habit convenience is a wise investment. For years, I couldn't bring myself to rent a gym locker, because I lived just six blocks away. The need to lug every-thing around, however, made going to the gym seem inconvenient, so I went less often. Finally, I realized: "Exercise is an important pri-ority. The locker isn't very expensive. I'll use it frequently, and it'll make life a lot easier. This is a good place to spend money." One reader reported that she'd assumed she disliked cooking but finally realized that she disliked grocery shopping. Now she pays a little more to order her groceries online, and that extra convenience means that she's willing to cook.

As I continued to look for ways to harness the power of the Strat-egy of Convenience for my habits, I noticed that more and more, people and institutions exploit the fact that habits stick better when they're pleasurable. It may be an illusion, but an activity seems easier—and therefore more convenient—when it includes an element of fun, satisfaction, or beauty.

Everyone knows that it's healthier to take the stairs than the el-evator or escalator, but most people don't bother. However, when a subway station in Sweden transformed its stairs into a piano keyboard that actually played notes as people walked on it, 66 percent more people took the musical stairs. When the Schiphol Airport put the image of a housefly above the drains of urinals, men began to aim at it—a change that reduced spillage rates by 80 percent. "Gamification" is used in the design of devices and apps to help people improve their habits. Doing something a few times for fun isn't necessarily enough to form a habit, but it's a start.

In the same way, attractive surroundings relieve drudgery, and well-made tools make work a joy—which helps to strengthen habits. As an underbuyer, and a disliker of errands, I tend to skimp, but it's worth the time, effort, and money to invest in good tools and pleasant work surroundings.

I stored tickets, invitations, event information, and school notices in one overstuffed shabby file marked "Upcoming." To make life easier, I decided to make twelve monthly files. My first instinct was to scrounge through the apartment to find twelve used folders, then I thought—no, nice new folders will make it more pleasant to maintain my filing habits. I may dislike shopping, but I do love to buy office supplies, and after an enjoyable trip to the office-supply store, I asked Eleanor to label the folders by month. I get a shot of pleasure every time I see her careful seven-year-old handwriting on the new folders, which makes me more likely to stick to my habit of regular filing.

The fact is, it's easier to make pleasant activities into habits. That's why despite the extreme paleness that comes with my red hair, I can't develop the habit of sunscreen; I dislike that sticky feeling on my skin. For years, I'd been trying to floss more regularly. (Which was important, because I've been informed that I have an unusually high rate of tartar buildup. Who knew?) Then my dental hygienist suggested, "Some people find it easier to use picks than to use floss. I'll throw in some Soft-Picks for you to try." This change made a big difference. I don't like the feeling of flossing, but using the picks gives all the uncouth satisfaction of picking my teeth. And that makes the habit feel more convenient, and so I do it.

As I looked for ways to make my habits more convenient and more pleasant, I realized that I should first consider whether I should maintain those habits *at all*. It's too easy to spend time on needless tasks, and some of my habits could be avoided altogether. Nothing can be more convenient than *that*. It's a Secret of Adulthood: The biggest waste of time is to do well something that we need not do at all. One woman complained that her family was in the habit of putting their clothes in the wash when they were inside out, and no matter how much she reminded them, she couldn't change their habits. Then she realized that she could change *her* habit, and now she washes and puts away the clothes inside out.

I decided to make bill paying more convenient. My mail habits were already pretty good: I toss junk mail right away and put real mail straight into my "special drawer," where I keep everything I need—stamps, checkbook, a return-address stamp—and I deal with mail every Sunday night. Still, I wanted to improve, and I realized I could switch to automatic payments. Then I wouldn't have to deal with those bills *at all*.

For the next few months, as I paid bills, I gradually switched most accounts to automatic pay. Often, it takes work to make things easier, but in the end, this kind of hidden, no-action habit requires *no* effort or time, but runs in the background.

A friend described how he set up his hidden habit. "We weren't saving enough for college. Finally, after worrying for years, I set up an automatic savings account, which deducts the money from my paycheck. Now I'm in the habit of saving without ever having to think about it."

It's a Secret of Adulthood: Make it easy to do right, and hard to go wrong.

One evening as I was puttering around the kitchen, I glanced over at Jamie, who was pulling a container of indeterminate leftovers out of the fridge. This familiar sight triggered me to think about the fact that people would be more likely to eat leftovers if the food was stored in an easy-to-open container, rather than in a hard-to-open container.

I sighed. All this thinking about the Strategy of Convenience, and habit formation in general, was taking up a lot of space in my mind. Especially given my Upholder Tendency, I had to remind myself to stay the master of my habits, and even of my thoughts about habits; I shouldn't let them take over.

I looked again at Jamie, who'd come over to stand next to me to get a bowl out of the cabinet. It was an utterly ordinary moment, yet for some reason I was struck by his presence, by the fact of our marriage. We'd spent almost half our lives together. No one was closer to me, and he was standing right beside me—yet suddenly he seemed very far away. He glanced up, and he seemed to have some idea of what I was thinking; he didn't say anything, but he smiled and took my hand.

I don't want habit to deaden me to Jamie's presence. I don't want to take him for granted, to listen to him with only half my attention, to look at him without seeing him. I want my habits to help free me to pay more attention to him, and to everything else that's important to me.

CHANGE MY SURROUNDINGS, NOT MYSELF

Inconvenience

For in truth habit is a violent and treacherous schoolmistress. She establishes in us, little by little, stealthily, the foothold of her authority; but having by this mild and humble beginning settled and planted it with the help of time, she soon uncovers to us a furious and tyrannical face against which we no longer have the liberty of even raising our eyes.

—MICHEL DE MONTAIGNE, "Of Custom, and Not Easily Changing an Accepted Law"

Just as I can strengthen *good* habits by making them *more* convenient, I can squash *bad* habits by making them *less* convenient. I didn't need to spend much time exploring the Strategy of Inconvenience, because it's the mirror image of Convenience—but it's too important not to have its own name.

Sometimes, the more I have to exert myself, the better. If I want to stop using the snooze button, I put the alarm clock across the room. A friend chose a resort based on the fact that he could get Internet service only in its business center. Another friend told me he has two computers. "One is for work, one for nonwork," he explained, "so if I want to start messing around, I have to physically get up from my chair and go to my other computer. I don't waste nearly as much time." The irony of "convenience foods" is that for the most part, they're exactly the foods that we should make *less* convenient. As author Michael Pollan advises, "Eat all the junk food you want as long as you cook it yourself."

A key for understanding many bad habits? *Impulsivity*. Impulsive people have trouble delaying satisfaction and considering long-term consequences; they find it difficult to plan ahead, and once they start a task, they struggle to stick with it. Also, when impulsive people feel anxious about performing a task, they often try to make themselves feel better by avoiding the task, by procrastinating. However, while some people are more impulsive than others, we all sometimes feel the urge to succumb to some immediate gratification—and often, that means breaking a good habit.

The harder it is to do something, the harder it is to do it impulsively, so inconvenience helps us stick to good habits. There are six obvious ways to make an activity less convenient:

- Increase the amount of physical or mental energy required (leave the cell phone in another room, ban smoking inside or near a building).
- Hide any cues (put the video game controller on a high shelf).
- Delay it (read email only after 11:00 a.m.).
- Engage in an incompatible activity (to avoid snacking, do a puzzle).
- Raise the cost (one study showed that people at high risk for smoking were pleased by a rise in the cigarette tax; after London imposed a congestion charge to enter the center of the city, people's driving habits changed, with fewer cars on the road and more use of public transportation).
- Block it altogether (give away the TV set).

For instance, when spending is inconvenient, we're less likely to make an impulse purchase. A friend controls his impulse spending by never carrying credit cards, so that he can't buy anything that costs more than the cash in his wallet. A reader noted, "For many years, I've had my salary paid into a savings account, and then moved money into my current account to spend. As there's usually a delay in the move, I have to plan ahead and perhaps delay/not purchase something until the cash is there. I've always attributed my ability to save to this system."

Many people want to cut back on a shopping habit, and one effective strategy is to make shopping as inconvenient as possible. Don't take a cart or a basket. Be quick, because the less time we give ourselves to shop, the less money we spend. For women, shop with a man (women spend less when they shop with men than they do when they shop alone, with another woman, or even with children). Don't touch or taste, which triggers the desire to buy. Disable one-click shopping on sites. Erase online bookmarks. Log out of shopping accounts after every visit, and use websites as a guest, so that information has to be entered every time. Little obstacles make a big difference, and it's easier to erase a bookmark than to stifle the impulse to buy something. Change our surroundings, not ourselves.

As always, though, it's true that different solutions work for different people. For many people, online shopping is a problem, but a reader noted: "I usually only buy things online. That way, I don't make impulse purchases. I have more time to think about and research them." (From that brief comment, I suspect that this reader is a Questioner.)

Going online is only too convenient, and getting more convenient all the time, so people who struggle to resist online shopping or "procrastisurfing" can benefit from apps such as Freedom or Self-Control, which make it inconvenient (or even impossible) for users to access email or visit websites for preset periods of time. One reader explained why this approach works: "I really only want to block one site—the *Daily Mail* celebrity gossip section. I just reset the site-block each day at a moment when I'm not particularly tempted, and I only need to summon the will-power to do this one click, then the choice is made."

Because the inconvenience of decision making makes us less likely to act, employers can use the Strategy of Inconvenience to prod employees to develop good financial habits. For instance, by setting helpful default options for retirement funds, employers "nudge" employees into participating. Employees could always change the default options, but it takes effort, so most people don't bother—which means that without any conscious decision or effort, they've got the hidden habit of saving for retirement.

In the areas of eating and drinking, people come up with all sorts of ingenious ways to exploit Inconvenience: "I eat with my nondominant hand." "I use chopsticks whenever I eat at home." "I keep the temperature of my freezer turned very low. When the ice cream is rock hard, I have to work to chip out a few spoonfuls." "Instead of putting platters on the table, I keep them in the kitchen, so I have to get up to get more food." "My wife insists on keeping cookies in the house, so I tie them up in a bag that's a pain to open." "Instead of taking wine, which I gulp down, I drink whiskey, which I have to sip." Many colleges have eliminated cafeteria trays; when students can't easily load up on food and must make multiple trips, they take less. One study found that going trayless cut food waste by as much as 25 to 30 percent, and I bet people eat less, too.

In one extreme example, when three armed men burst into the home of renowned socialite Anne Bass and demanded that she open her safe, they discovered a few hundred dollars, some jewelry—and chocolate. She explained to the puzzled robbers that she kept the chocolate in her safe so that she wouldn't eat it too quickly. She used the Strategy of Inconvenience.

Of course, sometimes we don't make a habit inconvenient because we don't really want to change. A friend said, "I have a bad habit of checking my phone while I'm driving. It's sitting on the seat next to me, and I hear it buzzing, and I can't resist. How do I increase my self-control, so I don't check it? How do I get more motivated by safety?"

"Forget about self-control and motivation," I suggested. "How about muting the phone and putting it on the floor of the backseat? You won't know it's buzzing, and you wouldn't be able to reach it anyway."

"Oh." He looked disappointed. And I realized that he didn't really want to stop the habit of checking his phone.

I'd been looking for ways to make aspects of my life more inconvenient as a way to help me stick to my good habits, when I was struck by the dreariness of this endeavor.

I called Elizabeth. "Do you think I'm a killjoy?" I demanded. "Am I turning into a humorless habits machine?"

She laughed, but paused before she spoke. "Well, yes and no. I really am interested in what you're thinking about, so I like to hear about it."

"But . . . ?"

"But yes, sometimes it can be kind of grim."

"Like when?"

"I mean, I find it amusing usually. But I remember when we were in Kansas City, we went to Winstead's diner, and you didn't let Eleanor get fries. I'm like, 'You cannot tell a little girl she can't have French fries. A burger and fries, that's the American meal!' But," she added, "it's true that Eleanor didn't care."

I was laughing. French fries! Always with Elizabeth, the French fries. We were both so predictable.

"But don't you remember," I protested, "I told Eleanor she could have French fries *or* a Frosty." A "Frosty" is the signature Winstead's chocolate milk shake. "And she picked the Frosty. I mean, fries *and* a Frosty?"

"Well anyway, sometimes your habits do seem—judgmental."

"You think I'm judgmental?" One of the nicest things about Elizabeth is that even though she has decided opinions and high standards of behavior, she somehow never seems judgmental.

"Actually, I think you've gotten less judgmental from doing this project. You have more appreciation of the fact that people are different from you."

"I used to think I was pretty typical, but now I see that I'm extreme. I can't judge people according to what works for me."

"That's good."

A STUMBLE MAY PREVENT
A FALL

───────

Safeguards

When conviction is present, and temptation out of sight, we do not easily conceive how any reasonable being can deviate from his true interest. What ought to be done, while it yet hangs only on speculation, is so plain and certain, that there is no place for doubt; the whole soul yields itself to the predominance of truth, and readily determines to do what, when the time of action comes, will be at last omitted.

—SAMUEL JOHNSON, *The Idler,* No. 27

One of the paradoxes of habits? Habits are surprisingly tough, and habits are surprisingly fragile.

For that reason, even though habits come fairly easily to me, I use safeguards to protect my good habits. Instead of *resisting* temptation, I try to *anticipate* and *minimize* temptation—both in my environment and in my own mind—and I plan for failure. I've got the habit of exercise, I've been exercising for years, and I feel physically uncomfortable if I go several days without exercise, and yet this habit always feels slightly at risk. There's a downward pull toward bad habits that requires us to maintain an active, concrete effort to protect our good habits—remarkably, even the good habits that we *enjoy.*

The Strategy of Safeguards keeps one lapse from turning into a full relapse.

The story of the wily Greek hero Odysseus is often invoked as an example of Safeguards. The goddess Circe warned Odysseus that as he and his men sailed near the land of the Sirens, they'd hear the beautiful singing that lured sailors to their deaths. So Odysseus, following Circe's advice, plugged the sailors' ears with wax and ordered himself bound to the mast so he couldn't succumb to temptation. We must play the role of both Circe and Odysseus by warning ourselves of temptations and challenges, and establishing the safeguards that will protect us.

The fact is, we're surrounded by temptation. One study estimated that people spend about one-fourth of their waking time resisting some aspect of desire—most commonly, the urge to eat, to sleep, to grab some leisure, and to pursue some kind of sexual urge.

To defeat a possible temptation, we must first recognize it. Catholicism includes a helpful concept, the "near occasion of sin"—a person, thing, or other external circumstance that's likely to entice us to go wrong. If we identify these near occasions of sin, we can take steps to avoid them. Therefore, the first step in the Strategy of Safeguards is the elimination of the cues that lead to those temptations. After we identify the siren calls that would prompt us to break our habits, we can figure out how to avoid them.

The simplest thing to do is to hide the reminder of temptation: the iPad, the bottle of wine, piles of clothes catalogs. *Out of sight, out of mind*—it really works.

Sometimes we can avoid a cue altogether. Unbeknownst to me, Eliza had developed the habit of stopping to buy candy on her way home from school, as I discovered only when she told me that she wanted to break the habit. We talked it through, and she came up with an obvious safeguard: "I won't walk home along Lex," she decided. Lexington Avenue offers several candy-buying opportunities on every block. "If I don't walk by the stores, I won't buy candy."

Unfortunately, cues lurk everywhere, and often we can't control or avoid them. A cue might be a place, a mood, a time of day, a transition, other people, or a pattern of behavior. Even a fleeting sight or sound or smell can be a trigger. In one study, people given sandwiches in nontransparent wrap ate less of the sandwich than people whose sandwiches came in transparent wrap. Television, with its relentless stream of ads, poses problems for those tempted by junk food; conversely, the absence of cigarette ads helps those trying to quit smoking. Hospitality expert Jacob Tomsky notes that, when checking into a hotel, some alcoholics ask for an empty minibar. Eliminating cues stops temptation before it starts, so it never overpowers us. As Montaigne observed, "The infancies of all things are feeble and weak. We must keep our eyes open at their beginnings; you cannot find the danger then because it is so small: once it has grown, you cannot find the cure."

Because it's impossible to eliminate all cues from our surroundings, we need additional safeguards. The next step, and a highly effective habit-formation tool, is to make detailed plans of action for keeping good habits, with what researcher Peter Gollwitzer calls "implementation intentions," also known as "action triggers" or "if-then" planning. "If _____ happens, then I will do _____."

With "if-then" planning, we try to plan for every habit challenge that might arise, so we don't make decisions in the heat of the moment—we've already decided how to behave.

Resolving ambivalence and indecision in advance, when we're in a cool and detached frame of mind, serves as a safeguard, because it means we can act quickly and without internal debate when the need arises. People who use if-then planning are much more likely to stick to their good habits than people who don't. While it's not possible to anticipate every situation that might arise, this mental preparedness is enormously helpful. As Dwight Eisenhower observed, "Plans are worthless, but planning is everything."

Over time, I created a list of some of my own if-thens:

If I want to get a lot of original writing done, I go to the library, where I don't have Internet.

If offered wine, I decline. (Almost always.)

If I'm writing, I shut down my email.

If I'm invited to dinner, I eat a snack before I go, so I won't be too hungry.

If I'm writing and need to verify some information, I write "look up" in my text to remind me to deal with it later, rather than allow myself to be distracted by the fun of research.

If-then planning is one of the most important tools within Safeguards, because it arms us to face any high-risk situation with a carefully considered plan. We can be prepared for the times when we go on vacation, travel, have a new baby, get a new job, move, go to a holiday party . . . the list goes on. Once we've put the effort into making an if-then plan, it takes much less energy to put it into operation.

If-then planning does demand mental energy, however, as well as a certain pessimism. This exercise is probably easiest for Upholders, who enjoy making and keeping rules. When Questioners become convinced that this approach is effective, they may embrace it as well. Obligers may find it difficult to stick to their if-then plans—"If I want to skip going to class, then I must email the teacher to explain my absence"—if no external accountability enforces it. Rebels resist binding themselves, so they usually won't make if-then plans.

The Strategy of Safeguards can help us avoid breaking good habits—and just as important, it provides a way to deal effectively with lapses, those times when we falter in maintaining a good habit. As the proverbs hold, "A stumble may prevent a fall" and "He that stumbles, and does not quite fall, gains a step." I remind myself that a stumble doesn't mean total failure. In fact, a stumble may be helpful, because it shows me where I need to concentrate my efforts in order to do better next time. Planning for a stumble during habit formation almost seems like giving ourselves permission to stumble—but it's not. It's a way to protect a habit.

When we do stumble, it's important not to judge ourselves harshly. Although some people assume that strong feelings of guilt or shame act as safeguards to help people stick to good habits, the *opposite* is true. People who feel less guilt and who show compassion toward themselves in the face of failure are better able to regain self-control, while people who feel deeply guilty and full of self-blame struggle more.

Instead of viewing our stumbles as evidence that we're weak or undisciplined or lazy, we can see our stumbles as part of the habit-formation process. Imagine a person who hasn't been taking his medicine. If he feels ashamed, he might avoid visiting his doctor; or he could tell himself, "It happens," "We've all done it," "I'll do it differently next time," or "What I do most days matters more than what I do once in a while." That kind of self-encouragement is a greater safeguard than self-blame.

Indeed, guilt and shame about breaking a good habit can make people feel so bad that they seek to make themselves feel better—by indulging in the very habit that made them feel bad in the first place.

This accounts for the striking poetic justice of bad habits.

As I learned in my high school English class when we studied Dante's *Inferno*, poetic justice dictates that the punishment be tailored to fit the crime. So in Dante's vision of the Ninth Circle of Hell, a fiend punishes the sowers of discord and schism by continually splitting apart their bodies. The poetic justice of bad habits is relentless and cruel, because *the punishment for a bad habit is . . . the bad habit*. As a friend said to me, "I feel too anxious to tackle my bad habits, but my bad habits are what make me anxious." One survey found that some women who worry about their finances use "retail therapy" to feel better—they shop in order to cope with their anxiety. Gamblers who worry about money distract themselves by gambling. When procrastinators fall behind, working on the task makes them so anxious that they have to stop working in order to feel better; as someone wrote on my blog, "I feel anxious because I'm not getting anything done, so

I get a massage to feel better. But I don't get anything done, because I'm busy with things like getting a massage." People who feel listless and dull watch TV to make themselves feel better, then they feel listless and dull because they've been watching hours of TV. The character Fat Bastard in the Austin Powers movies makes the same point: "I eat because I'm unhappy, and I'm unhappy because I eat."

The favorite medicine turns to poison, and temporary comfort becomes a source of more guilt, regret, and feelings of lack of control—which can lead to more indulgence in bad habits. It's a Secret of Adulthood: Make sure the things we do to make ourselves feel *better* don't make us feel *worse*.

To form good habits, we want to stumble as rarely as possible. A stumble may prevent a fall, true, but all falls begin with a single stumble. *So it's very, very important not to stumble.* That's the paradox: a stumble is no big deal, and yet a stumble is a very big deal.

Also, the more faithfully I adhere to my new habits, the more likely they are to stick. A study showed that when people were trying to form habits, perfect compliance wasn't necessary, but the earliest repetitions of the habit helped most to establish it. With time, the gains became smaller. The bottom line? I should start strong with my habits, and use safeguards to protect them, especially at the beginning.

Because stumbles occur more frequently as a new habit is being formed, it pays to be particularly vigilant in the early days, and in the context of well-known stumbling blocks: tension with other people, social pressure, loneliness or boredom or anxiety, and—perhaps surprisingly—positive emotions, such as joy or excitement.

Counterintuitively, minor temptations can be more challenging than major temptations. A student might not say, "I'm going to spend the afternoon at the beach with my friends," but he'd think, "I'll check out sports highlights for fifteen minutes before I start working," then fifteen more, then fifteen more, and pretty soon three hours have gone by. Little temptations sometimes slip past our guard.

The key is to catch ourselves in a stumble right away. Because of the colorfully named "what the hell" phenomenon, a minor stumble often becomes a major fall. Once a good behavior is broken, we act as though it doesn't matter whether it's broken by a little or a lot. "I didn't do any work this morning, so what the hell, I'll take the rest of the week off and start on Monday." "I missed my yoga class over spring break, so what the hell, I'll wait to start in the fall." A friend's wife used if-then planning to avoid this "what the hell" trap. As she made her plan to quit smoking, she told her husband, "After I give up smoking, if by some chance you see me having a cigarette, remind me that I've still 'quit,' I haven't fallen off the wagon altogether."

Dieters seem especially susceptible to this kind of pattern, where a minor misstep turns into a major binge, in what's known as the "abstinence violation effect": "I broke my diet by eating this one minicupcake, so now I'm going to eat the whole box." Also, when dieters figure that they've blown their diet, they tend to do a worse job of tracking their consumption, at the very time when the Strategy of Monitoring would be particularly helpful. By continuing to monitor consumption, a person gains a sense of awareness, and even more important, a sense of control. Counterintuitively, monitoring can even be reassuring. If I'm thinking, "Oh yikes, I just ate a *ton* of meatballs," I feel out of control. By entering "6 meatballs" into my food tracker, I take control. Six meatballs is a lot of meatballs, but it's just six meatballs.

A friend described how once she stumbles, she falls. "It's like I rush to gobble down as much forbidden food as I can that day," she told me, "because I know the next day I'll have to start to eat right again."

"People do tend to self-regulate day by day," I said.

"Or maybe I even wait until Monday, or the first of the month."

"How about this," I suggested. "Instead of feeling that you've blown the day and thinking, 'I'll get back on track tomorrow,' try thinking of each day as a set of four quarters: morning, midday, afternoon, evening. If you blow one quarter, you get back on track for the next quarter. Fail small, not big."

A friend explained how a colleague used the Strategy of Safeguards. "This older manager told me, 'Lots of people at this company have affairs, and I've seen lots of marriages break up as a result.' He'd kept his own marriage strong by following five habits, and he told me I should follow them, too."

"What are they?" I asked.

"Never flirt, even as a joke. Never have more than one drink with people from work. Never confide details from my personal life to people from work, and don't allow them to confide in me. Never allow myself to have a 'special friend' at work. Unless it's an unmistakably professional context, don't meet alone with a colleague or client. Like if a client calls with tickets for the U.S. Open, never go in a twosome."

I don't completely agree with all these suggested habits, but they're worth considering as possible safeguards. People often assume, "I would never have an affair"—that it's just a matter of good character and solid values. But in practice, temptation can sometimes arise over a long period of time and look quite different from what we expect. Slowly, a relationship changes. Or by contrast, a stressful or intense moment creates a sudden energy that, in the right environment, leads to an affair. If-then planning and habits can act as safeguards.

One thorny challenge within the Strategy of Safeguards is figuring out a way to allow ourselves to break a good habit occasionally, without losing the good habit altogether. After all, sometimes we *do* want to break a habit—to take advantage of a rare opportunity, say, or to celebrate. A very effective safeguard for that situation is the *planned exception*, which protects us against impulsive decisions. We're adults, we make the rules for ourselves, and we can mindfully choose to make an exception to a usual habit by planning that exception in advance. I generally work a full day, but on any day when I hand in a draft of a book, I spend the rest of the day reading in bed.

Say a person wants to learn Spanish, and to make progress as rapidly as possible, has created a habit of studying Spanish for an hour every morning. Then he goes on vacation, and he might think, when he wakes up on that first morning in a new hotel, "I'm supposed to study, but I'm on vacation, so I deserve a break." This kind of spur-of-the-moment decision to break a habit shows a lack of self-control—and we dislike feeling out of control of ourselves. By contrast, he could decide, in advance, "When I'm on vacation, I'm not going to study Spanish, then I'll start again as soon as I'm home." Very consciously, ahead of time, he makes a mindful exception, so that he's in control.

A planned exception works best when it's made for something *memorable*. A year from now, the Spanish student will think, "Oh, I remember all the fun I had on that great vacation." That's one reason consumption snobbery is a good strategy; it means we make exceptions only for the most worthwhile indulgences. A good test of a planned exception is "How will I feel about the exception *later*? Will I think, 'I'm so happy that I broke my usual habit to take advantage of that opportunity,' or 'Well, looking back on it, I wish I'd made a different choice'?"

Exceptions also work best when they're limited, or when they have a built-in cutoff point. Skip the gym to have extra time to prepare for the annual retreat, not the weekly staff meeting. Make an exception for Christmas Day, not the Christmas season—Christmas is a holi*day*, after all. I saw this approach's effectiveness when Elizabeth told me, "We're having Thanksgiving dinner with Adam's family this year, and I've decided that I'm going to eat stuffing. Stuffing makes me feel like I'm really *partaking* of the holiday."

"Great," I said. "First, you've decided in advance to make an exception, so you feel in control. Second, stuffing is a symbol for

Thanksgiving, so you're not depriving yourself of the quintessential Thanksgiving experience—and it's very helpful to avoid feeling deprived. Third, stuffing is self-limiting. How often can you eat stuffing? It's not an exception that will become a habit."

An impressive solution.

The Strategy of Safeguards requires us to take a very realistic—perhaps even fatalistic—look at ourselves. But while acknowledging the likelihood of temptation and failure may seem like a defeatist approach, it helps us identify, avoid, and surmount our likely stumbling blocks.

NOTHING STAYS IN VEGAS

Loophole-Spotting

So convenient a thing it is to be a reasonable creature, since it enables one to find or make a reason for everything one has a mind to do.

—BENJAMIN FRANKLIN, *Autobiography*

It's human nature: we seek loopholes. Even when we're deeply committed to a good habit, even when we *enjoy* that habit, we're often seeking possible justifications to excuse ourselves from it . . . just this once. With a little ingenuity, there's a loophole for every occasion.

A loophole is an argument for why we should be excused from following a good habit. We aren't mindfully planning the exception in advance, or acknowledging that we're making an exception; we're finding a loophole—usually on the spur of the moment—that lets us off the hook.

Loopholes often flit through our minds, almost below the level of consciousness. If we recognize them, we can judge them and stop kidding ourselves. It's when we deceive ourselves that our bad habits tyrannize us most.

Of the Four Tendencies, Obligers struggle most often against the temptations of loopholes. Rebels don't make excuses to justify doing what they want; Upholders and Questioners feel a greater pressure from their own inner expectations to resist loopholes. Obligers act when they're held externally accountable, so they look for loopholes to excuse them from that accountability. Nevertheless, no matter what our Tendency, loopholes can prove quite enticing, so in order to identify them more readily and help myself guard against them, I made a list of the ten major categories.

Moral Licensing Loophole: In moral licensing, we give ourselves permission to do something "bad" (eat potato chips, bust the budget) because we've been "good." We reason that we've earned it or deserve it.

> I've been losing weight steadily on this diet, so it will be okay for me to cut a few corners.
> I've been so good about meditating, I deserve a day off.
> I've done so many Christmas errands, I deserve to buy a little something for myself.
> I'm much better about this than I used to be.
> I saved so much by not buying _____ that I can buy _____.
> After all the work I've done today, I've earned a nice glass of wine.

In a popular, yet counterproductive, example of moral licensing, people use exercise to justify splurging on food or drink. "I went running today, so I've earned a few beers." The fact is, exercise doesn't help with weight loss; weight loss is driven by changes in diet.

Sometimes we don't even *wait* to earn or deserve something "bad"; we argue that we're entitled to be "bad" now because we plan to be "good" in the future. That variation of the Moral Licensing Loophole is . . .

———

Tomorrow Loophole: As part of my investigation of First Steps, I'd identified "tomorrow logic." *Now* doesn't matter, because we're going to follow good habits tomorrow. And, as Little Orphan Annie famously observed, tomorrow is always a day away.

> I'll be really frugal in January, so it doesn't matter if I blow the budget in December.
>
> I can spend the day hanging out with friends because starting tomorrow, I'm going to buckle down, which means I'm definitely on track to finish my paper on time.
>
> It doesn't matter what I eat now, because I'm starting a diet tomorrow. (Research shows that people who plan to start dieting tomorrow tend to overeat today.)
>
> There's no point in tidying up because this weekend I'm doing a thorough spring cleaning.
>
> I travel all the time for work, but I'll see more of my children during the summer.
>
> My boss complains that I'm always late, but starting Monday, I'm always going to be on time.

A reader commented, "I use the tomorrow loophole to make some very bad, often life-altering spending habits out of line with my true philosophy on money. I love to start over on a new day/week/year, and I will overindulge because I want to 'get it all out of the way today' before starting fresh and doing things properly tomorrow." Another reader wrote: "At work, I act as if tomorrow is a magical day when everything will go smoothly, and I'll have loads of free time. So I tell myself I'll start tomorrow."

Some people even fool themselves into thinking that extreme indulgence *today* will give them more self-control *tomorrow*. One reader posted, "I even go so far as to try to have a real blowout today, to get to the point of sickening myself, so that I will not be tempted by the bad food/behavior tomorrow—thus helping my tomorrow self to be better. It doesn't make sense, now that I write it down." Spending an entire day watching TV doesn't make a person feel less like watching TV, or more like working, the next morning.

False Choice Loophole: This is the loophole-seeking strategy I most often invoke. I pose two activities in opposition, as though I have to make an either/or decision, when in fact, the two aren't necessarily in conflict. Here are some of my own false choices:

I haven't been exercising. Too busy writing.

I don't have time to edit my draft, I've got too many emails to answer.

If I go to sleep earlier, I won't have any time to myself.

I'm so busy, I'll make those appointments once things calm down.

I can't make the bed or put clothes in the hamper, I have to arrive on time.

A reader posted on my blog: "Dieting doesn't actually reflect one of my core values, it can't. I firmly believe that life is too short, that we need to make the most of it—and for me, that means going out, seeing friends, exploring new countries, new places, new tastes—and that doesn't sit well with long-term, slow, steady weight loss. If The Boyfriend shouts up the stairs 'pub'—as he does quite frequently—I'm not going to say 'oooh, I can't, I need to eat lettuce tonight.' Sorry, but if I get knocked down by a bus tomorrow I'm not going to remember the lettuce as my head spins, but I will remember having fun chats and laughing with himself." She contrasts two choices—embracing life to the fullest and staying home to eat lettuce—but are these the only two alternatives?

Another reader commented, "I use the False Choice loophole all the time at work. I make to-do lists with some items that are easy and fun, and some that are way too ambitious, then I do the easy, fun things because 'I have to do them, they're on my list,' but then I don't have time for the hard things. This results in procrastination on the large or unpleasant tasks under the guise of being productive."

Lack of Control Loophole: Weirdly, we often have an illusion of control over things we can't control—"If I spend a lot of time worrying, the plane is less likely to crash," "If I play my lucky numbers, I'll win the lottery eventually"—but deny control over things we can control ("If my cell phone buzzes, I have to check it"). We argue that circumstances force us to break a habit, but often, we have more control than we admit.

"When I work in my favorite coffee shop," a friend told me, "I absolutely have to get a muffin. Their muffins are so good, I can't resist, but I really don't want to eat them."

"Why don't you work in a different coffee shop?" I asked.

"Oh, but that's my favorite coffee shop," she said earnestly.

"Right," I said. "Because you always have one of those delicious muffins when you go there."

"That's not why I go," she said. Then she laughed. "Well, now that you mention it, maybe it is."

Although we can't control every aspect of a situation, we usually can control it more than we tell ourselves.

I travel all the time.

It's too hot. It's too cold. It's too rainy.

I have an injury.

I'd had a few beers.

These chips have been specially engineered by the food industry to be irresistible.

My kids take up all my time.

I've never been able to resist this.

I started without realizing what I was doing.

With everything going on right now, I can't be expected to stick to a good habit. (There's a great running gag in the movie *Airplane*, in which the air-traffic control supervisor remarks, as he lights up a cigarette, "Looks like I picked the wrong week to quit smoking." Later, as he takes a drink, he adds, "Looks like I picked the wrong week to quit drinking." Then later, "Looks like I picked the wrong week to quit amphetamines" and "Looks like I picked the wrong week to quit sniffing glue.")

The Lack of Control Loophole is closely tied to another popular loophole . . .

Arranging to Fail Loophole: It's odd. Instead of fleeing temptation, we often plan to succumb. In what Professors Lee Beach and G. Alan Marlatt dubbed "apparently irrelevant decisions," we make a chain of seemingly harmless decisions that allow us covertly to engineer the very circumstances that we'll find irresistible.

I've long been obsessed by author J. M. Barrie's strange, brilliant skeleton of a book, *The Boy Castaways of Black Lake Island*, about three boys who set sail to seek the adventure of being capsized. I'm particularly haunted by its first line, "We set out to be wrecked"; to fail was the very purpose of their undertaking.

I'll just check my email quickly before I go to the meeting, and then make this one call . . . oh no, it's so late, there's no point in going to the meeting now.

I drove across town to that gourmet grocery store to buy broccoli, and I ended up buying their special cheesecake. Who could resist?

I'll buy some scotch to have in the house in case someone stops by.

My husband and I love to go on "all-inclusive" cruise vacations, and I can't resist the all-you-can-eat food.

I'll play a video game for fifteen minutes before I start working. Okay, another fifteen minutes.

I'm going to lie on the sofa so I can brainstorm ideas in comfort.

A friend told me, "I know a guy in L.A. who has some trouble with gambling. The last time I saw him, he said, 'I just lost a ton of money in Vegas.' I said, 'I thought you weren't supposed to go there anymore.' He said, 'I'm not, but I didn't go there to gamble.' I asked, 'So why were you there?' He said, 'I bought a new car, and I wanted to take it for a test drive.' He was absolutely serious."

We set out to be wrecked.

"This Doesn't Count" Loophole: We tell ourselves that for some reason, this circumstance doesn't "count." I lived in a group house after college, and my housemate's boyfriend one day said to me, in a patronizing tone, "Boy, I wish I had as much free time as you do, to read for pleasure." He practically lived with us, so I saw how he spent his time, and I answered, "But you have lots of free time, you watch a ton of sports on television." He said, "Oh, that doesn't count." But everything counts.

I'm on vacation.

It's holiday season. (On average, people gain one pound during the winter holidays, and most don't ever lose it; overweight people tend to gain more.)

What are weekends for?

I'm sick.

These are just the leftovers from my son's plate.

This is a one-time thing. (Samuel Johnson observed, "Those faults which we cannot conceal from our own notice, are considered,

however frequent, not as habitual corruptions, or settled practices, but as casual failures, and single lapses.")

I ordered it for both of us, which means you're eating half, even if
I eat the whole thing.

I've totally given up drinking. Except on the weekends and when
I'm out with friends.

I'm about to exercise, so this will burn right off.

I don't even want this.

This period of my life is so stressful that I can't be expected to do
anything except focus on my deadline/case on trial/relative in
the hospital.

This loophole is an occupational hazard for my sister Elizabeth.
For a TV writer, shooting a pilot is thrilling, but it's also extraordinarily stressful. She's been through this several times, and she told
me, "The temptation when shooting a pilot is to say, 'Nothing else
matters. We're shooting a pilot, this is completely separate from real
life, it doesn't count.'"

"Everything counts," I said with a sigh.

We can always mindfully decide to make an exception, but there
are no freebies, no going off the grid, no get-out-of-jail-free cards,
nothing that stays in Vegas.

Questionable Assumption Loophole: We make assumptions that
influence our habits—often, not for the better—and many of those
assumptions become less convincing under close scrutiny. A reader
posted a good example: "I set up weird mental blocks around my
time. For instance, if it's 9 a.m. and I have an appointment at 11 a.m.,
I'll think 'Oh, I have to go somewhere in two hours, so I can't really
start anything serious' and then end up wasting my whole morning
waiting for one thing to happen."

Our assumptions sound reasonable . . . but are they?

This is taking too long, I should be done already.

I can't start working until my office is clean.

I'm too busy to take the stairs. It's faster to wait in this long elevator line.

All creative people are messy.

I've already showered, so I can't work out.

We might need this someday.

I'm so far behind, there's no point in doing anything to catch up.

I need to get good value from this all-you-can-eat buffet.

My instructor will be angry with me because I've missed so many times.

I've been working out, so those extra pounds I've gained must be muscle.

This will help me concentrate.

Unless I can sweat for an hour, it's not worth exercising.

One very sneaky Questionable Assumption Loophole is the belief that a habit has become so ingrained that we can ease off: "Keeping track of travel expenses has become second nature to me," "I love my morning writing sessions so much, I'd never give them up." Unfortunately, even long-standing habits can be more fragile than they appear, so it pays not to get complacent. People tend to overestimate their dedication. As one reader posted: "I gave up Nutella in December 2011. A few years later I thought I would be able to handle the Nutella once more so I bought two jars on sale. I ate 4,000 calories of Nutella over 36 hours." I experienced this with driving. I'm a fearful driver, and for many years I didn't drive at all in New York City. Finally I tackled this fear and started driving again. I still very much dislike driving, but I *do* drive, and I aim to drive at least once a week to stay in the habit of driving so that I don't develop that fear again. More than once, however, I've caught myself thinking, "Wow, I'm so much less afraid to drive than I used to be. In fact, I don't think I have to drive once a week anymore." Hah!

Concern for Others Loophole: We tell ourselves that we're acting out of consideration for others and making generous, unselfish decisions. Or we decide we must do something in order to fit into a social situation.

It will hurt my girlfriend's feelings if I leave her to go for a run.

So many people need me, there's no time to focus on my own health.

It would be rude to go to a friend's birthday party and not eat a piece of cake.

I don't want to seem holier-than-thou.

When I try to change this habit, I get irritable, and my family complains.

I can't ask my partner to stay with the kids while I go to class.

At this business dinner, other people might feel uncomfortable if I don't drink.

I'm not buying this junk food for me, I have to keep it around for others.

A reader with a great deal of insight into her own loophole-seeking posted on my blog: "I blame my lack of motivation on the needs of others. When I get up early, I feel wonderful. It's a very creative and productive time for me. However, both my sweetie and I love using our pre-wake-up time as cuddle time. Although he's very supportive and encouraging of me to get up, my sleepy brain that doesn't want to get out of bed blames my lack of motivation on him—I don't want to let him down, etc. I do the same thing with my mother and eating healthy foods when I am at her home. Although she's supportive, I find myself reaching for the second cookie because 'I wouldn't want her to feel bad or think that I didn't like them.' I know that these are excuses—not reality—but I still end up feeling resentful towards other people."

———

Fake Self-Actualization Loophole: Often, a loophole is disguised as an embrace of life or an acceptance of self, so that the failure to pursue a habit seems life-affirming—almost spiritual.

> You only live once (YOLO).
>
> I'll be sorry if I don't at least try it.
>
> I should celebrate this special occasion. (How special? National Cheesecake Day? A colleague's birthday?)
>
> Life is too short not to live a little.
>
> I have to take advantage of this now or miss out forever. (Fast-food joints exploit this loophole; customers buy more when a limited-time offer is tied to a season, an event, or a specific holiday, such as pumpkin spice lattes or heart-shaped doughnuts.)
>
> It's too nice a day to spend doing this.
>
> I'm afraid of missing out (FOMO).
>
> I want to embrace myself, just as I am. (I try to remember to "Accept myself, and expect more from myself.")

When I was explaining my Abstainer approach to an acquaintance, she scolded me: "You only live once! Eat a brownie, enjoy life!"

"We only live once," I said, "but I'm happier when I skip the brownie." Which is true.

For most of us, the real aim isn't to enjoy a few pleasures right now, but to build habits that will make us happy over the long term. Sometimes, that means giving up something in the present, or demanding more from ourselves.

"One-Coin" Loophole: One of the most insidious of loopholes is the "one-coin" loophole—insidious because it's absolutely true. This loophole gets its name from the "argument of the growing heap," which I learned about in Erasmus's *The Praise of Folly*. According to a footnote, the argument of the growing heap is:

If ten coins are not enough to make a man rich, what if you add one coin? What if you add another? Finally, you will have to say that no one can be rich unless one coin can make him so.

In other words, even though one coin certainly isn't sufficient to make a man rich, a man only becomes rich by adding one coin after another.

This teaching story highlights a paradox that's very significant to habits and happiness: often, when we consider our actions, it's clear that any one instance of an action is almost meaningless; yet at the same time, the sum of those actions is very meaningful. Whether we choose to focus on the single coin or the growing heap will shape our behavior. True, any one visit to the gym is inconsequential, but the habit of going to the gym is invaluable.

Focusing on the one coin is a way to deny the conflict between our values: a person isn't choosing between the desire to stay close to his extended family and his desire to skip the weekly family brunch to sleep in—because one missed brunch is no big deal. But when he considers the accumulated cost of the missed visits, the conflict looks different.

> I haven't worked on that project for such a long time, there's no point in working on it this morning.
>
> I'm not going to wear my helmet. What are the chances I have an accident today?
>
> I should keep track of business expenses, but there's no point in keeping one receipt.
>
> Why work on my report today, when the deadline is so far off?
>
> A year from now, whether I went to a video arcade today won't matter.
>
> What's one beer?

By reminding ourselves that the heap grows one coin at a time, we can help keep ourselves on track. Also, the mere act of adding one coin to the heap strengthens a habit, just as each subtraction weakens it. So each coin is actually two coins: the healthy habit itself, and the protection and reinforcement of that habit. The habit of the habit is more important than the habit itself.

For this reason, it can be helpful to keep a habit symbolically, even if we can't keep it literally, to keep a habit in place. Someone who can't go for a run because his wife is sick can go for a short walk. Someone who can't write for an hour because the kids are home from school can write for ten minutes.

Usually, loopholes are invoked in the heat of the moment, in the eagerness to justify junking a habit. I spend the first hour of my day doing email, but one morning I had several very tricky, annoying emails to answer, and I wanted to walk away from my desk. As I sat there, I could feel my mind generate appropriate loopholes, just like a cell phone searching for a signal. "I'm usually so diligent," "One hour of email won't make a difference," and "If I don't answer these now, I'll feel more like answering them later" sprang into my mind without effort. Then I reminded myself that I'd already decided: "I spend this time answering email."

By catching ourselves in the act of invoking a loophole, we give ourselves an opportunity to reject it, and stick to the habits that we want to foster.

WAIT FIFTEEN MINUTES

———

Distraction

Conscious self-denial leaves a man self-absorbed and vividly aware of what he has sacrificed; in consequence it fails often of its immediate object and almost always of its ultimate purpose. What is needed is not self-denial, but that kind of direction of interest outward which will lead spontaneously and naturally to the same acts that a person absorbed in the pursuit of his own virtue could only perform by means of conscious self-denial.

—BERTRAND RUSSELL, *The Conquest of Happiness*

One evening, I mentioned to Jamie that I was investigating a new habit strategy. When I'm grappling with an idea, talking about it helps me to understand it better. Jamie doesn't always enjoy the role of sounding board, but this night he was game.

"What's the strategy?" he asked.

"The Strategy of Distraction."

"That sounds easy. I get distracted all the time."

"No," I answered, "this isn't the kind of distraction that happens accidentally. You have to do it *on purpose*, which can be hard."

Then Jamie was himself distracted from our conversation by his need to pack for a business trip, so I stopped my explanation, but I couldn't stop thinking about the Strategy of Distraction.

When we distract ourselves, we purposefully redirect our thoughts, and by doing so, we change our experience. Distraction can help us resist temptation, minimize stress, feel refreshed, and tolerate pain, and it can help us stick to our good habits.

Of course, it's not enough to be distracted; we must distract ourselves in the right way. Checking Pinterest isn't a good distraction for the person who wants to break the habit of late-night online shopping; reading a mystery would work better. Also, making a purely mental shift can be difficult, so distraction works best when it involves physical activity: walking around the block, woodworking, or cleaning out the kitty-litter box. Of course, if it's an enjoyable distraction, such as playing catch with a child, so much the better.

Using the Strategy of Distraction doesn't mean trying to *suppress* an unwelcome thought, but rather deliberately shifting attention. When we try to squash a particular thought, we may trigger the "ironic rebound," so that paradoxically, we think about it all the more. The more I try to avoid thinking about how exhausted I'll be if I don't fall asleep, the more insistent this thought becomes, until I'm so agitated that I can't possibly sleep. So I don't try to avoid thinking "I need sleep," but instead turn my attention to something else.

Although people often assume that cravings intensify over time, research shows that with active distraction, urges—even strong urges—usually subside within about fifteen minutes. So now whenever I'm tempted to break a good habit (or indulge in a bad habit, two sides of the same coin), I say to myself, "I can leave my desk—in fifteen minutes." The delay of fifteen minutes is often long enough for me to get absorbed in something else. If I distract myself sufficiently, I may forget about a craving entirely.

A friend told me that if she's tempted to splurge while shopping, she resists pulling the impulse purchase from the shelf. "I tell myself, 'If I still want it by the time I've finished shopping, I can go back for it.' But by that time, I've forgotten about it, or it's too much trouble to hunt it down. I only go back if I *really* want it." Also, telling myself, "If I want, I can do that, in fifteen minutes," often works better (even for an Abstainer like me) than telling myself "no." "No" can sometimes lead to the dreaded backlash effect, in which feelings of deprivation make the forbidden more enticing.

Waiting fifteen minutes proved effective against my growing "checking habit." When I was sitting at my desk at home with three monitors, or out in the world with my phone, I felt a more and more frequent urge to check my email, Facebook, Twitter, LinkedIn, Pinterest, and all the rest. By the time I'd checked everything, I could start all over again. I wanted to get this habit under control before it became an official Bad Habit.

This checking habit was inflamed by the phenomenon of "intermittent reinforcement." Usually my email isn't very rewarding, but occasionally—and I never know when—I get an email that's *great*. This kind of unpredictable, variable, instantaneous reinforcement is the hallmark of many powerfully habit-forming actions, such as playing slot machines. Checking is also rewarding because it offers the possibility of resolution, which people crave—I get replies to my emails, I learn the definition for "claustral," I see that 150 people commented on my post. And that feels good.

Checking certainly yields rewards from time to time, but I didn't want a habit of constant checking, and delay helped me nip this habit in the bud. Now when I feel myself reaching for my smartphone, or clicking over into email and social media on my desktop, I tell myself, "Wait fifteen minutes." Sometimes I still want to look, but often I'm already in the middle of something else, and the impulse has passed.

I've heard all sorts of funny variations of Distraction. One person does twenty jumping jacks before eating a snack; another drinks a glass of water between each glass of wine; someone else takes a few minutes to be very aware of the bottom of her feet. I've heard that taking a whiff of grapefruit or peppermint helps curb appetite. Many people keep their hands busy as a way to avoid snacking. "Giving myself a manicure keeps my hands busy," a friend explained, "and I can't eat anything out of a bag if my nails are wet."

Distraction can also make it easier to keep my good habits by taking my mind off my worries or giving me relief from the blues. If I can ease myself into a better state of mind, I'm better able to use self-command. No surprise, studies suggest that distraction works best if it directs our minds to something absorbing and pleasant, rather than distressing or highly arousing. *Shrek*, not *Schindler's List*.

I figured that the Strategy of Distraction could help me soothe the agitation I feel whenever I'm harshly criticized, and soon I got the opportunity to test it. Usually my reader email is kind, or at least constructive, but in the space of one week, one reader attacked my appearance, one reader told me I was a bad role model for my daughters, and one reader characterized my practice of providing bookseller links (with full disclosure of my affiliate relationships) as "getting kickbacks."

When I get those kinds of emails, my habit—which is challenging to keep—is to adopt a mild tone. Sometimes I even get a cordial response back. (One person sent me a harsh email, and *three years* later emailed me to apologize.) To make myself feel calmer before I responded, I used Distraction, poking around on the Science Daily site to help myself muster the self-control to give a civil answer.

Along the same lines, I've noticed that some people exploit their smartphones to distract themselves from negative moods. Because he was going to a funeral, a friend would miss an important meeting that we'd scheduled. "Call me tomorrow afternoon and tell me what happened," he said.

"I can't call you!" I told him. "You'll be coming out of your grandmother's funeral."

"I'd like for you to call. It will be a distraction."

The Strategy of Distraction can also help people fight the siren call of *potato-chip news*. I'm not drawn to potato-chip news myself, so it took me a while to understand this challenge.

"Potato-chip news" is news that's repetitive, requires little effort to absorb, and is consumable in massive quantities: true crime, natural disasters, political punditry, celebrity and sports gossip, or endless photographs of beautiful houses, food, clothes, or people. Its information is usually sensationalized to carry the maximum emotional effect—to make people feel shocked, frightened, envious, outraged, insecure, or indignant.

Most of us enjoy potato-chip news occasionally—to track the Oscars or the Olympics, for instance. But those who regularly spend hours indulging in it may find they're angry with themselves for watching, and distraught by what they're watching, yet unable to step away.

Many people consider spending excessive time on potato-chip news as a bad habit in itself, and it can also inflame other bad habits, because people get so agitated by it that they lose self-command and turn to bad habits for comfort. One person wrote, "I was so worried about the election that I ate half a pan of peanut-butter brownies in front of CNN." It's important to follow the presidential election, but still, we need to deal with remote events in ways that don't derail our attempts to manage ourselves.

Distraction can help. By mindfully shifting attention away from potato-chip news, people can break free from its time-sucking grip. They can read a novel, play with a dog, do Sudoku, anything to pull away from the screen. Sometimes people limit themselves to written news accounts or establish time limits. One person told me, "I've been 'shopping' on StreetEasy for over three years. I try to limit myself to visiting the site a couple of times a week, but it's hard."

Of course, one person's bad distraction habit might be another's good distraction habit. A friend reads the sports-and-pop-culture site Grantland to distract himself when he wants a beer on a work night; on the other hand, someone else said, "I've realized I can't take a five-minute break and go to ESPN.com. I read one thing, then another. Plus I'm from Cincinnati, so I care a lot about the Bengals, and if I read something about how the Bengals suck, it puts me in a really bad mood, and I can't work."

Although I'm not attracted by potato-chip news, I sometimes find myself falling prey to a related problem, the "bad trance." The bad trance often hits when I'm exhausted—as when, paradoxically, I feel both too tired and too wired to go to bed. Often, when I'm in the bad trance, I'm overindulging in something I don't even enjoy. I'm watching bad TV, finishing a boring book, eating food that's not delicious, clicking around a website that doesn't interest me, or most inexplicably, flipping through a magazine I've already read.

In a good trance, or flow state, time passes swiftly yet feels rich, and when I emerge, I feel energized and exhilarated. In a bad trance, time feels neither full nor empty, and I find myself sitting with my mouth half open, regretting the time I've wasted. Every once in a while, I do love to lie on a hotel bed and spend an hour channel surfing, but I don't want to make a habit of going into the bad trance. I watch for the symptoms—a feeling of lethargy that makes it hard to get out of my chair, coupled with a feeling of listless curiosity—and make the effort to distract myself from the lure of the trance.

One unexpected benefit of going to sleep earlier has been the marked decline in the frequency of my bad trances. When I'm not exhausted, and when I'm not up too late, I don't fall into this habit.

Distraction can be helpful, but it can also be distinctly *unhelpful*. For instance, the "ping" of new email kept interrupting my thoughts when I was working, and once I knew I had a new email, it was very hard to resist reading it. Intermittent reinforcement! So I used a few minutes of my next Power Hour to figure out how to turn the sound off.

Also, to avoid unhelpful distractions, I often leave my home office to write in the library near my apartment. I don't work in an office, so I'm not interrupted by coworkers, but at home even the *possibility* of interruption distracts me. At the library, I know that the phone won't ring, the doorbell won't buzz, the mail won't arrive.

A friend who works in his studio apartment figured out a way to avoid the distractions of napping and snacking. Every morning he makes his bed, eats breakfast, and "goes to work" for the day, which means he doesn't allow himself to sit on his bed or go into the kitchen, except at mealtime. Author Jean Kerr spent half her writing time in the parked family car, where she had no distractions from her four young sons, and where there was nothing to do except work.

Although working at the library solved my distraction problem, at one point I began to wonder if I "should" train myself to work better at home. Shouldn't I develop the self-control to resist the siren call of email, Facebook, Twitter, LinkedIn, and all the rest? Shouldn't I manage myself so I didn't have to pack up and go to the library?

Then I realized—no. My existing habits work very well: when I'm at home, I do work related to the online world, such as email and social media; to do the harder work of writing, I go to the library (or less often, a coffee shop). Why force myself to change? I love the library! It's a *treat* to work there. It's one block from my apartment, so I don't spend a lot of time going to and fro. It's helpful to walk out into the fresh air and sunlight, and to have a little break between "home" and "work."

Besides, I know myself. I'd need a lot of self-control to develop the habits to limit my Internet usage when I'm at home—but at the library, the Internet never tempts me. Why waste self-control energy unnecessarily? It's easier to change my surroundings than to change myself.

I've discovered another, quirkier focus booster. When I sit down to write, I always have the urge to stick something in my mouth—gum, a snack, a hot drink—because it helps me concentrate. I can satisfy this urge, I've learned, by chewing on a plastic coffee stirrer. I picked up this idea from Jamie, who loves to chew on things. His favorite chew toy is a plastic pen top, and gnawed pen tops and little bits of plastic litter our apartment. Every time we go to a movie, he grabs a straw to chew while we watch. He also chews on plastic stirrers, and I decided to try it myself. I've been *astonished* at how helpful this small habit is. I keep stirrers in my office and backpack, and whenever I sit down at my computer, I pop one between my teeth, and it helps me to focus. Chewing on a plastic stirrer is probably the adult equivalent of using a pacifier, but it works. Perhaps it's the placebo effect—but after all, the placebo effect is quite effective. I do worry that it might not be a good idea to chew away on plastic. Oh well.

Paradoxically, I find that a brief period of distraction can sometimes help me avoid being distracted. When I'm trying to focus for a long time, it's helpful to take brief, refreshing breaks (emphasis on the *brief*). When a friend gets stuck, she juggles. "It's the perfect break," she explained. "It's fun, it's active, it takes a lot of concentration, yet it's mindless. And I can't do it for very long, so my break can't be very long."

I realized I have a habit like that myself, which I'd been treating as a bad habit, but it's not a *bad* habit, it's a *good* habit—my habit of wandering through the library stacks to look at whatever titles catch my eye. I love doing this, and I've found a surprising number of good books this way. I'd always considered it an inefficient use of time, but actually it was a perfect distraction.

The fact is, I can't write for three hours straight, or for even forty-five minutes. I need a lot of breaks. It's a Secret of Adulthood: To keep going, I sometimes need to allow myself to stop.

NO FINISH LINE

Reward

The reward of a thing well done is to have done it.

—RALPH WALDO EMERSON, "New England Reformers"

I'd been practicing meditation for several months without a single day off, and I no longer felt slightly ridiculous as I lowered myself onto my cushion every morning. For the most part, though, I didn't see any change in myself, and that five minutes of meditation was becoming more frustrating and boring. One morning, after I'd settled myself into position and set the alarm on my phone, I had a powerful urge to stand right back up.

I didn't, but my attempts at an empty mind that morning were foiled by my reflections about why I hadn't jumped up. I sat in the early-morning light, not meditating, thinking about my habit. I was sticking with it for two reasons. First, I knew I shouldn't break a good habit on a whim. *Decide, then don't decide.* Second, because I'd made a habit of meditating, skipping the meditation would make me feel as though I'd started the day on the wrong foot. This is the power of habit—the iron that helps bind me to my good habits, and to my bad habits as well.

Maybe meditating was changing me imperceptibly. Maybe my struggle to meditate showed just how much I needed meditation. Maybe if I stuck to it, I'd experience a breakthrough. *Or maybe not.*

As an Upholder, an argument like "You've been so diligent, take a day off!" didn't really tempt me. But I did briefly think, "Maybe I should give myself a reward for sticking with meditation." That line of thought seemed dangerous for some reason, but I didn't know why. Wasn't a reward a good way to keep myself motivated?

And so on and so on until, with relief, I heard the "crickets" alarm go off, and I could stand up.

This train of thought, plus a brief conversation with a friend, made me focus on the issue of reward—and its risks. My friend announced, "I've been dieting, but the minute I hit my goal weight, I'm going to reward myself with a luscious slice of chocolate cake." Even beyond the obvious fact that her plan seemed to undermine the whole purpose of the diet, this struck me as a bad idea. But why?

The Strategy of Reward is a very familiar and popular method to encourage good behavior. It's so familiar and popular, in fact, that it's easy to assume it's effective. Go for a run, have a beer.

But do habits work like that? Rewarding good behavior sounds like a sensible idea—*on the surface*. But the more I thought about rewards—about the research I'd read, and more important, what I'd observed in people's behavior—the more skeptical I became. As explored by writers such as Alfie Kohn in *Punished by Rewards* and Daniel Pink in *Drive*, rewards have very complex consequences.

In fact, I eventually concluded, rewards can actually be *dangerous* for habit formation. If I want to make a habit, I must use rewards in a very careful, limited way. I noted the irony: studying the Strategy of Reward meant studying why we should mostly *avoid* using reward.

A reward obstructs habit formation, for three reasons.

First, a reward teaches me that I wouldn't do a particular activity for its own sake, but only to earn that reward; therefore, I learn to associate the activity with an imposition, a deprivation, or suffering. This well-documented—but too often ignored—consequence of rewards relates to the difference between outer and inner motivation.

We're *extrinsically motivated* when we do an activity to get an external reward (a carrot) or to avoid an external punishment (a stick);

we're *intrinsically motivated* when we pursue an activity for its own sake. Drawing on intrinsic motivation makes us far more likely to stick to a behavior, and to find it satisfying.

Organizational theorists Thomas Malone and Mark Lepper identified several sources of intrinsic motivation:

Challenge: we find personal meaning in pursuing a goal that's difficult but not impossible.

Curiosity: we're intrigued and find pleasure in learning more.

Control: we like the feeling of mastery.

Fantasy: we play a game; we use our imagination to make an activity more stimulating.

Cooperation: we enjoy the satisfaction of working with others.

Competition: we feel gratified when we can compare ourselves favorably to others.

Recognition: we're pleased when others recognize our accomplishments and contributions.

The Four Tendencies can help us figure out which intrinsic motivators might resonate most for us. For an Upholder, a habit that's a source of control might have special appeal; for a Questioner, curiosity; for an Obliger, cooperation; for a Rebel, challenge.

Despite the greater power of intrinsic motivation, people frequently rely on extrinsic motivation—the easy carrot or stick—to try to prod themselves or others into action. But it turns out that extrinsic motivation undermines intrinsic motivation, so rewards can turn enthusiastic participants into reluctant paid workers, and transform fun into drudge work.

One study showed that children who got a reward for coloring with magic markers—an activity that children love—didn't spend as much time with markers, later, as children who didn't expect a reward. The children began to think, "Why would I color if I don't get a reward?" Furthermore, rewarded children produced drawings of significantly lower quality than children who expected no reward. I visited a major corporation that, to encourage employees to attend health lectures, bestows points that can be redeemed for prizes; so why would employees go if they don't get points? As my sister the sage once told me, "You want volunteers, not recruits."

Many assume that offering a reward will help people to jump-start a healthy habit, which will then persist after the reward fades away. Not so. Often, as soon as the reward stops (and sometimes before it stops), the behavior stops. When people get paid to exercise, take medication, or quit smoking, they do so, but once the reward has been gained, the behavior may stop, too. If an employer gives people $120 for taking a health-risk assessment, why would they take it again for free? If I tell Eliza that she can watch an hour of TV if she reads for an hour, I don't build her habit of reading; I teach her that watching TV is more fun than reading. With some behaviors, of course, it's safe to assume that they'll continue even if the reward stops. I gave Eleanor an M&M every time she successfully used the potty, but I was pretty confident she'd continue to use the potty even after I cut off her M&M supply.

Rewards pose these dangers, and to make matters worse, we often choose a reward that directly undermines the habit—as with my friend's reward of chocolate cake. When I told her that I thought rewarding herself with cake was a bad idea, she protested, "But what will be my reward for losing ten pounds?"

I laughed. "Losing ten pounds!"

Perverse rewards undermine our efforts and teach us to despise the very behavior we want to embrace. I love the TV show *Friends*, and one episode captures this tension. Chandler has started smoking again, and Phoebe points out, "But you've been so good for three years."

Chandler, cigarette in hand, explains, *"And this is my reward."*

The second reason rewards pose a danger for habits is that they require a *decision*. A habit, by my definition, is something we do without decision making; making a decision such as "Do I get my reward today?" "Do I deserve this?" "Have I done enough to earn the cash bonus?" or "Does this time count?" exhausts precious mental energy, moves attention away from the habit to the reward, and in the end, interferes with habit formation.

With my own habits, I've decided not to decide. I do an action without debate, without evaluation, and without reward. Just as I don't reward myself for brushing my teeth or buckling my seat belt, I don't consider Power Hour, exercise, or posting to my blog to be exceptional accomplishments that merit a reward. These actions are habits that run on automatic.

The third danger posed by rewards? This one took me much longer to recognize: the risk of the "finish line." Setting a finish line does indeed help people reach a specific, one-time goal, but although it's widely assumed to help habit formation, the reward of hitting a finish line actually can *undermine* habits.

I constantly work to understand what's happening right in front of me, and when I first noticed that finish lines tend to disrupt habits, I was perplexed. I noticed this phenomenon after several people told me the same thing, practically in the same words, that I'd heard from a college friend. He'd told me, "When I was training for the marathon, I was great about running. I loved it. I took it so seriously that I drove the people around me crazy. I thought of myself as a runner and thought I'd be running forever. Then I finished the marathon, I took the two weeks of rest you're supposed to take . . . and somehow three years have gone by."

This pattern puzzled me. Shouldn't working toward a specific goal create a habitual practice and supply an emotional satisfaction that would strengthen the habit? Shouldn't the reward of crossing a finish line give people more psychic energy to persevere? I was surprised— almost to the point of disbelief—to observe that finish lines didn't have that effect.

Finally, it became perfectly obvious. A finish line marks a *stopping point*. Once we stop, we must start over, and *starting over is harder than continuing.* I'd seen this in my study of the Strategy of First Steps. The more dramatic the goal, the more decisive the end—and the more effort required to start over. By providing a specific goal and a temporary motivation, and requiring a new "start" once reached, hitting a milestone may interfere with habit formation.

It's absolutely true that a reward may help people reach a *specific goal*—but in the area of habit formation, the aim is to adopt a habit *forever,* to change the way we live for the better. Not to finish this grant proposal, but to write every day forever; not to run a marathon, but to exercise forever. In a study of people trying to quit smoking, people offered a prize for turning in weekly progress reports had worse long-term quitting rates than people who had no intervention, and programs that rewarded people for wearing their seat belts resulted in lower long-term seat-belt wearing than programs without rewards.

Aside from the energy required to start over once we've crossed the finish line, the very fact that we've achieved a finish line creates its own problem. Once we decide that we've achieved success, we tend to stop moving forward. As a perfect illustration, a guy told me, "I set a goal for myself, '6 by 30,' " he said. "I wanted to get a six-pack before my thirtieth birthday, which was right around the time I was getting married."

"Wait," I interrupted, "let me guess how this turns out. You reached the goal but haven't maintained it."

"Pretty much," he admitted. And he's a behavioral economist!

Though it's easy to assume that if we consistently repeat an action, it becomes a habit, often it doesn't work that way. I know someone who joined National Novel Writing Month, where participants write 1,667 words a day to complete a 50,000-word novel in a month. He effortlessly kept pace with the program and thought he was building a writing habit, but once the month ended, he stopped writing. He'd been striving toward a finish line, not building a habit. A blog reader observed, "Hitting the finish line usually means dropping the Lenten habit I've adopted. Pray the rosary every day? I planned to keep it up, but I stopped after Easter."

A finish line divides behavior that we want to follow indefinitely—to run, to write, to practice—into "start" and "stop," and all too often, the "stop" turns out to be permanent. I was amazed to read that within six months of delivery, 60 to 70 percent of women who stop smoking during pregnancy have started to smoke again. They drop the smoking habit for months, and they kick the chemical addiction out of their system, but when they cross the finish line, they start smoking again.

The reward of the finish line has a particularly bad effect for people on a "diet." Despite its popularity—in 2012, about one in five American adults was on a diet—dieting has an abysmal track record. According to a review of studies of the long-term outcomes of calorie-restricting diets, one-third to two-thirds of people who dieted eventually regained more weight than they initially lost. Why? Perhaps because people are encouraged to set a goal weight, and once they've hit that finish line, they slide back into their old eating habits. As one reader explained: "I followed the Atkins diet to fit into a dress for a wedding, wore the dress, then ate whatever I wanted. The weight came back, but it was really hard to start Atkins again. I didn't have the wedding to keep me motivated." Maintaining a healthy weight requires us not to follow a temporary diet, but to change our eating habits *forever.*

True, some people do seem to have the energy for successive fresh starts, at least if the goals seem valuable enough to them. A friend told me she'd had knee surgery and endured the months of required physical therapy.

"The rehab must have been tough," I said. "I know you've never liked going to the gym."

"No. And now I go regularly."

"How were you able to stick to it?" I asked.

"I had a goal—to go skiing with my children. I knew that if I didn't do the rehab, I'd never be able to do that."

"If you hadn't had that goal, don't you think you might have stuck with it anyway? After all, without rehab, you'd have lost the full function of your knee. That's pretty important."

"I don't know," she admitted. "Would I have done it, several times a week, for all those months? I don't think so. Maybe I would have gone once a week."

"But for you, the goal of family skiing did the trick."

"Yes, and last week, we all went skiing together."

"Now that you've crossed that finish line, will you keep going to the gym?"

She paused. "I think so, because I have a new goal. I want to get in great shape."

"It's good you have a new goal, but be careful," I warned. "From my research, I'd say that you're in a danger zone. Your reward marks a stopping point—which means you're starting again, and starting is hard. So pay close attention to the habit."

A few months later, I was curious to hear whether she'd been able to use her new goal successfully. When I asked her if she was still going to the gym, she answered, "Yes! Because my new goal—to fit comfortably into the clothes I wore on my honeymoon—keeps me motivated."

I admire my friend's tenacity, and this approach works for her. I've noticed that some people are serial goal setters, rather than habit formers. Also, she's a Questioner, so perhaps a succession of finish lines helps to satisfy her desire for justification and sound reason. To me, constantly setting and committing to new goals sounds like too much effort; I find it easier just to commit to a habit. That's the Upholder perspective.

And many people do indeed find it helpful to sprint toward a finish line. The intense but limited efforts of a Blast Start can help us jump-start a new habit or pour new energy into an existing habit. For instance, many people successfully focus on a specific habit for thirty days to help themselves launch into a new behavior. Having done that, they should be careful, however, to recognize the special challenge posed by a finish line, so that they can put extra effort into maintaining their good habits after crossing that line. The real test of a thirty-day Blast Start is what happens on *day 31*.

If they want the new behavior to become a habit, they should use if-then planning from the Strategy of Safeguards to decide, in advance, how to proceed after hitting the finish line—perhaps by continually setting themselves new goals, just as my friend with the bad knee replaced one goal with another, or by deciding what the everyday habit should be.

Because rewards can undermine habit formation, I didn't want to focus on rewards to motivate myself; nevertheless, a habit must be rewarding in some way, or I wouldn't bother to do it at all.

My challenge, therefore, was to make my habits *rewarding* without sabotaging myself with *rewards*. How?

By finding my reward *within the habit itself*, with a reward that takes me deeper into the habit. If I look outside a habit for a reward, I undermine the habit. If I look within the habit for the reward, I strengthen the habit. A natural consequence of doing a lot of writing is getting a new, improved laptop (I wear out laptops; the keys start popping off). Once a week, when I do strength training, I walk there and take a taxi home. It's an indulgence to take a taxi instead taking the subway, but I decided, "A natural consequence of a demanding workout is feeling tired, and because I'm so tired, I get to take a taxi."

I pitched a friend on this approach after he told me, "I want to cut back on my drinking, so I'm giving up drinking for a month. As a reward, I'll buy myself an iPad."

"Can I suggest thinking about it in a different way if you want to change your habits for the long run?" I asked.

"Sure."

"If you quit drinking, you'll save money, right?"

"Absolutely. I spend a ton at restaurants and bars."

"So, a *natural consequence* of not drinking is that you'll have more spare cash. You can choose to spend the money on an iPad, or whatever. Getting the iPad isn't a *reward* for not drinking; it's a natural consequence of giving up drinking and having that money."

"I don't get what you mean."

"Say you want to start packing lunch for work. Instead of thinking, 'As a reward for preparing and bringing in my own lunch, I'll splurge on a lunch at an expensive restaurant on Friday,' you think, 'Now that I'm bringing in lunch every day, I'm going to splurge on a fabulous set of knives, so my habit of cooking is more fun.'"

"What's the difference?"

"A 'reward' changes your attitude toward a behavior. At some level, it causes you to think 'I'm not drinking because I want an iPad.' But if you think 'I'm not drinking because I want to feel healthier, more energetic, and more in control. Added benefit: I have extra money to buy things I want.' That's a different state of mind, and might shift the way you view drinking in the future."

The reward for a good habit is the habit itself. I visited a Fortune 10 company with a brilliant wellness policy: any employee who uses the company gym at least seventy-five times annually gets the next year's membership for free. This offer struck me as a terrific combination of the Strategies of Monitoring, Accountability, Convenience—because something feels more convenient when it's free—and Reward. The company's reward for exercise is *more exercise*. (Which reminds me of the old joke: Making partner in a law firm is like winning a pie-eating contest, and being told that the prize is . . . more pie.)

In addition to the particular benefits conveyed by a habit, the mere fact of sticking to a healthy habit gives me a rewarding sense of growth; adding one coin to the growing heap is very satisfying. My UP band gives me a sense of advancement, without the risks presented by a finish line. Continuous progress is the opposite of a finish line.

JUST BECAUSE

——

Treats

One of the secrets of a happy life is continuous small treats.

—Iris Murdoch, *The Sea, the Sea*

I'd started many habits over the past several months, and, Upholder that I am, I embraced them, and I planned to follow them indefinitely. No finish lines. Nevertheless, while I was being more productive and more mindful, I sometimes felt burdened by these new activities. All this effort could be tiresome, even for someone like me.

Which is where the delightful Strategy of Treats comes in. Unlike a reward, which must be earned or justified, a "treat" is a small pleasure or indulgence that we give to ourselves *just because we want it*. We don't have to be "good" to get it, we don't earn it or justify it.

"Treats" may sound like a self-indulgent, frivolous strategy, but it's not. Because forming good habits can be draining, treats can play an important role. When we give ourselves treats, we feel energized, cared for, and contented, which boosts our self-command—and self-command helps us maintain our healthy habits. Studies show that people who got a little treat, in the form of receiving a surprise gift or watching a funny video, gained in self-control, and I know that I find it easier to face Power Hour if I had coffee with a friend during the day. It's a Secret of Adulthood: If I give more to myself, I can ask more from myself. Self-regard isn't selfish.

By contrast, when we don't get any treats, we feel depleted, re-sentful, and angry, and justified in self-indulgence. We start to crave comfort—and we'll grab that comfort wherever we can, even if it means breaking good habits.

To strengthen my good habits, I decided to create a menu of healthy treats—but that can be more challenging than it sounds. So many popular treats come at a cost: the museum visit requires a long trip across town, the new shoes are expensive, the martini tonight will make the morning tougher. My favorite treat is reading, and reading requires time and concentration, which aren't always easy to muster. A reader of my blog noted, "I love to play the piano, but it takes focus, and some days I've already spent out my focus quota."

I began by collecting examples of other people's inventive treats: browsing through art books, cookbooks, or travel guides; taking photographs on a walk; napping; having a session of "fur therapy" (petting a dog or cat); wandering through a camping store; looking at family photo albums; keeping art postcards in the car visor for a quick diversion in stalled traffic; going to a comedy club; going to baseball games; listening to podcasts; coloring in a coloring book; visiting an amusement park; learning a new magic trick.

It's important to have some treat options that aren't very demand-ing. A friend told me, "Every day after I get my kids off to school, I go back to bed for twenty minutes. I may go to sleep, or else I just lie there. I'm still at work by 9:00 a.m., and that little indulgence makes me so happy." A friend living in London told me his treat: "My cal-endar is packed, but twice a day, for fifteen minutes, I sit and drink an espresso and read the *International Herald Tribune*, and I don't check email, I don't do work. I don't want any additional breaks, but I'm furious if I don't get those two." Another friend said, "I wonder if there's something a person could do with this sexually. Depending on their situation." He laughed. "I don't even want to say out loud what I'm thinking."

"No, don't spell it out!" I protested. "But it's true that treats that come through the body seem to have a special power."

Sometimes treats might not look like treats. Writer Jan Struther observed, "Constructive destruction is one of the most delightful employments in the world." I find that true, and tasks like shredding mail, emptying out files, or even peeling hard-boiled eggs can feel like a treat. Funnily enough, clearing clutter is also a treat for me, when I'm in a certain mood. On my blog, people wrote about their own untreatlike treats: ironing, writing code, doing Latin translation.

As a treat for herself, for her birthday, one of Jamie's colleagues walked to work—six miles. "Did she do it to prove to herself she could do it?" I asked. "Or as a treat?"

"Oh, she wanted to do it," Jamie assured me. "For fun."

Although I love hearing what other people consider treats, I remind myself to "Be Gretchen." Just because an activity is a treat for *someone else* doesn't mean it's a treat for *me*—and vice versa. A friend said, "I love CrossFit, that's a treat for me." Maybe I could reframe my yoga class, or exercise generally, as my "treat," I thought. Then I realized—nope. I do enjoy it, *in a way*, but it's not a treat. A friend told me that her favorite treat was to shop for gifts—a task that for me is arduous enough to qualify for Power Hour. I wish my bank of fun included activities like sketching, playing tennis, cooking, doing puzzles, or playing a musical instrument, but they're not treats for me.

I made a list of my own treats. One of my favorites is a visit to the library. I love keeping a log of books I want to read, looking up the call numbers, and wandering through the stacks to pick them out. Returning library books is an odd little treat, too (perhaps that's my Finisher nature). I love copying out my favorite passages from books and adding them to my various collections of quotations. I view sleep as a big treat, which is why I don't resent the idea of going to bed earlier, the way some people do. For me, it feels like a luxurious indulgence.

Beautiful smells are a reliable treat and can be enjoyed in an instant, with no cost, no effort, and no planning. In a flash, I get pleasure from the fresh smell of a grapefruit, or the comforting fragrance of clean towels, or the promising smell of a hardware store. I remind myself to *notice* such treats, to register the fact that I'm experiencing a scent that I love.

After all, we make something a treat by calling it a "treat." It's all too easy to overlook how much we enjoy something. When we notice our pleasure, and relish it, the experience becomes much more of a treat. Even something as humble as herbal tea or a box of freshly sharpened pencils can qualify as a treat. "Look," I tell myself as I light a scented candle, "I'm giving myself a treat." Sometimes we can even reframe a challenging habit as a treat, which makes it much easier to keep. A reader observed, "When I thought of exercise as something I 'should' do, it was hard to get into a routine. Eventually, I decided to count my daily walk or cross-country ski as a treat—my time for myself in a day otherwise filled with responsibilities. Somehow, that made it much easier to make it a priority."

The treats of childhood retain a special power. As a child, I was rarely allowed to drink soda or to buy a book instead of checking it out from the library. What do I do now, with abandon? Drink diet soda and buy books (the book-buying treat is wholly separate from the library-visiting treat). So perhaps we parents need to think hard about what we identify as treats for our children.

A friend thought she should renounce her treat. "I really love coffee, but I know I should stop drinking it," she told me.

"Why?" I pressed. "Does it keep you up at night? Does it make your stomach hurt?"

"No, it doesn't affect me."

I couldn't resist launching into a defense of coffee. "You need some treats, and as treats go, coffee is great. Even if you buy very expensive coffee, it's not *that* expensive, in absolute terms. It boosts your energy and focus. If you don't add anything crazy, it doesn't have any sugar, carbs, fat, or calories, but it does have antioxidants, vitamins, minerals, and even fiber, weird as that sounds. Caffeine is fine if you're drinking it in the human range. Plus, there's pleasant ritual connected with it—you can go out for coffee with a friend."

"But I drink so much. I should at least cut back."

"But *why*?" I pressed. "Enjoy it! Samuel Johnson said, 'All severity that does not tend to increase good, or prevent evil, is idle.' A habit isn't bad unless it causes some kind of problem."

I don't think I convinced her.

Putting time, money, or energy toward treats may be easier or harder, depending on a person's Tendency. Rebels readily give themselves treats. As an Upholder, I have a strong sense of self-preservation, and I'll say to myself, "I'm at the end of my rope. I'm going to stop working and read Jung's *Memories, Dreams, Reflections* for an hour."

Because they want to have good reasons for their actions, some Questioners may be more willing to give themselves treats if they believe that getting treats isn't frivolous or arbitrary.

For instance, a Questioner might benefit from thinking, "I'm getting a massage, which increases immune function" or "I'll go to the football game with my brother, and that will strengthen our family ties." Other Questioners like to consider treats as "investments." A Questioner wrote: "I'm getting a haircut at the expensive place, not the $20 place, because having a professional cut and color helps my career. (Maybe a little bit just because I like it so much better.)" To be sure, some Questioners may conclude that "because I want to" is a sufficient justification for a treat.

Obligers, by contrast, may have trouble giving themselves treats if they feel that the time, energy, or money is more properly owed to someone else. But it's important for Obligers to have treats. They're susceptible to burnout, and too many moments of self-deprivation, or too much work for the benefit of others, may lead them to feel resentful, neglected, or deprived. Touching on Obliger rebellion, one Obliger wrote: "I don't give myself treats, finding it much easier to give treats to others. Every so often, however, a level of anger surfaces . . . I have no problem treating myself when I am in these rare times of 'Obliger resistance.' " Another Obliger explained how he uses his Obliger character to convince himself to enjoy at least one regular treat: "I'm reluctant to give myself treats but happy to provide treats to others. I just never feel right taking that time away from the other things and people that I'm responsible for. I do manage to take one night a week for myself (I'm a member of a skating team), which is a classic Obliger thing to do as I wouldn't get out if people weren't counting on me."

Framing a treat in terms of its benefit to others is a good way for Obligers to manage to give themselves treats: "If I spend a few hours playing golf, I'll be more patient at home and at work." A reader wrote, "I just spent more on a make-up product than I have in my entire life, because I recently resolved to pay more attention to my appearance. I decided to do this because I thought it would help me feel more attractive, which would be good for my marriage. Notice that the ultimate goal is improving my relationship, not just feeling better for my own sake."

People who are around Obligers can help ward off Obliger burn-out, and Obliger rebellion, by encouraging them to treat themselves (healthfully) and by providing external accountability to make sure they follow through. "You said you wanted to take a nap, and you'll be irritable if you don't. Go lie down. We won't expect to see you for an hour."

The four Tendencies may have different views about whether to schedule treats regularly, or whether to indulge in spontaneous treats. As an Upholder, I prefer a scheduled treat; I like being able to anticipate and depend on getting that treat. A Rebel prefers a spontaneous treat. A Questioner would follow whatever course would enhance the pleasure of the treat. An Obliger would need external accountability to get that treat, which would usually require scheduling.

By helping us to feel energetic and happy, healthy treats can play a key role in fostering good habits, but we must guard against the temptations of unhealthy treats. The pleasure lasts a minute, but then feelings of guilt, regret, loss of control, and other negative consequences kick in. A reader posted on my Facebook page: "My treats are *never* good for me. If I'm feeling good, I think I deserve something that's not good for me. If I'm feeling bad, I think I deserve something that's not good for me." Another reader added, "Skipping class is a treat that has a bad effect on me. I do it to feel better, but it makes me feel so much worse."

Three categories of treats, in particular, are dangerous. First, food. Indulging feels good for a moment, but it may leave us feeling worse in the long run. One study found that women are more likely to eat chocolate when feeling anxious or depressed, but this treat just makes them feel more guilty. People who struggle with their relationship to food may do better to find nonfood treats, period.

Second, shopping. For many people, shopping is a treat—perhaps surprisingly, research suggests that people are more likely to impulse-shop when they're feeling *good* than when they're feeling *bad*. Shopping is a chance to have a small adventure; to enjoy the world by looking, touching, tasting, and smelling; to feel the thrill of the hunt, the bargain, and the crossed-off items on the to-do list. However, spending too much time or money on shopping can make people feel worse. Some manage to enjoy an anxiety-free shopping treat by limiting themselves to window-shopping or bargain hunting at flea markets or garage sales. A reader wrote: "I do sometimes 'sport shop' for entertainment or relaxation or emotional pick-up. I set a money limit before going into a store to browse." Another reader fills up her online cart, then abandons it without making a purchase. One reader posted: "I pop into an antiques store while I am out running errands. I almost never buy anything, but stylishly arranged stores with beautiful things are such pleasant places—like small art museums." Another explained, "I shop online a lot, sometimes too much. Recently, if I see something I like, I will pin it to a Pinterest board instead of buying it right away. This often satisfies the 'need' to buy the item and gives me the small jolt of happiness that comes along with getting something new. Just knowing I've saved it somewhere is satisfying." But as with food, people who struggle to curb their spending may do better to find nonretail activities.

The third category of dangerous treats? Screen time, particularly television (however viewed). Americans spend about half their leisure hours watching TV. Although I don't watch much TV, I'm determined to keep it a treat instead of a default activity, which it can become all too easily. Television stays a treat, I concluded, if:

- I anticipate with pleasure watching a particular show (I'm not just flipping through the channels).
- I watch with someone else.
- I turn off the TV when the episode is over.
- I feel energized, not listless, when the episode is over.

Screens of all kinds tend to drain energy, if used too long; they consume time that could be spent in other activities; they make it easy to stay up too late; they make it easy to eat mindlessly. Technology is a good servant but a bad master. Like habit itself.

Although treats make it easier to stick to good habits, if we make a habit of a treat, it may stop feeling like a treat. In "treat creep," a rare treat gradually turns ordinary, or a small indulgence grows larger over time. Philosopher Immanuel Kant permitted himself only one pipe per day, but as years passed, his pipe bowls became much larger. Taking a bath with fancy bath salts once a week is a treat; taking that bath every day might make it a background activity of life. I can tear through all of the magazines in my stack, one right after the other, or I can dole them out as treats. Things can be part of an ordinary day, or we can consider them treats.

Of course, whether a particular habit is "good" or "bad" is a matter of opinion.

"If you're cultivating good habits," a friend told me, "you should give up your habit of drinking so much diet soda."

"Nope!" I answered. "I don't consider it a bad habit. *Regular* soda is terrible, but I never touch the regular stuff."

"It can't be good for you."

"Well," I said with a shrug, "I don't smoke, I hardly drink, I eat low-carb, and I don't believe that diet soda is harmful. Would I be better off drinking plain water? Maybe. But this is my treat."

Perhaps because of my Upholder nature, marching through my daily calendar sometimes feels like an energy-boosting treat.

One day, in fact, my sister said to me, "I had an epiphany. You would have made a great monk."

Elizabeth knows me very well. "It's *so strange* that you say that," I replied. "Just last week I was reading *The Rule of St. Benedict.*" This extraordinarily influential, thousand-year-old guide sets out the rules for monks living in monasteries. "I love the monastic approach to the day. Every hour with its own name and its own activity, all laid out."

Not everyone (e.g., certainly no Rebel) is attracted by the idea of having each day ordered, but I love the monkish *horarium,* or "table of hours," the highly specific routine that runs on an annual cycle, with variations for the days of the week and the seasons. Every part of the day has its own character and purpose, with time set aside for prayer, manual work, rest, eating, sleeping. Few decisions, no hurry, time for everything.

I was particularly intrigued by the hours that monks set aside for *lectio divina*, or spiritual reading. This is another kind of treat. To be happy, even we non-monks need to make time for transcendent matters—such as beauty, creativity, service, faith—but too often these get pushed aside for more urgent demands, and life begins to feel empty and purposeless. Scheduling *lectio divina* is a way to make sure that the spiritual gets attention—whether a person decides to read holy books and attend religious services, as a monk would do, or adapts this habit to make regular time to leaf through art books, read biographies of great figures, spend time in nature, go to concerts, volunteer, or meditate. For some people, politics is a spiritual concern, tied to transcendent values such as justice, opportunity, and freedom. And from what I've observed, sports seems to have a spiritual value for some people—with its aspects of devotion, loyalty, hope, and perseverance.

Once we've truly adopted a habit, it comes easily, without decision making. But until that point—and many habits, alas, can never be completely taken for granted—giving ourselves a little boost with treats helps us maintain our self-command. Goethe pointed out, "Whatever liberates our spirit without giving us mastery over ourselves is destructive." And whatever liberates our spirit while giving us mastery over ourselves is constructive.

SITTING IS THE NEW SMOKING

Pairing

In the acquisition of a new habit, or the leaving off of an old one, we must take care to launch ourselves with as strong and decided an initiative as possible . . . Never suffer an exception to occur till the new habit is securely rooted in your life. *Each lapse is like the letting fall of a ball of string which one is carefully winding up; a single slip undoes more than a great many turns will wind again.*

—WILLIAM JAMES, *Psychology: Briefer Course*

For me, the Strategy of Pairing was such a familiar approach to habit formation that it took me a long time to notice it. I'd used it often in my own life, and it came so naturally to me that I didn't give it much thought. When I happened to mention it, however, people responded with so much interest and enthusiasm that I realized it deserved to be studied as its own strategy. In the Strategy of Pairing, I couple two activities, one that I need or want to do, and one that I don't particularly want to do, to get myself to accomplish them both. It's not a reward, it's not a treat, it's just a *pairing*.

For example, I'd briefly explained the Strategy of Pairing to an acquaintance, and a few months later, she reported that it had transformed her habits.

"I have to tell you," she said with enthusiasm, "thanks to what you said, I've been going to the gym regularly. It's *amazing*. I could never get myself to go, and now I go all the time."

"Really?" I said, pleased that she was giving me credit, even if undeserved, for this before-and-after. "Uh, remind me . . . what exactly did you try?"

"I'm using the Strategy of Pairing. Now I watch certain TV shows only while I work out. That's why I go! I *want* to go to the gym, because I have all these shows I'm addicted to."

"Excellent!" I said. "Are you ever tempted to sneak in an episode at home, too?"

"No, because I know that if I did it once, I'd do it all the time. *Only at the gym* is my rule. I was sick for a few days, and I thought, 'I can't go to the gym, and I'm just lying here, so wouldn't it be okay to watch my show?' But I didn't let myself."

I've used pairing to help me stick to the habit of exercise myself. Although I've shaped myself into a dedicated if low-intensity exerciser, I still sometimes feel the pull of my couch-potato nature, and pairing helps me keep my gym habit strong. I love reading magazines, and Jamie and I still subscribe to lots of old-fashioned print magazines—nineteen, the last time I counted—and I allow myself to read them *only* at the gym, when I'm on the cardio machines. (The fact that I can easily read magazines while I exercise may suggest that I'm not exercising very hard—and I'm not. But at least I'm showing up.) My sister does the same thing with her home treadmill and the *Real Housewives* shows. "It really makes me *want* to do the treadmill," she explained. During college, I used pairing to get myself to exercise: I wouldn't let myself take a shower unless I'd exercised. I'd go a day, or maybe two, without a shower, but pretty soon I really wanted that shower.

Pairing can work in all kinds of circumstances. When I lived in San Francisco after college, I took a good walk every morning, because I bought my morning bagel from a bagel store half a mile from my apartment. If I wanted the bagel, I had to go for the walk. (I find it much more satisfying to walk with a purpose: to go to a favorite coffee shop, to hike to the top of the mountain.) I know someone who does "car praying": he says his daily prayers during his commute home from work. Someone else watches TED talks while shaving. A friend who travels frequently for work has a rule that she never works on an airplane; she only reads novels. That habit makes her business travel much more fun, and she keeps the habit of reading. A reader wrote: "I do 'Commercial Cleaning.' When a commercial comes on, I do a chore—wash six dishes, put a load in the dryer, dust the dining room. Once the commercials are over, I sit down again. It's amazing how I can get so much done in little spurts. Plus I don't consider myself such a slug at the end of the day." A man told me that he keeps his pillbox next to the coffeemaker and doesn't allow himself to make his morning coffee until he's taken his daily medication.

No surprise, Upholders and Questioners find the Strategy of Pairing easier to use than the other Tendencies do. Depending on the situation, Obligers may find it difficult to use this Strategy because there's no external accountability. There's no one to say, "Nope, you can't make coffee until you've taken your medicine." Nevertheless, some Obligers do seem to be able to use it successfully. Rebels are unlikely to try this approach.

I'm always on the alert for exciting new habit-formation ideas, and my friends often pitch me their favorites. A highly organized friend suggested a pairing. "Give my habit a try," she told me. "When I walk from one room to another at home, I carry something with me. I don't put it away, necessarily, I just move it closer to its destination."

"But how will that make a difference?" I asked, skeptical.

"You'll see."

She sounded so confident that I decided to give it a shot. And this simple pairing—walking and carrying—is surprisingly effective. Things get put away much more easily, without a lot of special effort or extra trips. I'm walking from the bedroom to the kitchen, so I bring my giant mug. I'm walking from the front door to my bedroom, so

I bring the book that needs to be shelved. It seems like a small thing, but it definitely cuts down on the clutter in my apartment.

Pairing provides the satisfaction of multitasking, since by definition, two things are getting done at once. A friend emailed me soon after she started using the Nike FuelBand: "If I spend a half hour in the park with my dog in the morning, I want it to be useful in addition to just exercising the dog, and now I'm more conscious of how many steps I'm taking. I also started listening to audiobooks while walking the dog, so now I'm making that time count in three ways."

We can also use the Strategy of Pairing to discourage ourselves from following an undesirable habit. We might pair eating with the civilized habit of sitting down at a table—which means not eating directly from a container, and not eating at a desk, in the car, on the street, or standing in front of the fridge. If I watched TV by myself, I might binge-watch through a favorite series in a few nights, but because I only allow myself to watch those shows with Jamie, and Jamie refuses to watch more than one episode at a time, I never forsake all life responsibilities in order to watch TV.

I looked for other ways to apply the Strategy of Pairing. First, as part of my ongoing effort to move more, to strengthen my Foundation, I'd been trying to go for a long walk each weekend—but it felt like a real burden.

One of my twelve Personal Commandments is "Identify the problem." What was the problem? I got bored during these walks. I decided to pair my walks with time with friends and emailed two friends to suggest a regular walking date. Both were game. One friend can go only occasionally; the other can go more regularly, though it usually takes a few emails to set up. I actually don't mind the slight logistical hassle; because the walks aren't quite predictable, they feel more like a treat. Over time, in fact, I realized that although I'd formed this habit to get more exercise, it's actually more important as a habit pair to strengthen my relationships. The time with a friend is more valuable than the steps logged on my UP band.

Nevertheless, I couldn't always walk with company. Eleanor listens to audiobooks all the time—mostly the Harry Potter books, the Little House books, the Narnia books, and a history series called The Story of the World—and inspired by her example, I bought the audiobooks of Philip Pullman's His Dark Materials trilogy. Listening to these books made me *so happy*. Once I even walked an extra five blocks, just to listen longer.

I wanted to do more walking—and less sitting. As a writer, I spend most of my day in a chair, but I'm so restless that I imagined that I was on my feet a reasonable amount—to get something to drink or eat, or to go to the bathroom, or to check something in a book. However, when I set my UP band to vibrate whenever I sit still for forty-five minutes, I learned that I was doing a *lot* more sitting than I'd assumed.

This matters, because studies suggest that plain old sitting is a bad habit. Sitting is the new smoking; studies show that the average American sits for at least eight hours a day, and while we sit, our metabolism changes for the worse. Sitting for several hours a day seems to raise people's risk of early death, even for people who exercise. Plus I noticed that walking around boosted my concentration and energy level.

To combat over-sitting, I decided to pair talking on the phone with standing: if I want to use the phone, I must stand. For years, I've wanted a treadmill desk—a treadmill with a desk on it, so that I could walk while on the computer or phone—but my office is too tiny to hold one, so standing is the next best thing. I don't talk on the phone a lot, but often enough that this pairing means that I do add a fair amount of movement to my days.

Pairing is effective—sometimes, *too* effective. It's easy to allow a bad habit to form by creating a pair. Some familiar bad-habit pairs: "I always get drunk on Saturday nights." "I always read an email as soon as I get it." "I always go shopping when I'm traveling." Once the pair is formed, breaking it up feels like deprivation.

A friend loved eating candy at the movies so much that when she decided to change her eating habits, she had to quit going to the movies. Another friend had paired his morning cup of coffee with a cigarette, so when he decided to quit smoking, he switched to tea.

But just as pairing can create bad habits, it can also be used to contain a bad habit. A reporter told me, "I had a bad habit in college. Every time I finished an exam, I let myself eat a croissant. I *love* croissants."

"But that sounds okay," I said. "It's a good pair, because you got to have croissants sometimes, but since you didn't take that many exams, you didn't get them often. It was self-limiting. It's not like you were going to take an extra exam just to get another croissant. You figured out a way to stay in control of your croissant habit."

"True."

"Also, taking an exam is no fun, but this pairing made it more pleasant."

I'd been thinking about the power of the Strategy of Pairing, and at one point, I had an inspiration. Few things bring me as much pure happiness as encouraging someone to form a good habit—and I can *occasionally* be a bit pushy about it. So I'm sure my long-suffering sister wasn't surprised to see an email pop up in her inbox:

From: Gretchen

As you know I've long been obsessed with treadmill desks. I want one desperately but alas, can't fit one into my office and still be able to open the door. A bit of a drawback. However YOU should get one!

I visited my friend A. J. to see his treadmill desk. He said he works on it all the time. He got used to it very quickly, and loves it—says he feels so much more energetic, feels sluggish on the days when he can't use it. He walks SEVEN MILES most days, and he walks very slowly. It's very quiet—less noise than an a/c.

The fact is, it's very tough for you to exercise these days. You've got a lot on your plate, and you're only going to get MORE. This might be a way to cross exercise off your to-do list without even noticing it. While you work, you walk.

I would LOVE to buy this for you. I never did get you a birthday present. Please consider it! I wish I had the gumption just to order it, and beg your assistant to help get it situated in your office, but I fear that springing a treadmill desk on someone is like giving them a kitten they didn't ask for.

Think about it . . .

From: Liz

What an amazing offer!!! Let me ponder!

Several hours later, I got another email from her, with a report not just about her decision, but also about that of her longtime writing partner and co-show-runner, Sarah:

From: Liz

So . . . drumroll . . . With much excitement and gratitude I'm accepting your incredibly generous gift! I truly think this treadmill desk is gonna be a game changer. It's exactly what I need. I've already told everyone at work I plan to become an obnoxious bore on the subject.

Another drumroll . . . Sarah has decided to get one too! She said she can't lounge on a couch while I'm walking all day. Our plan is to put the 2 treadmill desks in my office, in front of a whiteboard. We'll keep two mini desks in her office. We're convinced we're going to lead a major TV writer trend.

THANK YOU! I love it already!

Less than a week later both treadmills had arrived, and I called Elizabeth to hear the report.

"So?" I demanded. "How is it?"

"It's really great!" she said. "We used them all day."

"Was it hard to get used to it?"

"Not at all. We were in my office a lot, rewriting a script, so I was walking for about three and a half hours. I wasn't going fast, sometimes as slow as 0.8 miles per hour—but I still walked 4.55 miles in total. I'll be able to go faster when I'm more used to it, and depending on what I'm doing."

"More than four and a half miles? That's great."

"I'm really into the *distance*, Sarah's really into the *number of steps*. As soon as she saw the number of steps she was walking, she instantly took to it. We're going to keep track and see how far we go."

"You could track it on a map! Like, 'We've walked to San Francisco.' So satisfying."

"Yes. Already I feel very righteous, seeing the numbers mount up. Plus it makes work much better. Our notes call with the studio about the script lasted forty minutes, and I walked the whole time. And on top of that I told Sarah that I thought we'd snack less if we were on the treadmill."

"That makes sense," I said. "People are sensitive to the slightest bit of inconvenience. Having to get off the treadmill makes it that much harder to run to the kitchen. How do you feel?"

"My legs definitely got tired, but I think I'll adjust. The most important thing, though, is whether it will help lower my A1C level. For me, it's *all* about the blood sugar."

After some time passed, I checked in with Elizabeth again. She'd instantly embraced the habit of the treadmill desk, and was logging about five miles daily. She still didn't know exactly how it was affecting the all-important A1C level, because this test had to be done in her doctor's office.

"Last time, my A1C level was terrible," Elizabeth told me, "and bringing that number down is the most important thing for me. If the treadmill desk deals with that, it's a game changer. Especially for people who have type 2 diabetes. I'm surprised people aren't *issued* treadmill desks, because compared to the cost of medicine and doctor visits, they're a bargain. Or I'd think that Google-type companies would offer them to their employees. Plus it helps with stress. When things blew up at work, I reacted better than I would have otherwise, and when I leave work, I know that no matter what else did or didn't happen, I've walked five miles."

Until Elizabeth got the treadmill desk, she hadn't been able to make a habit of exercise. Now that she could use the Strategy of Pairing—bolstered by the Strategies of Convenience, Monitoring, and Foundation—the habit had kicked in hard.

Also, Elizabeth is an Obliger. She told me, "I've realized that it's easier for me to exercise when it feels like obligation to my diabetes."

Once again, I saw that when people frame their habits in the way that makes the most sense to them, they succeed better. It would never occur to me to characterize exercise as "an obligation to diabetes," but I could immediately see why that formation resonated with her.

Because of her health issues, getting more exercise was a truly significant habit for Elizabeth, and I was thrilled that I'd helped her to form that habit, but sometimes it struck me that my preoccupation with the subject of habits was . . . petty. Was it ridiculous to devote so much time to thinking about how to eat better, or sleep more, or clear out my to-do list faster?

Life was too solemn, too splendid to be frittered away in such trivial concerns. But while concentrating on my habits might seem small-minded, in the end, mastering those habits would allow me to put these questions out of my mind, to transcend them. I could turn all my attention to worthier matters, and yet be assured of the solidity of the architecture of my everyday life.

These small, everyday actions had their own value; the pressure of my daily habits would mold my future. These habits were little things on their own, but their combined weight was massive. I thought again of one of my favorite lines from Samuel Johnson: "It is by studying little things, that we attain the great art of having as little misery and as much happiness as possible."

UNIQUE,
JUST LIKE
EVERYONE ELSE

As the saying goes, I'm unique, just like everyone else. While we can learn about ourselves by looking in a mirror—as in the "Self-Knowledge" section—we also learn about ourselves by considering ourselves in comparison to others. This section encompasses the Strategies of Clarity, Identity, and Other People, which, by placing us in the context of other people, illuminate our individual values, interests, and temperament. And when we understand ourselves better, we can do a better job of shaping our habits.

CHOOSE MY BALE OF HAY

Clarity

People pay for what they do, and still more, for what they have allowed themselves to become. And they pay for it very simply: by the lives they lead.

—JAMES BALDWIN, *No Name in the Street*

One of the great puzzles of habit is the fact that some habits form too easily, while others don't seem to stick. Why? There are many answers, but sometimes, I realized, the problem is a lack of *clarity*. I feel ambivalent: I want to do something, but I also don't want to do it; or I want one thing, but I also want something that conflicts with it; or everyone seems to agree that some habit is important, but it's not important to me.

It took me a long time to grasp the importance of the Strategy of Clarity; I'm always eager to focus on the concrete, and "clarity" seemed somewhat abstract. But it turns out that clarity is an extremely important element of habits, and extremely practical, too.

Two kinds of clarity support habit formation: *clarity of values* and *clarity of action*. The clearer I am about what I value, and what action I expect from myself—not what other people value, or expect from me—the more likely I am to stick to my habits.

Research suggests that when we have conflicting goals, we don't manage ourselves well. We become anxious and paralyzed, and we often end up doing nothing. When I reflected on the habits that I'd struggled with over the years, I realized how often my hesitation and backsliding were due to the lack of *clarity*. Should I use free time on school-day mornings to work on my emails or to read aloud to Eleanor? Should I work every Saturday afternoon, or should I devote that time to leisure? Should I encourage Eliza to do her homework in the kitchen, in the company of the family, or should she study in her room, away from noise and distractions? I feel ambivalent, and my uncertainty about these competing claims depletes my energy. Like Buridan's Ass, the donkey that starves because it can't decide between two bales of hay, I become paralyzed by indecision.

As I talked to people about habits and happiness, certain pairs of conflicting values kept cropping up:

I want to give 110 percent to work.	I want to give 110 percent to my family.
I want to work on my novel.	I want to exercise.
I want to get more sleep.	I want some time each day to talk to my sweetheart, watch TV, and have fun.
I want to spend less time in the car.	I want my children to participate in many after-school activities.
I want to be very accessible to other people.	I want time alone to think and work.
I want to be frugal.	I want to join a gym.
I want some time to relax when I get home from work.	I want to live in a house that's clean and orderly.
I want to meet new people and see my friends.	I want more solitude.
I want to plan for the future by saving for retirement.	I want to enjoy the present by traveling.
I want to drink less.	I want to be the life of the party.

As these pairs illustrate, often when we experience a lack of clarity, it's because two important values conflict. They're *both* important, so we agonize about which value to honor in the habits we pursue.

When I face values that seem to conflict, I first remind myself to consider whether this conflict might be a false choice. Can I choose both?

A mother in Eleanor's class told me, "I couldn't go to my exercise class because my son wanted me to read to him." She seemed pleased with herself, and I imagine she thought, "I'm willing to sacrifice my own desires to be attentive to my son." (I suspect that she's an Obliger.)

Though I gave a noncommittal response, to me that seemed like a false choice. I wanted to say, "Being a good parent is a very high value, but what value should be served in *that particular situation*? Maybe you can exercise *and* read to your son, by reading to him during a non-exercise time."

When we push ourselves to get clarity, when we identify the problem, sometimes we spot new solutions. I heard about a couple who went to marriage counseling because they were fighting constantly about chores, and whether a clean house or ample leisure time was more important. They kept arguing—until they decided to quit marriage counseling and spend the money on a weekly cleaning service. A friend loves taking long bike rides on the weekends, but he also wants to spend time with his family. For a long time, whatever he did with his day, he wished he'd done something else. When he pushed himself to state plainly the nature of the conflict, he saw a solution. On Saturdays and Sundays, he gets up at 5:00 a.m., rides for six hours, and spends the rest of the day at home.

It's easier to stick to a habit when we see, with clarity, the connection between the habit and the value it serves. I make my bed, because I know that the habit makes me feel calmer. I give my daughters hello and good-bye kisses, because that habit makes me feel more loving.

It's probably true that the worldly values of pleasure, vanity, and fastidiousness are just as persuasive as higher values. I bet more people brush their teeth to prevent bad breath than to prevent cavities. A fitness trainer told me, "Men tend to come in because they want to improve a skill, like their tennis game, or regain something they've lost, like being able to walk up stairs without puffing. Women want to look better. Everyone adds health justifications later."

When it's not apparent that a habit has value, people are less likely to follow it. People often stop taking their medication when they don't see an obvious connection between the medicine and their condition—as sometimes happens with people taking medication for high blood pressure. Although I'd always vaguely intended to get the flu vaccine as a family, we never did until Elizabeth learned that her diabetes might have been triggered by a bad case of the flu. A few days of the flu? Flu vaccines didn't seem worth the bother. Risk of diabetes? We get the vaccine every year.

Clarity is one reason that the Strategy of Scheduling is so helpful. It's important to have time to write; to have time with my family; to read. Instead of spending my day in a chaos of warring priorities, and feeling as though whatever I do I'm leaving important things undone, I can use the clarity of Scheduling to guarantee that I have time and energy to devote to each activity that matters.

Clarity also helps shine a spotlight on aspects of ourselves that we may wish to conceal. We should pay special attention to any habit that we try to *hide*. The desire to prevent family or coworkers from acting as witnesses—from seeing what's on the computer screen or knowing how much time or money we're spending on a habit—is a clue that in some way, our actions don't reflect our values. One reader wrote, "I go on secret shopping sprees, and hide the bags in the storage room. I don't want anyone to know what I spent."

One way to attack a hidden bad habit—secret smoking, secret shopping, secret monitoring of an ex-sweetheart on Facebook—is to force it out into public view. We may choose to give up the habit if we can't keep it secret. Or we may be reassured to realize that others share our habit. One reader wrote, "My secret habit was watching the Hallmark Channel. I confessed, laughing but embarrassed, to a friend, and she said, 'Me, too!'"

True, we might hide a habit for other reasons. A reader posted: "I'm a closet writer. Whenever anyone asks me what I've been up to, I never tell them that writing a novel is occupying half my time. I somehow feel dishonest, but there's something about telling people I'm writing that makes me feel overly exposed." Many people keep secret blogs.

We should also pay special attention to anything we feel compelled to *explain*. Paradoxically, unnecessary self-justification can be a feature of denial. Once I found myself telling Jamie about the many reasons that I hadn't gotten any work done that day—though he didn't care how much or how little work I'd completed. When I stopped talking, I realized that my desire to explain myself to him stemmed from a need to hide something from myself. I didn't want to admit that I'd violated my work habits.

A friend told me a poignant story. "I got in line at the grocery store," he recounted, "and I realized that I knew the woman ahead of me. She didn't notice me, and before I could say anything, she started a conversation with the cashier. She pointed to the food she was buying—really junky food, like chips, frozen blintzes, cookies—and said, 'My kids make me buy all this stuff, they love it.' But she doesn't have any kids! She doesn't even have a *cat*. I felt so bad about overhearing it that I switched lines."

In Tory Johnson's memoir *The Shift*, she writes, "From the day I got my driver's license, I developed a habit of pigging out at drive-throughs. When I rolled up alone to the window, I would pretend I was ordering for a few people by saying out loud, 'What was it they wanted?' As if the clerk at the window cared."

Clarity requires us to acknowledge what we're doing.

Clarity of values also makes it possible to identify *red-herring habits*. A red-herring habit is a habit that we loudly claim to want to adopt, when we don't actually intend to do so. Often, red-herring habits reflect other people's values or priorities. "I'm going to start cooking every night." "I'm going to quit buying lottery tickets." Like tomorrow logic, red-herring habits are dangerous, because they allow us to fool ourselves about our actual intentions.

As an Upholder who takes all announced aims very seriously—perhaps too seriously—I get concerned when I suspect that I'm hearing someone declare a red-herring habit.

I became aware of red-herring habits when I sat next to a man at a dinner party. "I'm going to start exercising," he said in an unconvincing tone. "I really need to."

"Why *don't* you exercise?" I asked gingerly.

"I don't have time, and I travel so much. Also my knee bothers me."

"It sounds like maybe you don't really want to exercise."

"Oh, I have to," he answered. "Periodically my wife and kids try to get me started. I'm going to start soon."

I understood. He didn't want to exercise, but he was using a red-herring habit to pretend—to his family and himself—that he was going to start exercising. One of these days. Ironically, if my dinner partner had said, "My family is pressuring me, but I have no intention of exercising," the act of acknowledging his choice, and its consequences, might have led him to decide that he *did* want to exercise. By repeating a red herring, he avoided admitting his true intention, which allowed him to deny what he was doing.

A friend used the Strategy of Clarity to avoid this trap. "I know it would be good to exercise," she told me, "but I have two kids, I work full-time, and if I tried to exercise, it would be one more thing to worry about. When my kids are older, I'll deal with it."

"Great!" I said.

She looked relieved but also suspicious. "I thought you would try to convince me."

"To me, it seems better to say, 'At this point, I'm not going to worry about exercising' than to keep saying 'I should exercise' but then never do it. Either way, you're not exercising, but because you have clarity about what you're doing, you feel in control. And you won't drain yourself feeling bad about it." Also, I predict, her feeling of self-control will help her do better if she does decide to start exercising, because she won't tell herself, "I've been trying and failing for years to do this."

What red-herring habits do I have? I should entertain more. My mother loves to entertain, and does it beautifully. I keep telling myself, "I will entertain!" But then I don't. I keep saying, "I should put my dishes in the dishwasher instead of the sink." But I just put my dishes in the sink.

Some red-herring habits I've already abandoned: "I'm going to make my daughters write thank-you notes." "I'm going to read a poem every night." "I'm going to keep a record of everything I read on Goodreads." "I'm going to use my good china." Someday, I vow, I will use my good china. But in the meantime, it's *such a relief* to give up this and other red-herring habits.

People in the Four Tendencies show different patterns with red-herring habits. Upholders form fairly few red-herring habits, because they tend to take expectations very seriously, and act on them unless they're clearly optional (like reading a poem every night). Questioners sometimes espouse red-herring habits when they're not actually convinced that the proposed habit is sufficiently justified to deserve follow-through. Obligers claim red-herring habits when they feel the pressure of others' expectations, but with no framework of accountability to push them into action. Rebels have no trouble saying, "Nope, I'm not going to do that," so red-herring habits don't trouble them much.

———

By providing clarity—or not—our words can make it easier or harder to keep a habit. People who use language that emphasizes that they're acting by their own choice and exercising control ("I don't," "I choose to," "I'm going to," or "I don't want to") stick to their habits better than people who use language that undermines their self-efficacy ("I can't," "I'm not allowed to," or "I'm supposed to"). There's a real difference between "I don't" and "I can't."

The very words we choose to characterize our habits can make them seem more or less appealing. "Engagement time" sounds more interesting than "email time"; "playing the piano" sounds more fun than "practicing the piano"; and what sounds more attractive, a "personal retreat day" or a "catch-up day" or a "ditch day" or a "mandatory vacation day"? (People of different Tendencies would choose different terms.) Would a person rather "take a dance class" or "exercise"? Some people like the word "quit," as in "I've quit sugar"; some are put off by its overtones of addiction. A woman told me, "I try not to use the words 'forever' and 'never,' but I like the word 'permanent.'"

Many people report that they want to "feel less stressed." But "stress" is a vague word, and because it doesn't pinpoint any concrete problems, it doesn't suggest any solutions. When I say "I'm stressed out," I blur the connection between the way I *act* and the way I *feel*. So, instead of saying "I'm stressed," I press myself to identify exactly what's bothering me. "I work at home, so I feel as though I should be working all the time." "I'm working with someone who drains my energy." "I want us to have fun family adventures, but we all need a lot of downtime at home, too." "I can't decide what opportunities to pursue." "My laptop isn't syncing properly with my desktop." "I get flustered when both my daughters talk at me at the same time." "I feel awkward in this social situation." Once I've spelled out the problem in words, the greater clarity usually helps me to spot a solution.

Besides clarity of values, another kind of clarity supports habit formation: *clarity of action*. The more specific I am about what action to take, the more likely I am to form a habit. A habit to "be more mindful," for instance, is too vague to be a habit, but "have a moment of gratitude every time I walk into my apartment building" or "take a photo of something interesting every day" are concrete actions that can become habits.

Clarity of action is often a problem with medicine. Studies suggest that up to 55 percent of adults don't take their medicines as prescribed, and several of the top reasons for this failure reflect a lack of clarity: if people wonder "Why should I bother to take these pills, anyway?" or "When am I supposed to take those pills?" or "Did I take my pills today?" they're less likely to take them. That's why some of the old familiar pill bottles have been replaced by blister packs with compartments clearly labeled with the day of the week.

To achieve greater clarity in my actions, I often invoke a "bright-line rule," a useful concept from law. A bright-line rule is a clearly defined rule or standard that eliminates any need for interpretation or decision making; for example, observing the Sabbath, or using *The New York Times Manual of Style and Usage* to decide grammar questions, or never buying bottled water, or answering every email within twenty-four hours, or calling home every Sunday night are bright-line rules.

One familiar bright-line rule is the habit of making purchases only from a prepared list as a way to eliminate impulse shopping. A reader explained, "I shop from a list, not only for groceries, but for clothing and cosmetics as well. This is not only to save money, but to avoid clutter."

I already adhere to many bright-line rules. I never use that instrument of torture, the snooze alarm. Eleanor and I leave for school at exactly 7:50 every morning. Jamie and I disagree about one bright-line rule: I think that once you decide to go to an event, you go; Jamie has a more fluid view (I'm an Upholder; he's a Questioner).

People have their own idiosyncratic bright-line habits. I met a guy who told me that he was "vegetarian before dinner." A friend told me, "When I got married, I decided to say yes to sex whenever possible because our relationship would be better with more sex."

Another friend told me, "My habit is never to have more than *three*. Of whatever. Three beers, three TV shows."

"How did you come up with this?" I asked. "Why three?"

"I don't remember," she said. "I've followed this rule for as long as I can remember. What's scary is how faithfully I followed it as a kid." Unconventional, but effective.

As an underbuyer, I very much dislike buying new clothes, and when I do have new things, I have to fight the impulse to "save" them, to keep them crisp and unused by continuing to wear my shabby clothes. I decided to make a bright-line habit of throwing away anything that had a hole.

To my surprise, this habit turned out to be an utter failure. I simply *cannot* throw something away simply because it has a hole. I'd coach myself, "This is my new habit! Come on, into the trash with that sock!" But I couldn't do it. Bright-line rules work only if we follow them.

One morning, as I was walking home after dropping Eleanor off at school, I had one of those rare moments of reflection when I step back from my daily concerns to take a more sweeping view of my actions. I was pouring energy into changing my habits, yet when I asked myself, "What change would add more happiness to my life?" none of my habits addressed an issue at the top of my list: I wanted to see my sister more often.

The problem, I realized, was that I didn't have a time dedicated to Elizabeth. I see my parents frequently because I've set aside specific times to visit, at Christmas and in August. No decisions, no planning—just pick the dates and buy the plane tickets. I see my parents at other times as well, but I *always* see them at those times.

Elizabeth and I didn't have this kind of standing plan. Every other year we overlap in Kansas City for Christmas, and occasionally I go to Los Angeles for work, but that wasn't enough. Our plans never crystallized. When would we do it? Where would we go? Which family would travel? Too many decisions. No clarity, no action.

Having identified the problem, I considered possible solutions. Elizabeth's and Adam's work schedules as TV writers are highly unpredictable; summer is a very busy season for them; they have a young child. My family was on a much more predictable schedule. I came up with a proposal, and I called Elizabeth to discuss it.

"Listen," I said, "I really wish we could get our two families together more often. I think we should have a standing plan, where we get together once a year."

"That would be great, but when?"

"This is what I've figured out. You and Adam don't have much control of your schedule, so we plan for Presidents' Weekend, because that's a three-day weekend, and Eliza and Eleanor actually get four days. It may turn out that you have to work, but you'd have as good a chance then as with any other three-day weekend. We pick some great hotel within driving distance from L.A., so you don't have to buy airplane tickets. That way, if you have to cancel at the last minute, you won't lose a ton of money, and you won't spend much time making arrangements. Even if you three can't make it, the four of us will come anyway, and we'll have fun either way. So it's simple, with no stress if you have to cancel."

"But that means you guys have to fly all the way out here."

"Now that Eliza and Eleanor are older, it's not a big deal. It's a lot easier for us to travel than for you. And we'll enjoy California."

"And we do this every year?"

"If it works, we can stick to it. No decisions. Easy is more important than fabulous."

Elizabeth and Adam both thought this sounded like a great idea, so I bought a guide to southern California, we picked the Santa Barbara area as our destination, and we made our reservations. Flash forward: Elizabeth had to cancel because of work, then at the last minute, her schedule changed again, and she, Adam, and Jack were able to come. It worked perfectly.

After that, I realized that I could tie other yearly habits to trigger dates like Presidents' Weekend. For instance, Labor Day now triggers me to schedule the family flu vaccine. St. Patrick's Day triggers me to review finances with Jamie (green). A friend and I share the same birthday, and each year, we have lunch to celebrate; I almost never see her otherwise, but knowing that I'll see her once a year helps maintain our friendship.

Trigger dates also save me from feeling guilty. Because I won't worry about holiday shopping until after Thanksgiving, I don't feel guilty about not shopping earlier. Clarity.

Around this time, I called Elizabeth for an update on the treadmill desk. It had made her life better than before, to a gratifyingly dramatic degree.

"I love it!' she said. "I've walked almost two hundred miles."

"That's amazing."

"I've figured out it's really a key to controlling my blood sugar. When I was on jury duty and on vacation, my blood sugar went way up, even though I was eating the same way. Now I know that I have to exercise."

"How much do you walk each day?"

"It depends on what's happening at work. If we have notes calls, I get lots of treadmill time. Some days, I walk more than seven miles. Plus work is more satisfying when I'm getting exercise accomplished at the same time. There's something about the treadmill that makes you feel, 'I'm up for this challenge! I'm striding toward success!' Instead of feeling like I'm under an avalanche, I feel in control."

"And it's easy to get yourself to do it?"

"Once it's your desk, it's your desk. It's not a hard habit to keep."

I'M THE FUSSY ONE

Identity

One regrets the loss even of one's worst habits. Perhaps one regrets them the most. They are such an essential part of one's personality.

—OSCAR WILDE, *The Picture of Dorian Gray*

Just as I'd been slow to grasp the importance of the Strategy of Clarity, I'd been studying habits a long time before I began to appreciate the importance of *identity*. My idea of "this is the kind of person I am" is so bound up in my habits and actions that it's hard for me to see. But eventually, I realized that my sense of identity makes it easier or harder to change a habit.

My friend Maria helped me understand the power of identity.

I knew Maria because her son had been in Eliza's kindergarten class. She had a cheerful energy and an air of mischief that made me want to get to know her better—and in fact, a few years later, we started working together to make the videos for my blog. One day, after we'd finished making the latest set of videos, we started talking about habits. Purely by coincidence, of course.

"Any habits that you'd like to change?" I proposed. "Want to be a habits guinea pig for my notions?"

"As a matter of fact, I'd like to cut back on my drinking," Maria said. "I enjoy drinking, especially wine, but I pay the next day. Even if I've just had a glass of wine or two, I don't feel great. Also, normally

I have crystal-clear recollections of conversations, but when I drink, it's hazier. Last week I had a great conversation with my brother at dinner, and we were really connecting—but when I try to remember exactly what we both said, I can't. Plus," she added, "I have this feeling that if I nailed this down, other things would be easier—exercise, food, things like that."

"True," I said.

As an Abstainer, I felt obligated to point out the Abstainer option, but Maria wasn't interested.

"No." She shook her head. "I don't want to give up alcohol. The thing is, I'm Italian, I love great food and wine, I want to enjoy myself. And I think people expect it of me. I have a friend who says, 'Are you having a glass of wine? Okay, I will, too.' People expect that I'll always be tons of fun."

"You are *always* tons of fun!" I said. "You *know* you are."

"Yes," she admitted with a laugh. "I am tons of fun."

"Also, people will probably hardly notice how much you're drinking—unless they're using you to pace themselves, like 'Oh, Maria's having another glass of wine, so I can, too.' Research shows that people eat and drink more or less depending on what the people around them do. And you want to do what's right for *you*."

"I do love to have a great time," she said, "but all that drinking isn't making me feel good."

"So you need to figure out how much and when you want to drink."

After considering different scenarios, Maria decided on the habits she wanted to adopt. She wouldn't drink wine with dinner at home; for an ordinary dinner at a restaurant with friends, she'd limit herself to one glass of wine; for special celebrations, she'd allow herself several glasses. Maria and I emailed back and forth about her attempts to form a new habit, and at first I mostly focused on Maria's rules for herself—*when* and *how much* she'd drink. (We Upholders always want to know the rules.) We also discussed whether she could come up with a substitute drink—something festive but nonalcoholic. Maria invented a "family drink" of sparkling water with pomegranate juice and lime to drink with her husband, Tom, who was also trying to cut down. I loved the idea of a family drink for the end-of-day drink ritual.

Over time, however, it became clear that for Maria, her *sense of identity* was a far more significant obstacle than sticking to the rules. Even though Maria had highlighted this issue during our very first conversation, I hadn't realized its significance. Her identity as an Italian, as someone who loves good meals, as the "fun one," was her real challenge.

> From: Maria
>
> I feel like I am denying my personality . . . an Italian enjoying cooking and wine. I don't miss the taste, I do miss the celebratory feeling and the relaxation that accompanies a glass of wine. However, I do feel better not having that random drink or two on week nights at home. Last night I had to convince Tom not to open a bottle of wine because I knew I would want one! He agreed. I do have satisfaction that I am in control.

Identity exerts a powerful force over our habits. When I told a friend about my low-carb eating, she shook her head and said, "That would never work for me. I don't want to be the fussy one, the one who says, 'I don't eat this' or 'I don't do that.'"

"You could make exceptions, like if you're a guest at someone's house."

"Is that what you do?"

"No," I acknowledged, "I stick to it. I don't care if people think I'm fussy, I *am* fussy. Also," I added, "I worried about my weight for so many years, it's worth it to me to be fussy, not to have to worry about it anymore."

"Not me, I'm 'the girl who eats anything.'"

"It's only a problem if that non-fussy identity conflicts with something else—like eating in a different way. It's not hard for me, because I get a big kick out of telling people, 'I'm one of those low-carb fanatics you read about.'"

Now that I'd identified it, I began to see the role of identity in many habit-related situations. "My husband and I desperately need to go to bed earlier," a friend told me. "We stay up too late, and we have to get up early because of the baby. We're exhausted. We keep saying we're going to go to bed earlier, and we never do."

"What's your routine?"

"At about eleven, we go into the kitchen, have some nuts or cheese or something, and talk."

"That sounds nice."

"Yes," she said. Then she added what sounded like the key to the issue: "We know we should be responsible parents and go to sleep. But we're holding on to this last piece of our adult lives, before the baby. It just feels so . . . *domesticated* to go bed before midnight. Even though we really need the sleep."

The fact is, changing a habit is much more challenging if that new habit means altering or losing an aspect of ourselves. I regret the loss of even the most trivial identity-defining habits. For instance, for years I didn't own a purse. I liked being "the kind of woman who doesn't own a purse," and I delayed buying a purse, even though in many situations carrying a purse would have been far more convenient than lugging my backpack around. Relinquishing this part of myself caused me a pang, even though it was such a tiny part of my identity.

Research shows that we tend to believe what we hear ourselves say, and the way we describe ourselves influences our view of our identity, and from there, our habits. If I say, "I'm lazy," "I can't resist a sale," "I'll try anything once," "I never start work until the last minute," or "I'm lucky," those ideas become part of my identity, which in turn influences my actions.

Often, too, we can describe the same attribute in either positive or negative terms, which can help us shape the habits we want: Am I conscientious or rigid? Spontaneous or impulsive? Gourmet or glutton? Fun-loving or slacker? Artistic or disorganized? Energetic or restless?

For years, I thought of myself as someone who "hates exercise," but at some point, I realized that I hated *sports*—I'm spectacularly uncoordinated, I don't like games, and I don't find competition fun. But I don't mind *exercise*—running, cardio machines, weight training. Thinking of myself as someone who "enjoys exercise" allowed me to change the way I viewed my nature, and that helped me to become a regular exerciser. In one study, one group of registered voters was asked, "How important is it to you to vote?" while another group was asked "How important is it to you to be a voter?" The second group was more likely to vote in the next election, because voting had been cast as an expression of identity—"This is the kind of person I am"—not just a task to be done.

It can be thrilling to add a new element to our identity. I loved becoming "a New Yorker," "a parent," "a blogger," "a driver," and "a happiness expert." Novelist Haruki Murakami, an avid long-distance runner, wrote about this process: "[Running an ultra-marathon] should add a few new elements to your inventory in understanding who you are. And as a result, your view of your life, its colors and shape, should be transformed. More or less, for better or for worse, this happened to me, and I was transformed." Identity can help us live up to our own values: "I'm not someone who wastes time at work," "I'm no shirker," "If I say I'll show up, I show up."

Of course, it's important to follow through on the habits that relate to our sense of identity, as opposed to letting the identity substitute for the habits. Watching CNBC doesn't mean I'm making smart choices with my retirement account. Wearing running shoes isn't the same as running. Buying vegetables isn't the same as eating vegetables. Reading *Outside* magazine doesn't mean I go camping. Writing about happiness won't make me happier unless I stick to my happiness resolutions. I had dinner with a friend who told me, "I've stopped eating sugar, but that chocolate mousse looks so delicious that I'm going to break my rules."

"When did you give up sugar?" I asked.

"Last week," he said. He'd only gone without sugar for a few days, but in his mind, he was now a person who "never ate sugar."

Sometimes, telling others about a decision to alter an aspect of our identity can help us stick to our habits. Maria used the Strategy of Distinctions to realize that she does better when she makes public resolutions.

> From: Maria
>
> I was at a meeting and two people drank red wine, and two didn't, I being one of them. Of course when I said no, there was a big "oh why not?"
>
> I actually wanted to explain what I'm doing, and I also felt I had to, to prevent myself from changing my mind and deciding to have a glass after all. Once I made a statement about it I felt I couldn't go back. Explaining reinforced the decision to say no.

Sometimes we adopt a habit to signal the identity we want others to see. Artist David Salle told reporter Janet Malcolm, "I had to train myself not to arrive exactly on the dot. It was absurd and unseemly to be so punctual. It was particularly unseemly for an artist to be so punctual." (Less absurd, I wanted to ask, than for an artist to be deliberately unpunctual to live up to other people's notions of how an artist should behave?) Or we may adopt a habit to signal an identity we *wish* we had. A friend told me: "I drank a little and smoked a little pot in high school—not because I wanted to, but because it was the quickest way to signal, 'I'm fun! I'm not a goody-goody!' Even though really I was."

Companies and institutions can change our habits—for better and for worse—by persuading us to link certain habits to identities to which we aspire. In their invaluable book *Made to Stick*, Chip and Dan Heath describe how an antilittering campaign successfully changed the littering habits of Texans, after messages such as "Please Don't Litter" and "Pitch In" failed with the target demographic (the typical litterer was a man, between the ages of eighteen and thirty-five, drove a pickup, and liked sports and country music). For the campaign, famous Texans such as George Foreman, Stevie Ray Vaughan, Willie Nelson, and various sports figures made TV spots with the message "Don't mess with Texas." The campaign convinced viewers that a *true Texan*—a proud, loyal, tough, virile Texan—doesn't litter. During the campaign's first five years, visible roadside litter dropped 72 percent. Our habits reflect our identity.

From what I've observed, the Strategy of Identity is particularly helpful for Rebels. Rebels generally have a tough time accepting the constraints imposed by habits, but because they place great value on being true to themselves, they embrace a habit if they view it as an aspect of their identity.

For instance, a Rebel might want to be a respected leader. The identity of "leader" might help him to choose to keep habits—such as showing up on time or going to unnecessary meetings—that would otherwise chafe. He will *choose* to behave this way.

A Rebel wrote on my blog: "For me, the most important characteristic of a Rebel is the freedom to be authentic to the person I am at this moment. My desires and needs shift, and I want the autonomy to pursue that. But I also have a strong sense of self—certain values and characteristics that define who I am and that don't change. For example, I've always defined myself as a great mother. I wasn't going to be the kind of mom that I had—I was going to be a dedicated mom who shows love. And I do." Another Rebel noted, "If a habit is part of who I am, then that habit isn't a chain holding me to the ground, it's permitting me to be authentic to myself."

We can get locked into identities that aren't good for us: "a worka-holic," "a perfectionist," "a Southerner," "the responsible one." As part of the Strategies of the Four Tendencies and Distinctions, I'd worked to identify different personality categories to which I belonged, but those kinds of labels should help me understand myself more deeply, not limit my sense of identity. Someone wrote on my site, "Food and eating used to play a big part in my identity, until I realized that my baking and being a 'baker' was resulting in being overweight. So I had to let that identity go." A Rebel friend clearly loves the idea of herself as the hard-partying fun girl, and when I overheard someone jokingly tell her, "You're not an adult," she repeated with delight, "No, I'm no adult!" She likes the identity of being a non-adult, but that identity could become a problem. Anyone who identifies with the idea of youth—as a wunderkind, as a prodigy, as a Young Turk, as an ingenue—will eventually be forced out.

When I began to think about my identity and my habits, I saw several instances in which my identity was getting in my way.

I identify as a reader, and as part of that identity, I'd developed the habit of finishing every book I read, because a "real" reader finishes books. Right? And I'm not alone. According to the book recommen-dation site Goodreads, 38 percent of readers *always* finish a book. I vowed to adopt the habit of putting down a book as soon as I lost in-terest. What a relief. When I let myself abandon a boring book, I have more time to read what I love, and I feel more energized and happy, because I enjoy myself more.

But I had another identity-related habit that required more inter-nal debate.

For months, I'd been trying to meditate—which had required me to change my identity, because for years, I'd identified as "a person who resists meditation." But then I'd decided to try it.

I'd stuck with it this far, but it was time to reconsider. My Upholder Tendency and habit inertia had pushed me to continue with meditation, but except for a few times when I'd felt better able to calm myself, it didn't seem to make any difference. For me, meditation was difficult and boring, and seemingly fruitless. A bad mix.

I decided to stop meditating.

But once I made that decision, I discovered that I was reluctant to relinquish the new part of my identity. I was tempted to stick with meditation merely because I wanted to be a "person who meditates." Which is not the same thing, at all, as wanting to meditate.

No, I would quit. It wasn't a good fit for me. I was sorry that I hadn't embraced it, but as always, I reminded myself to do what's right for *me*.

Once again, I was "a person who *doesn't* meditate." Be Gretchen.

NOT EVERYONE IS LIKE ME

Other People

Associate with people who are likely to improve you.

—SENECA, *Letters from a Stoic*

I'm a gold-star junkie. I love praise, appreciation, and knowing that I've helped someone. For that reason, I loved to hear about Elizabeth and her treadmill desk. Thinking about a good habit that I'd helped *her* to form gave me far more pleasure than thinking about my own new-and-improved habits—especially when she'd told me that the treadmill desk had allowed her to get better control of her blood sugar. And now it wasn't just the treadmill. She called with a further update.

"Listen, I went to InForm Fitness!" My beloved strength-training gym had opened a branch in L.A. I'd forwarded the announcement email to Elizabeth, but she hadn't replied, so I figured she wasn't interested.

"Excellent! What did you think?"

"It's *hard*. But I see what you mean. Twenty minutes, once a week—how can I justify not doing it?"

Elizabeth gave me full credit, which delighted me, but Jamie wasn't as free about doling out the gold stars. We were getting dressed one morning when I saw him contemplating himself in the mirror.

"I've lost several pounds," he said. He didn't need to lose weight, but I'd noticed that he was looking leaner.

"Do you eat differently now that I eat low-carb?" I'd restrained myself from imposing my low-carb philosophy on Jamie or my daughters—who continue to eat sweets, bread, potatoes, and the like, within reason—but admittedly, I did talk about it a lot.

"Sure," he said with a shrug.

"Really, you do?" I was pleased to think that he'd been paying attention. "How?"

"Well, I don't really eat much bread anymore," he said, as he pulled a gray suit off the hanger. "On the weekends, I used to buy a quarter loaf of that raisin bread and eat it. Now I don't. I don't get bagels on the way to work. I don't eat as much granola."

"Is it because of the way I eat, or because of the logic of eating low-carb, or you just don't want to anymore?"

"A little of all of that," he said noncommittally. As usual, he wasn't very interested in plumbing the depths of his habits.

Then, not long after this conversation, my mother-in-law mentioned that she and my father-in-law had also started to cut back on their carbs—partly because of me, partly because of the Taubes book, partly because it seemed like a good idea.

It's a Secret of Adulthood: I can't make people change, but when I change, others may change; and when others change, I may change.

Up until now with my habits project, I'd focused on strategies that I use as an individual; now I wanted to explore how people's habits interact, in two directions. Other people's actions and habits exert tremendous influence on me, as mine do on them.

First, I considered how other people affect my habits. I tend to think of myself as a separate actor, working on my habits on my own, but what others do, say, and think rubs off on me. For instance, in a phenomenon known as "health concordance," couples' health habits and statuses tend to merge over time. One partner's health behaviors— habits related to sleep, eating, exercise, doctor visits, use of alcohol, cigarettes, and marijuana—influence those behaviors in a partner. If one partner has type 2 diabetes, the other partner faces a significant increase in the risk of developing it, as well. If one partner gives up cigarettes or alcohol, the other is more likely to quit. As a reader wrote: "I stopped drinking, and my husband has cut down a lot, too. Partly out of laziness, partly because 'social' drinking isn't social anymore."

Jamie's unwavering commitment to exercise has helped me stay dedicated. I also caught his habit of reading multiple books at one time, and buying books even when I have a huge pile I haven't read yet. (Before we were married, I read one book at a time, and never allowed myself to acquire more than five unread books.) Also, some of my habits bothered Jamie so much that I gave them up. For some reason, he objected to my snacking in bed.

Because we're quite susceptible to "goal contagion," we may rapidly pick up someone else's habits, so it's helpful to be around people who are good role models. Other people can have a tremendous influence. In fact, I've found that I'm more likely to be persuaded by seeing one person's successful action than by the most impressive research. It's a data point of one—but for me that's a *very persuasive data point*. Once I thought about it, I was startled to realize how often I'd picked up a strong habit based on someone's passing remark. I saw a Twitter comment about Scrivener, the software program for writers, and now I use Scrivener every day. I read a short *New York Times* article that praised the Jawbone UP band, and now I use it every day. I switched from eating roasted, salted almonds to eating raw almonds after a friend told me, "Salt makes you hungry." I don't even know if that's true, but it changed my habit. In *The First 20 Minutes*, Gretchen Reynolds notes, "I stand on one foot when I brush my teeth at night. . . . [which] may be one of the most transformative actions I've picked up from researching this book. My balance and physical confidence have improved noticeably." I thought—well, I can do *that*. I decided to practice my balance when I rode up and down the elevator of our apartment building. Left foot on the way down; right foot, up.

Unfortunately, while people can be a good influence, they can also be a bad influence; by indulging in a behavior that we're trying to resist, they may tempt us to follow. "Look at what he's doing! I want to do it, too." Or we may want to avoid feeling out of step: "Everyone's doing that, I don't want to be a wet blanket." Someone told me, "I try to keep to a strict budget, and the biggest challenge to that habit is the way my friends spend money. They buy a lot of unnecessary things, and then I start to behave like them unconsciously."

In fact, people may actively undermine our efforts to change. Someone's new habit may make them feel abandoned, or jealous of the healthy habit and its consequences, or guilty in the face of someone else's efforts, or hurt if the habit makes them feel rejected or judged.

Or maybe they're just annoyed by some minor inconvenience it creates. "I'd like to have the habit of exercising on weekend mornings," one friend said. "I tried it a few times, but my family complained. I wasn't there to make breakfast, to get everyone organized, all that. What do I do?"

"Here's something I've noticed," I said. "If I do something only occasionally, people don't adjust. If I make a habit of something, they adapt." A friend had the same experience: "When I started shutting my office door for a few hours every morning, my coworkers learned to deal with it."

The presence of other people can influence our habits in another way: when we're in a social situation, usually we want to fit in. This basic desire, to be in step with others, can become a stumbling block for good habits. As a friend explained, "I want to keep the atmosphere positive, for things to go smoothly. If I'm sitting across from someone at dinner—especially a client—I don't want to order an appetizer salad as my entrée. Or if they order drinks, I feel like I should get a drink."

"Do you think people actually notice?" I asked. "And if they notice, do they care? Would *you* care?"

She hesitated. "I wouldn't care. But I think it does change things. Wouldn't it bother you?"

"No, I don't really think about it," I told her.

I'm very susceptible to picking up habits from other people, but I must admit, whether it's because I don't mind violating these particular social norms, or because I don't have very good manners generally, I don't worry much about what people think of my eating and drinking habits. For a long time I was baffled by other people's anxiety in this area, but eventually I realized that my attitude is more unusual than I'd thought.

Before I started researching habits, I'd assumed I was fairly average; in fact, I'd come to realize, I'm fairly freakish. *Not everyone is like me.* I'm an Upholder and a total Abstainer, of course. Also, as I discovered when I took the Newcastle Personality Assessor, which measures personality according to the Big Five model (openness to experience, conscientiousness, extroversion, agreeableness, and neuroticism, or OCEAN), for a woman I score "low" on agreeableness, which measures a person's tendency to be compassionate and cooperative and to value getting along with others. I suspect that my low agreeableness partly accounts for my willingness to appear fussy or out of step in social situations. Also, in all modesty, my lack of concern stems from modesty: I just can't imagine that others are paying much attention to me.

Surprisingly, or perhaps not surprisingly, I've found that the more matter-of-fact I am about my habits, the more readily people accept them—and me.

This observation brought me to the next question: How do I affect other people's habits? I'm an odd mixture. In certain situations, I shrink from prodding people to do things they resist doing—perhaps to a fault. One of my parental duties is to nudge my daughters to develop habits or to try activities that they may not want to do, and I worry that I let them off the hook too easily. I tolerate Eliza's habit of leaving wet towels scattered around. Eleanor learned to ride a bike late because I didn't make her practice regularly. My daughters—and Jamie and I—don't have very good table manners, because I don't enforce them.

On the other hand, it's often hard for me to resist playing the expert or giving a lecture about habit change. I have to remind myself that I can't convince people, they must convince themselves, and the more I push, the more I may inflame opposition. Also, I remind myself, the approach that works for me may not work for someone else. For instance, Elizabeth embraced the treadmill desk, but she never did go back to a low-carb way of eating. "I want to eat carbs sometimes," she told me, "though I do eat healthfully at work, *always*. And I *never* eat French fries." She found the approach that works for her.

Given my know-it-all nature, and my love for making suggestions, restraining myself from giving habit advice requires a lot of effort. It has proved much easier for me to give up sugar than to resist badgering people with advice about how to give up sugar. But I won't help anyone change a habit if I inspire a backlash of resistance.

Knowing where a person falls in the Four Tendencies is enormously useful when I'm trying to suggest a habit. Most people are Questioners or Obligers, and for a Questioner, an emphasis on reasoning, results, and logic is most persuasive; for Obligers, forms of external accountability are the biggest help. With Rebels, it's most useful to explain why a certain habit might be desirable, but make no attempt to encourage the Rebel to try it. They must choose on their own.

Also, I can help provide mental energy to support someone else's efforts. People fall into three gears when it comes to supporting (or opposing) other people's healthy habits.

Drive: People in "drive" mode add energy and propulsive force to our habits. They can be very helpful as they encourage, remind, and join in. However, if they're too pushy, they may be a nuisance, and their enthusiasm can rouse a spirit of opposition. They may very well push a Rebel away from a good habit.

Reverse: Some people press others to reverse out of a healthy habit. They may do this from a sense of love, such as the food pushers who argue, "You should enjoy yourself!" or "I baked this just for you!" Or their behavior may be more mean-spirited, as they try to tempt, ridicule, or discourage us from sticking to a healthy habit.

Neutral: These folks go along with our habits. They support us whatever we do. Sometimes this is useful, but sometimes this support makes it easier to indulge in habits when we know we shouldn't.

I asked if Maria thought anything I'd suggested had helped her with the habit of drinking less. I'd definitely been in drive mode with her.

"Yes, it helped," she said. "You talked to me in a nonthreatening way, you gave me ideas I could adjust, you followed up—and that helped. I'd think, 'I guess I'll have to tell Gretchen.'"

"Do you think your habit has improved?"

"For sure. Our conversations made me aware of what I was doing. In the past, I overdrank because I didn't think ahead, or register what I was doing. I just said, 'Who cares, I want to have fun!' Now I drink more slowly, and really savor it."

In some cases, as with Maria, I did help people with their habits. In other cases, not so much. For example, I'd made a few trips back to Marshall's apartment to help him finish clearing his clutter, but our efforts didn't seem to make much difference to him—other than to make his apartment more pleasant.

On my last visit, I said, "Wow, this place looks good." I wished I'd taken a *before* photo of Marshall's apartment so we could compare it to the *after*.

"Yes. There's not much left to do."

"Let me ask you," I said. "Does this make any difference in your ability to work on your own writing projects?" I gestured vaguely around his apartment. "It would make a difference to *me*, but does it make a difference for *you*?"

He thought about it. "Well, I don't think so. But that's because what I need to figure out is so much bigger: what to do with my life. I do like to be home more than I did, because there's not so much stuff. Also now I have the habit of constantly getting rid of my clutter and things I don't need—which I think is very helpful to sanity generally."

So that was good.

Arguably, with some people—namely, children—I might be able to enforce a behavior with enough consistency to make it catch hold as a habit.

Eliza and Eleanor are the two people I most want to influence (I'd like to influence Jamie, but don't have the same sway over him). Countless habits shape family life: Do we recycle? Do we always show up on time, or run a little late? Do we use curse words? Do we wear seat belts? Do we go to the doctor regularly? Do we kiss hello and good-bye? These kinds of background habits have great influence over children and their assumptions about how the world works.

Also, because people "catch" habits from each other, one important way to influence Eliza and Eleanor is for me to have good habits myself. If I want Eliza and Eleanor to be orderly, I should be orderly. If I don't want them to spend too much time staring into screens, I should turn off screens myself.

As I considered the habits I wanted for my children, I vowed that I wouldn't press too hard. When adults pressure children to adopt certain habits, sometimes those habits stick—but other times there's a backlash. As a friend told me, "When I was a child, my mother insisted that I hang up my clothes. Now I *never* hang up my clothes." With children and adults alike, when people are strongly warned not to do a particular thing, they often want to do it more than ever (the lure of the forbidden); when they get milder suggestions, they react with less resistance over the long run.

One night, Eliza and I had a long conversation about homework. She lay on her bed while I prowled around the room in search of clutter to clear. I stashed bottles of blue nail polish, threw away empty gum wrappers, put books on the shelves, and put away clothes as we talked. (I find light clutter clearing very relaxing. Eliza tolerated this activity.)

"I just hate the feeling that my whole weekend is ruined by homework," she complained. "I want time to hang out."

"But why is it worse on the weekend than during the week?" I asked, as I put loose pencils into a pen cup.

"The work isn't such a big deal," she explained. "But it seems like homework takes up the whole day."

I thought about this. I knew the feeling of having a whole day consumed by two hours of work.

"Listen," I said, "I have a crazy idea." I sat down next to her to emphasize the earnestness of my suggestion. "How about this? I get up every day at six a.m. There are no distractions, I get so much work done, I love it. Six o'clock is too early for you, but what if you got up at seven on Saturday or Sunday? That's the time you usually get up, so it wouldn't be too hard. You can work in my office with me. I bet you'd get a lot done. Then the rest of your day would be freer."

"But I like to sleep late on the weekends!"

"You really love that, I know. It would be a pain to get up. But then your day would be so open. And you could still sleep late one morning."

"Well . . . maybe," Eliza said, much to my surprise.

"Really?" I was excited to think she might try it. "Great!"

"I'll *try* it. I'm not agreeing to do it forever."

She agreed in theory, but when Sunday morning came, I wasn't sure what would happen when I knocked on her bedroom door at

7:00. After some mumbling, she got up. And it worked. Now, on Sunday mornings, Eliza joins me in my little office.

I do several things to help her maintain this habit. I make sure she's awake by 7:00; once I forgot to wake her, and she slept until 7:45 and wailed, "I feel like the whole morning is gone!" Before I wake her, I tidy my office so she has plenty of room; I turn on the space heater or the air conditioner; I bring her breakfast on a tray. Most important, though, I sit next to her and work myself. I'm a role model of industry, and I suspect she's less likely to jump to YouTube or Instagram if I'm sitting right there. This successful habit represents the combined strength of the Strategies of Scheduling, Accountability, Convenience, and Other People.

But I'm just one influence among many. Does Eliza get up early to work just because I suggested it? Doubtful. Is Eleanor neat because she sees me being neat, or because I try to make her be neat—or because she was born that way? I don't give myself too much credit or blame for my children's habits. Perhaps—like writing, leadership, and a sense of humor—good habits are something that must be learned, but can't be taught.

The Strategy of Other People covers how others influence my habits, and how I influence others' habits. I also hit on a quirky way to apply it—to *myself*. In an odd but effective trick, I view myself from the outside. When I think of myself in the third person, many things become clearer.

I hit on this technique after struggling to identify the right metaphor to describe the tension between my two selves—between now-Gretchen and future-Gretchen, between my want-self and my should-self. Jekyll and Hyde? The angel and devil on my shoulders? The charioteer driving two horses? The elephant and the rider? The ego, the id, and the superego? The spectator and the agent?

In a flash, I saw that there's me, Gretchen (now-Gretchen, want-

Gretchen), and there's my *manager*. I think I was inspired by Elizabeth's Hollywood workplace lingo.

I imagine myself as the client, a fabulous celebrity—and like all fabulous celebrities, I have a manager. I'm lucky, because my manager understands me completely, and she's always thinking about my long-term well-being.

These days, when I struggle with a habit, I ask myself, "What does my manager say?" I was considering scheduling an hour a day to work on an e-book. I vacillated until I asked myself, "What does my manager say?" and my manager answered, with a faint air of exasperation, "Gretchen, you don't have time for that right now." It can be a relief to be told what to do; I agree with Andy Warhol, who remarked, "When I think about what sort of person I would most like to have on a retainer, I think it would be a boss. A boss who could tell me what to do, because that makes everything easy when you're working."

I'm the client, and my manager is the executive who works for me—very appropriate, because my manager is my *executive function*. There's no need to rebel against my manager, because I am the boss of my manager. (Not to mention, I *am* the manager.)

My manager reminds me to follow my good habits: "Gretchen, you feel overwhelmed. Get a good night's sleep." "You're tired, but you'll feel better if you go for a walk." She stands up for me when other people are too demanding. Just as the rock band Van Halen famously required bowls of M&M's for backstage, with all the brown candies removed, my manager says, "Gretchen really feels the cold, so she can't be outside too long." "Gretchen is writing her new book now, so she can't give a lengthy response to that email." On the other hand, she doesn't accept excuses like "This doesn't count" or "Everyone else is doing it."

As an Upholder, however, I've learned to be a bit wary of my manager. I know how she thinks. She's very impressed by credentials and legitimacy. She's sometimes so focused on my future that she forgets that I need to have a little fun right now. My manager is helpful, but in the end, I'm the one who must "Be Gretchen."

I'd been trying to help Jamie with his sleep habits, because I'd been listening to him complain every morning about how badly he'd slept, but one day he proposed a new habit himself.

"You have all those rules for me about sleep," he said one night. "But we should have a habit to help us do something more important. I mean, sleep is important, but something more meaningful."

"Absolutely! What?" I asked, delighted at this show of habit initiative from Jamie. I try not to expect him to join in my preoccupations. I realize how tiresome I can become.

"Let's set aside some time to talk each night, to tell each other about our day, really share what we're up to."

"I would *love* to do that." I was touched. For him to propose that we schedule a nightly sharing session was a real departure from his usual let's-not-make-everything-too-complicated approach. "When? We need to be specific."

"How about after Eleanor goes to bed?" he suggested.

Now, most nights—I can't say we do this *every* night—we have a conversation about our days, and this small habit makes us feel more connected to each other. In the chaos of everyday life, it's easy to lose sight of what really matters, and I can use my habits to make sure that my life reflects my values.

EVERYDAY LIFE IN UTOPIA

Conclusion

There is no more miserable human being than one in whom nothing is habitual but indecision, and for whom the lighting of every cigar, the drinking of every cup, the time of rising and going to bed every day, and the beginning of every bit of work, are subjects of express volitional deliberation. Full half the time of such a man goes to the deciding, or regretting, of matters which ought to be so ingrained in him as practically not to exist for his consciousness at all.

—WILLIAM JAMES, *Psychology: Briefer Course*

On our flight home from a family trip, a chatty flight attendant remarked, as I declined to take anything from the snack basket, "After the holidays, a lot of people turn down the cookies and the pretzels."

"How long does that last?" I asked.

She smiled. "About as long as most New Year's resolutions."

I was intrigued by this real-world evidence of the failure of a yearly mass attempt at habit change. As many New Year's resolvers will agree, few experiences are as discouraging as repeatedly failing to keep a commitment to an important habit.

The most important thing I'd learned during my study of how we change our habits? *We can build our habits only on the foundation of our own nature.*

When I'd begun this inquiry, I understood very little about myself and my aptitude for habits. Now that I know I'm an Upholder, an Abstainer, a Marathoner, a Finisher, and a Lark, and have spent a lot of time thinking about what is, and isn't, important to me, I'm much better able to shape my habits.

By understanding myself better, I've also come to understand other people better. When I'd started my investigation, I felt quite confident doling out advice after a five-minute conversation with a stranger—and I hadn't realized how much my suggestions reflected my own temperament. Now I'm much less dictatorial. The opposite of a profound truth is also true, and often, opposing strategies work. We might try to make a habit more social, or more competitive, or more challenging—or less so. We might decide to go public with a new habit—or keep it private. We might abstain altogether, or indulge in moderation. No simple, universal solutions exist.

What's more, if we don't consider these differences among individuals, it's easy to misunderstand whether and why a habit-formation strategy is effective.

A friend told me, "For good health habits, the key is to have confidence in your doctor. My mother did home dialysis for years, and people were amazed that she could do that. But she had so much confidence in her doctor."

Hmm. I had a different theory. "Let me ask you," I ventured, "would you describe your mother as a disciplined person?"

My friend smiled in recognition. "Oh, yes."

"Say, if you'd told her you needed to bring a signed note to school next Friday, she'd remember?"

"Every time."

"Did she also take time for things that were important to her? Not just to other people?"

My friend nodded.

"Maybe your mother was the *kind of person* who could follow through with something difficult like home dialysis. Maybe that was the key, not the confidence in her doctor."

"Well," my friend admitted, "maybe so."

When we clearly understand the various levers—both internal and external—that move habits, we can make change much more effectively.

In my investigation of habits, I'd focused on the individual. The only person we can change is ourselves, and how we command *ourselves* is always the question that most interests me. Nevertheless, as I wrapped up my catalog of habit-formation strategies, I became increasingly interested by the possibilities for change on a larger scale—how companies, organizations, institutions, and designers of devices and other products can use habit insights to shape people's habits.

For instance, I spoke at a prominent tech company, and afterward got a tour. In current corporate fashion, there was a big bowl of candy by the reception desk, a display of energy bars and juices near the doors, heavily stocked kitchens throughout the buildings, and a giant cafeteria—and everything free.

"Let me ask you," I said to my guide, "do people gain weight when they start working here?"

"Oh, yeah! We all talk about it."

In law school, we took "issue-spotter" exams, which were actually kind of fun. An issue-spotter exam presents a long tale of legal woe, and students must spot every issue that arises—the law-school version of a child's "find the hidden pictures" puzzle. As I was shown around the corporate campus, I amused myself by trying to spot every change I'd make to help people foster healthier habits. What steps would make it easier for employees to eat more healthfully without even thinking about it? First, at the reception desk, I'd put all the candy in an opaque container with a lid, with a small sign that said "Candy." I'd put doors on the office kitchens. I'd change the bins that stored candies and nuts, so instead of pouring out their contents in a stream, the bins would dispense one small serving at a time (or better, I'd put those items in small, prepackaged Baggies). By the end of my tour, I'd written a ten-point memo in my head.

If this company changed the food environment at work, it could make a big difference in its employees' habits. But the fact is, for everyone, it's almost always easier, cheaper, and more fun to offer chocolate-covered pretzels than cucumber slices. And that's a challenge.

I loved my new habits—to commemorate my new way of eating, Jamie gave me a Christmas ornament in the shape of a strip of bacon—but the habits that give me the most satisfaction are the habits I've helped other people to form. My father loves his new way of eating: he now weighs what he weighed when he played high school football, his statin and blood pressure medications were cut in half, and what's more, his doctor has started eating low-carb. Eliza loves (well, maybe "loves" is the wrong word) finishing a big pile of homework on Sunday mornings. Elizabeth *loves* her habit of walking at her treadmill desk. When I checked in with her, she said, "My A1C level is great. I'm at the high end of 'normal.'"

"Is that good?"

"Yes, sometimes I've been nowhere *near* the normal range. So that's a relief."

"What's working?"

"I think it's a lot of things. The treadmill desk, for sure. Losing weight and cutting out a lot of crap that I was eating. The weekly strength training. It all feeds into each other. Also," she added, "Adam has been working out more, too."

Habits multiply, for better or worse, within individuals. They also spread from one person to another. As Maria observed about cutting down on alcohol, "It starts to be self-reinforcing. When I drink more wine than usual, I feel like—ugh." Elizabeth's habit of exercise helped her to exercise more—and helped her husband to exercise, too. On the other hand, the less we do, the less we feel like doing. If my office is a wreck, I don't feel like cleaning up.

As I reflected on the changes I'd seen in my habits and in other people's habits, it struck me that only rarely do we achieve a dramatic, picture-perfect *before* and *after*. Sometimes we do make a complete transformation; it's not an utter fantasy. But usually we end up in a place that's better than before. And that's enough.

Some habits become completely automatic; others require some effort, always. What matters is to be moving in the right direction. There's a great satisfaction in knowing that we've made good use of our days, that we've lived up to our expectations of ourselves. The true aim is not to *break* bad habits, but to *outgrow* them. With the bright light of attention, we can recognize and acknowledge them, and leave them behind.

Often, when we try repeatedly to form a habit that we desire, we fail because we want to reap its benefits without paying the price it demands. I think constantly of that stark line from John Gardner, so significant for habits, when he observed, "Every time you break the law you pay, and every time you obey the law you pay." Keeping a good habit costs us: it may cost time, energy, and money, and it may mean forgoing pleasures and opportunities—but not keeping a good habit also has its cost. So which cost do we want to pay? What will make our lives happier *in the long run*?

Around the time that I completed my habit-formation framework, I had a brief conversation with Eleanor that reminded me why I'd bothered with this long inquiry in the first place.

Every Sunday, we have family Movie Night. One evening, I

chose *Lost Horizons*, though I worried Eleanor might be a little bored or confused by the 1937 movie's story of a man who's spirited away to Shangri-La, a mysterious, idyllic village hidden deep in the Himalayas. To my surprise, she loved it—so much, in fact, that after I showed her my copy of the novel, she was inspired to write a sequel.

She labored away in a notebook, then came to read me what she'd written. I enjoyed her account of the romantic engagement and wedding of Robert and Sondra, but she really caught my attention after she'd finished.

"Oh," she said, "I forgot to tell you the title of my book."

"What?"

She paused for effect, then said, "*Everyday Life in Utopia*."

What a phrase, what an idea! *Everyday life in Utopia*. "Eleanor," I told her truthfully, "I absolutely *love* that title. That is *genius*."

I couldn't get those words out of my head. I wanted to buy a T-shirt with that slogan printed on it. I wanted to tattoo it across my ankle. I wanted to paint it on the wall in my office.

It struck me, in fact, that all of my work on habits and happiness was meant to help us construct, as much as possible, just that: everyday life in Utopia. Everyday life with deep, loving relationships and productive, satisfying work; everyday life with energy, health, and productivity; everyday life with fun, enthusiasm, and engagement, with as little regret, guilt, or anger as possible.

My study of habits has made me less judgmental, but also more opinionated—more convinced than ever of the enormous value of good habits. Before I started, I hadn't been making the most of my opportunities to create the life I wanted. Now, all that I'd learned about habits was helping me to make my life better than before, and step by step, to make my life more nearly my Utopia.

Tomorrow, without making any decisions, without exerting any willpower, I'll wake up at 6:00 a.m., kiss Jamie while he's still asleep, work on the computer for an hour, wake Eliza and Eleanor, fix the family breakfast (I'll have three scrambled eggs, no oatmeal), stand on one leg in the elevator, walk Eleanor to school, sit down at my clutter-free desk again . . . and so on. Those habits wouldn't make everyone happy, but they make me very happy.

Everyday life in Utopia.

Acknowledgments

Many thanks to everyone who shared their experiences with me—I'd never be able to imagine such thought-provoking, fascinating examples of how people deal with their habits. Most of my ideas about habits come from talking to the people around me, so I deeply appreciate the contribution of my family, friends, colleagues, and readers who told me their own stories of habit formation—and who patiently listened to me talk about my theories. A special thanks to my "recruits." I hope they got as much from the experience as I did.

My deepest heartfelt thanks go to my brilliant agent, Christy Fletcher, whose judgment and advice play an essential role in everything I do. And thanks also to everyone at Fletcher & Company.

I felt very lucky to get to work with the extraordinary people at Crown: Tina Constable, Mary Choteborsky, Molly Stern, and the whole outstanding team there. Thanks, too, to Lisa Highton at Two Roads Books (UK) and Nita Pronovost and Kristin Cochrane at Doubleday (Canada), and all the great people there.

Many thanks to Beth Rashbaum, who gave me invaluable editorial guidance. Thanks as well to my friends A. J. Jacobs, Michael Melcher, Oliver Burkeman, Rosemary Ellis, Kamy Wicoff, and Warren St. John, who generously offered me their time and energy to give me valuable comments.

As always, a special thanks to Jamie, Eliza, and Eleanor, and my whole family, who give me everyday life in Utopia.

Quiz: The Four Tendencies

Are you an Upholder, a Questioner, a Rebel, or an Obliger? Take this quiz. Check off every statement that describes you.

By design, the Four Tendencies overlap, so you'll have checks in more than one category; if you're like most people, you'll find that one category will more accurately describe your attitudes.

This quiz isn't dispositive; it's just meant to help you get a clearer reading on yourself. Having the same number of checks in two categories doesn't mean that you're split between those types. Think about the Tendencies and figure out the one that best describes you.

Upholder Tendency

____ I feel uncomfortable if I'm with someone who's breaking a rule—using a cell phone when a sign reads "No cell phones"—even if that person isn't going to get in trouble and isn't bothering anyone else.

____ I can meet a self-imposed deadline, even one that's set somewhat arbitrarily.

____ I've made New Year's resolutions in the past, and I usually have good success in keeping them. (Note: this question is specifically about *New Year's* resolutions.)

____ It's just as important to keep my promises to *myself* as it is to keep my promises to *other people*.

____ Other people sometimes feel annoyed by my level of discipline. I've been accused of being rigid.

Questioner Tendency

_____ If I want to make a change in my life, I'll make it right away. I won't make a New Year's resolution, because January 1 is a meaningless date.

_____ It's very important for me to make well-reasoned decisions; in fact, other people sometimes become frustrated by my demand for information and sound reasons.

_____ It really bothers me when I'm asked to do something for what seems to be an arbitrary reason.

_____ I like to hear from experts, but I decide for myself what course to follow. Even if I'm given a very specific instruction (say, with an exercise routine), I'll tweak it according to my own judgment.

_____ I can start a new habit without much effort, if it's something that makes sense for my aims. Otherwise, I won't do it.

_____ I question the validity of the Four Tendencies framework.

Obliger Tendency

_____ People often turn to me for help—to edit a report, to take over a carpool run, to speak at a conference at the last minute—because they know I'll pitch in, even when I'm swamped myself.

_____ I've given up making New Year's resolutions, because I never keep them.

_____ I'll do something to be a good role model for someone else, even if it's not something that I'd do for myself: practice piano, eat vegetables, quit smoking.

_____ I get frustrated by the fact that I make time for other people's priorities, but struggle to make time for my own.

_____ In my life, I've adopted some good habits, but I often struggle without success to form others.

Rebel Tendency

____ I don't make New Year's resolutions or try to form habits. I won't cage myself like that.

____ I do what I want to do; I'm true to myself, not other people's expectations.

____ If someone asks or tells me to do something, I often have the impulse to refuse.

____ Other people sometimes become frustrated because I won't do what they want me to do.

____ I enjoy a challenge as long as I choose to accept it and can tackle it in my own way.

____ If I'm expected to do something—even something fun, like a woodworking class—I have the urge to resist; the expectation takes the fun out of an activity that I enjoy.

Resources to Request

I hope that *Better Than Before* has given you many ideas about your own habits. For more, you may want to investigate my website, www.gretchenrubin.com, where I regularly post about my adventures in habit formation, as well as suggestions and further research on habits and happiness.

I've created many additional resources on the subject of habits. You can request the items below by emailing me at gretchenrubin1@gretchenrubin.com or by downloading them through my blog:

- A copy of the template I made for my daily time log, as mentioned in the chapter on the Strategy of Monitoring.
- A copy of my Habits Manifesto.
- A copy of my Starter Kit for launching a *Better Than Before* habits group, as discussed in the chapter about the Strategy of Accountability; accountability groups help people swap ideas, build enthusiasm, and most important, hold each other accountable.
- A one-page discussion guide for book groups; or a discussion guide for teams and work groups; or a discussion guide for spirituality book groups and faith-based groups.

You can also email me at gretchenrubin1@gretchenrubin.com or sign up on my blog to get these free daily or monthly newletters:

- My monthly newsletter, which includes highlights from the daily blog and the Facebook page

- The daily "Moment of Happiness" email, which provides a great habits or happiness quotation
- My monthly Book Club newsletter, where I recommend three books (one book about habits or happiness, one work of children's literature, and one eccentric pick)

If you'd like to volunteer as a Super-Fan, email me at gretchen rubin1@gretchenrubin.com. From time to time, I'll ask for your help (nothing too onerous, I promise) or offer a little bonus.

I've written extensively about happiness, and you can also request many resources related to happiness, such as my Resolutions Chart, a Starter Kit for launching a happiness project group, discussion guides for *The Happiness Project* and *Happier at Home* for book groups and spirituality and faith-based groups, Paradoxes of Happiness, some "Top Tips" lists, my comic called "Gretchen Rubin and the Quest for a Passion," and a copy of my Patron Saints. Email me at gretchen rubin1@gretchenrubin.com or download these resources from my blog.

For more discussion about habits and happiness, you can join the conversation on . . .

Twitter: @gretchenrubin
LinkedIn: GretchenRubin
Facebook: GretchenRubin
YouTube: GretchenRubinNY
Instagram: GretchenRubin
Pinterest: GretchenRubin

If you'd like to email me about your own experience and views, you can reach me through my blog, www.gretchenrubin.com. All email does come straight to me. I look forward to hearing from you about this endlessly fascinating subject: the practice of everyday life.

—*Gretchen Rubin*

Start a Better Than Before *Habits Group*

One very effective way to change your habits is to start or join a *Better Than Before* habits group. Being part of a group is a terrific way to create accountability, make new friends or deepen existing friendships, and ensure that your life reflects your values.

I've heard from many people who want to launch or join *Better Than Before* habits groups, so I created a starter kit to help get the ball rolling. If you'd like a copy, email me through my blog, gretchen rubin.com, or at gretchenrubin1@gretchenrubin.com.

Some groups consist of people who know each other already—colleagues at a law firm, college friends, a church study group, members of a family—and some groups consist of strangers who come together just to work on habits. Group members don't need to be working on the same habit; it's enough that they share the aim of *habit change*. Even two people give each other an invaluable boost in accountability and support. Finding an "accountability partner" can make a real difference. Because Obligers need external accountability to stick to their habits, belonging to a *Better Than Before* group would be especially helpful to them.

No technology can replace face-to-face encounters with other people. Nevertheless, if it's not possible to get together physically, technology provides many solutions. There are dozens of apps, devices, and platforms to help you connect with other people.

Remember, though, to get the benefit of being part of a group, you must participate. It's not enough to lurk or listen. You must speak up, hold others accountable, help to keep the group on track, ask questions, and show up. If someone recommends a book, read it; if someone suggests an app, give it a try.

In the tumult of everyday life, it can be easy to overlook the things that really matter. By setting aside this time to work on your healthy habits, you can make your life happier, healthier, and more productive. Together, we can help each other to do better than before.

Suggestions for Further Reading

Akst, Daniel. *Temptation: Finding Self-Control in an Age of Excess*. New York: Penguin, 2011.

Baty, Chris. *No Plot? No Problem! A Low-Stress, High-Velocity Guide to Writing a Novel in 30 Days*. New York: Chronicle Books, 2004.

Baumeister, Roy F., and John Tierney. *Willpower: Rediscovering the Greatest Human Strength*. New York: Penguin, 2011.

Baumeister, Roy F., Todd F. Heatherton, and Dianne M. Tice. *Losing Control: How and Why People Fail at Self-Regulation*. New York: Academic Press, 1994.

Beck, Martha. *The Four-Day Win*. New York: Rodale, 2007.

Benedict, Saint. *The Rule of St. Benedict*. New York: Penguin, 2008.

Blumenthal, Brett. *52 Small Changes: One Year to a Happier, Healthier You*. Amazon Encore, 2011.

Boice, Robert. *How Writers Journey to Comfort and Fluency*. Westport, CT: Praeger, 1994.

Currey, Mason. *Daily Rituals: How Artists Work*. New York: Knopf, 2013.

Deci, Edward L., with Richard Flaste. *Why We Do What We Do: Understanding Self-Motivation*. New York: Penguin, 1995.

Duhigg, Charles. *The Power of Habits: Why We Do What We Do in Life and Business*. New York: Random House, 2012.

Dunn, Elizabeth, and Michael Norton. *Happy Money: The Science of Smarter Spending*. New York: Simon & Schuster, 2013.

Elster, Jon. *Strong Feelings: Emotion, Addiction, and Human Behavior*. Cambridge: MIT Press, 1999.

————. *Ulysses Unbound: Studies in Rationality, Precommitment, and Constraints*. Cambridge: Cambridge University Press, 2000.

Eyal, Nir. *Hooked: How to Build Habit-Forming Products*. Self-published, 2014.

Fogg, B. J. *Persuasive Technology: Using Computers to Change What We Think and Do*. New York: Morgan Kaufman, 2003.

Halvorson, Heidi Grant. *Succeed: How We Can Reach Our Goals*. New York: Hudson Street Press, 2010.

————, and E. Tory Higgins. *Focus: Use Different Ways of Seeing the World for Success and Influence*. New York: Hudson Street Press, 2013.

Harris, Dan. *10% Happier: How I Tamed the Voice in My Head, Reduced Stress Without Losing My Edge, and Found Self-Help That Actually Works*. New York: It Books, 2014.

Heath, Chip, and Dan Heath. *Switch: How to Change When Change Is Hard*. New York: Broadway Books, 2010.

————. *Decisive: How to Make Better Choices in Life and Work*. New York: Crown Business, 2013.

Herbert, Wray. *On Second Thought: Outsmarting Your Mind's Hard-Wired Habits*. New York: Crown, 2010.

Higgins, E. Tory. *Beyond Pleasure and Pain: How Motivation Works*. New York: Oxford University Press, 2012.

Iyengar, Sheena. *The Art of Choosing*. New York: Twelve, 2010.

Jacobs, A. J. *Drop Dead Healthy: One Man's Humble Quest for Bodily Perfection*. New York: Simon & Schuster, 2012.

James, William. *Writings 1878–1899: Psychology: Briefer Course*. New York: Library of America, 1992.

————. *Writings 1902–1910: The Varieties of Religious Experience: A Study in Human Nature*. New York: Library of America, 1988.

Johnson, Samuel. *Selected Writings of Samuel Johnson*. London: Harvard University Press, 2009.

Johnson, Tory. *The Shift: How I Finally Lost Weight and Discovered a Happier Life*. New York: Hyperion, 2013.

Kahneman, Daniel. *Thinking, Fast and Slow*. New York: Farrar, Straus & Giroux, 2011.

Kohn, Alfie. *Punished by Rewards: The Trouble with Gold Stars, Incentive Plans, A's, Praise, and Other Bribes.* New York: Houghton Mifflin, 1993.

Langer, Ellen. *Mindfulness.* New York: Addison-Wesley, 1989.

Logue, A. W. *The Psychology of Eating and Drinking.* 3rd ed. New York: Brunner-Routledge, 2004.

Manejwala, Omar. *Craving: Why We Can't Seem to Get Enough.* Center City, MN: Hazelden, 2013.

Marlatt, G. Alan, and Dennis M. Donovan, eds. *Relapse Prevention: Maintenance Strategies in the Treatment of Addictive Behaviors.* 2nd ed. New York: Guilford Press, 2005.

McGonigal, Kelly. *The Willpower Instinct: How Self-Control Works, Why It Matters, and What You Can Do to Get More of It.* New York: Penguin, 2012.

Merton, Thomas. *The Silent Life.* New York: Farrar, Straus & Cudahy, 1957.

Miller, William, and Janet C'de Baca. *Quantum Change: When Epiphanies and Sudden Insights Transform Ordinary Lives.* New York: Guilford Press, 2001.

Murakami, Haruki. *What I Talk About When I Talk About Running.* New York: Knopf, 2007.

Pantalon, Michael V. *Instant Influence: How to Get Anyone to Do Anything—Fast.* New York: Little, Brown, 2011.

Patterson, Kerry, Joseph Grenny, David Maxfield, Ron McMillan, and Al Switzler. *Change Anything: The New Science of Personal Success.* New York: Business Plus, 2011.

Pink, Daniel H. *Drive: The Surprising Truth About What Motivates Us.* New York: Riverhead, 2009.

Prochaska, James O., John C. Norcross, and Carlo C. DiClemente. *Changing for Good: A Revolutionary Six-Stage Program for Overcoming Bad Habits and Moving Your Life Positively Forward.* New York: Harper, 1994.

Rath, Tom. *Eat Move Sleep: How Small Choices Lead to Big Changes.* New York: Missionday, 2013.

Reynolds, Gretchen. *The First 20 Minutes: Surprising Science Reveals How We Can Exercise Better, Train Smarter, Live Longer.* New York: Hudson Street Press, 2012.

Roenneberg, Till. *Internal Time: Chronotypes, Social Jet Lag, and Why You're So Tired*. Cambridge: Harvard University Press, 2012.

Russell, Bertrand. *The Conquest of Happiness*. New York: Norton, 1930.

Smith, Adam. *The Theory of Moral Sentiments*. New York: Prometheus, 2000.

Steel, Piers. *The Procrastination Equation: How to Stop Putting Things Off and Start Getting Stuff Done*. New York: Harper, 2011.

————. *Good Calories, Bad Calories: Fats, Carbs, and the Controversial Science of Diet and Health*. New York: Anchor, 2008.

Taubes, Gary. *Why We Get Fat: And What to Do About It*. New York: Anchor Books, 2010.

Teicholz, Nina. *The Big Fat Surprise: Why Butter, Meat and Cheese Belong in a Healthy Diet*. New York: Simon & Schuster, 2014.

Thaler, Richard H., and Cass R. Sunstein. *Nudge: Improving Decisions About Health, Wealth, and Happiness*. New York: Penguin, 2008.

Underhill, Paco. *Why We Buy: The Science of Shopping*. New York: Simon & Schuster, 1999.

Vanderkam, Laura. *168 Hours: You Have More Time Than You Think*. New York: Portfolio, 2011.

Vohs, Kathleen D., and Roy F. Baumeister, eds. *Handbook of Self-Regulation: Research, Theory, and Applications*, 2nd ed. New York: Guilford Press, 2011.

Wansink, Brian. *Mindless Eating: Why We Eat More Than We Think*. New York: Bantam, 2006.

Young, Lisa. *The Portion-Teller: Smartsize Your Way to Permanent Weight Loss*. New York: Crown Archetype, 2005.

Notes

Note about anecdotal sources: I've changed some people's identifying details, edited emails and reader posts for clarity and length, and rearranged the chronology of some events.

DECIDE NOT TO DECIDE: *Introduction*

"Researchers were surprised to find" Roy Baumeister and John Tierney, *Willpower: Rediscovering the Greatest Human Strength* (New York: Penguin, 2011), 239.

People with better self-control For a helpful discussion of the benefits of strong willpower, see Baumeister and Tierney, *Willpower,* 9–12, 260; Kelly McGonigal, *The Willpower Instinct: How Self-Control Works, Why It Matters, and What You Can Do to Get More of It* (New York: Avery, 2012), 12; Terrie Moffitt et al., "A Gradient of Childhood Self-Control Predicts Health, Wealth, and Public Safety," *Proceedings of the National Academy of Sciences* 108, no. 7 (2011): 2693–98.

Yet one study suggests Wilhelm Hoffman et al., "Everyday Temptations: An Experience Sampling Study of Desire, Conflict, and Self-Control," *Journal of Personality and Social Psychology* 102, no. 6 (June 2012): 1318–35; Baumeister and Tierney, *Willpower,* 3–4.

when people were asked to identify their failings Baumeister and Tierney, *Willpower,* 2; see also the Values in Action Project, Christopher Peterson and Martin Seligman, eds., *Character Strength and Virtues* (Washington, DC: American Psychological Association, 2004).

freedom from decision making is crucial Kathleen Vohs et al., "Making Choices Impairs Subsequent Self-Control: A Limited-Resource Account of Decision Making, Self-Regulation, and Active Initiative," *Journal of Personality and Social Psychology* 94, no. 5 (May 2008): 883–98.

people feel more in control Wendy Wood, Jeffrey Quinn, and Deborah Kashy, "Habits in Everyday Life: Thought, Emotion, and Action," *Journal of Personality and Social Psychology* 83, no. 6 (2002): 1281–97.

stress doesn't necessarily make us likely Wendy Wood, David Neal, and Aimee Drolet, "How Do People Adhere to Goals When Willpower Is Low? The Profits (and Pitfalls) of Strong Habits," *Journal of Personality and Social Psychology* 104, no. 6 (2013): 959–75.

as it speeds time, habit also deadens Wood, Quinn, and Kashy, "Habits in Everyday Life."

about 40 percent Ibid.

If I consider my life honestly Christopher Alexander, *The Timeless Way of Building* (New York: Oxford University Press, 1979), 67–68.

Poor diet, inactivity, smoking Centers for Disease Control and Prevention, National Center for Chronic Disease Prevention and Health Promotion (August 2012), http://www.cdc.gov/chronicdisease/overview/index.htm.

THE FATEFUL TENDENCIES WE BRING INTO THE WORLD: *The Four Tendencies*

"Surprisingly few clues are ever offered" John Updike, *Self-Consciousness: Memoirs* (New York: Knopf, 1989).

"Running seems like the most efficient" Leslie Fandrich, "May Exercise Plans," May 2, 2013, http://bit.ly/1lzbCWa.

DIFFERENT SOLUTIONS FOR DIFFERENT PEOPLE: *Distinctions*

Research shows that morning people For a fascinating investigation of the issues related to chronotypes, see Till Roenneberg, *Internal Time:*

Chronotypes, Social Jet Lag, and Why You're So Tired (Cambridge: Harvard University Press, 2012).

Larks are likely to be happier Renee Biss and Lynn Hasher, "Happy as a Lark: Morning-Type Younger and Older Adults Are Higher in Positive Affect," *Emotion* 12, no. 3 (June 2012): 437–41.

people lean toward being "promotion-focused" For an extensive discussion of this distinction, see Heidi Grant Halvorson and E. Tory Higgins, *Focus: Use Different Ways of Seeing the World for Success and Influence* (New York: Hudson Street Press, 2013).

start with modest, manageable steps Charles Duhigg, *The Power of Habit: Why We Do What We Do in Life and Business* (New York: Random House, 2012), 112.

"tiny habits" For a discussion, see B. J. Fogg's website, www.tinyhabits. com; see also Teresa Amabile and Steven Kramer, *The Progress Principle: Using Small Wins to Ignite Joy, Engagement, and Creativity at Work* (Cambridge: Harvard Business Review Press, 2011).

some people do better when they're very ambitious See, for example, James Claiborn and Cherry Pedrick, *The Habit Change Workbook: How to Break Bad Habits and Form Good Ones* (Oakland, CA: New Harbinger, 2001), 160.

"I have a great respect" Jeff Goodell, "Steve Jobs in 1994: The Rolling Stone Interview," *Rolling Stone*, June 16, 1994, republished January 17, 2011.

what habits work for them Mason Currey, *Daily Rituals: How Artists Work* (New York: Knopf, 2013).

WE MANAGE WHAT WE MONITOR: *Monitoring*

roadside speed display "The Problem of Speeding in Residential Areas," in Michael S. Scott, *Speeding in Residential Areas*, 2nd ed., Center for Problem-Oriented Policing, U.S. Department of Justice, 2010, http:// www.popcenter.org/problems/pdfs/Speeding_Residential_Areas.pdf.

people estimated that in the course Gretchen Reynolds, *The First 20*

Minutes: Surprising Science Reveals How We Can Exercise Better, Train Smarter, Live Longer (New York: Hudson Street Press, 2012), 97; see also David R. Bassett, Jr., et al., "Pedometer-Measured Physical Activity and Health Behaviors in U.S. Adults," *Medicine & Science in Sports & Exercise* 42, no. 10 (October 2010): 1819–25.

70 percent of Americans were overweight Centers for Disease Control and Prevention, FastStats, "Obesity and Overweight," http://www.cdc.gov/nchs/fastats/overwt.htm.

keeping a food journal Jack F. Hollis et al., "Weight Loss During the Intensive Intervention Phase of the Weight-Loss Maintenance Trial," *American Journal of Preventive Medicine* 35, no. 2 (August 2008): 118–26.

Americans, on average, walked 5,117 steps Bassett et al., "Pedometer-Measured Physical Activity."

wearing a pedometer and trying to hit a goal "Counting Every Step You Take," *Harvard Health Letter,* September 2009.

article about the Jawbone UP band David Pogue, "2 Wristbands Keep Tabs on Fitness," *New York Times*, November 14, 2012.

poor judges of how much we're eating Brian Wansink, *Mindless Eating: Why We Eat More Than We Think* (New York: Bantam, 2006), 60.

"unit bias" Andrew Geier, Paul Rozin, and Gheorghe Doros, "Unit Bias: A New Heuristic That Helps Explain the Effect of Portion Size on Food Intake," *Psychological Science* 17, no. 6 (2006): 521–25.

the bigger the package Wansink, *Mindless Eating*, 59–60.

people avoid the smallest and largest Kathryn Sharpe, Richard Staelin, and Joel Huber, "Using Extremeness Aversion to Fight Obesity: Policy Implications of Context Dependent Demand," *Journal of Consumer Research* 35 (October 2008): 406–22; see also Pierre Chandon, "How Package Design and Packaged-Based Marketing Claims Lead to Overeating," *Applied Economics Perspectives and Policy* 35, no. 1 (2013): 7–31.

When people preplate their food Wansink, *Mindless Eating,* 56.

current research suggests that weighing each day John Tierney, "Be It Resolved," *New York Times,* January 6, 2012.

people weigh their highest on Sunday Anna-Leena Orsama et al., "Weight Rhythms: Weight Increases During Weekends and Decreases During Weekdays," *Obesity Facts* 7, no. 1 (2014): 36–47.

being "too tired" is the most common reason Piers Steel, *The Procrastination Equation: How to Stop Putting Things Off and Start Getting Stuff Done* (New York: Harper, 2010), 147.

for every hour of interrupted sleep Lauren Weber, "Weary Workers Learn to Count Sheep Using Special Lighting, Office Nap Pods," *Wall Street Journal*, January 23, 2013.

My friend Laura Vanderkam Laura Vanderkam, *168 Hours: You Have More Time Than You Think* (New York: Portfolio, 2011).

thirty people were asked to estimate Dilip Soman, "Effects of Payment Mechanism on Spending Behavior: The Role of Rehearsal and Immediacy of Payments," *Journal of Consumer Research* 27, no. 4 (March 2001): 460–74.

Americans ate less than a fifth Gary Taubes, *Why We Get Fat: And What to Do About It* (New York: Anchor, 2011), 67.

FIRST THINGS FIRST: *Foundation*

While some experts advise focusing Roy Baumeister and John Tierney, *Willpower: Rediscovering the Greatest Human Strength* (New York: Penguin, 2011), 38.

people who work on one positive habit See, e.g., Megan Oaten and Ken Cheng, "Longitudinal Gains in Self-Regulation from Regular Physical Exercise," *British Journal of Health Psychology* 11 (2006): 717–33; Charles Duhigg, *The Power of Habit: Why We Do What We Do in Life and Business* (New York: Random House, 2012), 97–109; James O. Prochaska, John C. Norcross, and Carlo C. DiClemente, *Changing for Good: A Revolutionary Six-Stage Program for Overcoming Bad Habits and Moving Your Life Positively Forward* (New York: Harper, 1994), 57.

Being mildly but chronically short of sleep Eve Van Cauter et al.,

"The Impact of Sleep Deprivation on Hormone and Metabolism," *Medscape Neurology* 7, no. 1 (2005), http://www.medscape.org/view article/502825.

Among its most helpful benefits Oaten and Cheng, "Longitudinal Gains in Self-Regulation."

The people who get the biggest boost Gretchen Reynolds, *The First 20 Minutes: Surprising Science Reveals How We Can Exercise Better, Train Smarter, Live Longer* (New York: Hudson Street Press, 2012), 9–11.

about half have dropped out Shirley Wang, "Hard-Wired to Hate Exercise?" *Wall Street Journal*, February 19, 2013.

exercise doesn't promote weight loss For a helpful discussion of this issue, see Reynolds, *First 20 Minutes*, 80–95; Gary Taubes, *Why We Get Fat: And What to Do About It* (New York: Anchor, 2011), chap. 4.

it takes twenty minutes for the body David Lewis, *Impulse: Why We Do What We Do Without Knowing Why We Do It* (Cambridge: Harvard University Press, 2013), 146.

Many people point to studies See, e.g., "NWCR Facts," National Weight Control Registry, http://www.nwcr.ws/Research/.

a study of existing research Andrew W. Brown, Michelle M. Bohan Brown, and David B. Allison, "Belief Beyond the Evidence: Using the Proposed Effect of Breakfast on Obesity to Show 2 Practices That Distort Scientific Evidence," *American Journal of Clinical Nutrition* 98, no. 5 (2013): 1298–308; Anahad O'Connor, "Myths Surround Breakfast and Weight," *Well* blog, *New York Times,* September 10, 2013.

In one study of dieting women Angela Kong et al., "Self-Monitoring and Eating-Related Behaviors Are Associated with 12-Month Weight Loss in Postmenopausal Overweight-to-Obese Women," *Journal of the Academy of Nutrition and Dietetics* 112, no. 9 (September 2012): 1428–35.

we don't have to drink eight glasses Reynolds, *First 20 Minutes*, 63–64.

the habit of bed making Duhigg, *Power of Habit*, 109.

IF IT'S ON THE CALENDAR, IT HAPPENS: *Scheduling*

almost one in ten Americans had meditated Patricia M. Barnes, Barbara Bloom, and Richard L. Nahin, "Complementary and Alternative Medicine Use Among Adults and Children: United States, 2007," *CDC National Health Statistics Report #12,* December 10, 2008.

Happiness expert Daniel Gilbert Daniel Gilbert, *Stumbling on Happiness* (New York: Knopf, 2006), 223–33.

The Miracle of Mindfulness Thich Nhat Hanh, *The Miracle of Mindfulness: An Introduction to the Practice of Meditation* (Boston: Beacon Press, 1999).

Real Happiness Sharon Salzberg, *Real Happiness: The Power of Meditation* (New York: Workman, 2010).

Salzberg suggests starting with twenty minutes Ibid., 35.

thinking about the Isaiah Berlin essay Isaiah Berlin, *The Hedgehog and the Fox,* 2nd ed. (Princeton, NJ: Princeton University Press, 2013).

"Beware of all enterprises" Henry David Thoreau, *Walden* (New Haven, CT: Yale University Press, 2004), 22.

researchers at University College London Phillippa Lally et al., "How Are Habits Formed: Modeling Habit Formation in the Real World," *European Journal of Social Psychology* 40 (2010): 998–1009.

"Either *once only, or every day*" Andy Warhol, *The Philosophy of Andy Warhol (From A to B and Back Again) (*New York: Harvest, 1977), 166.

"Anything one does every day" Gertrude Stein, *Paris France* (New York: Liveright, 2013), 19.

which helps explain why sexual indiscretions Roy Baumeister, "Yielding to Temptation: Self-Control Failure, Impulsive Purchasing, and Consumer Behavior," *Journal of Consumer Research* 28 (March 2002): 670–76.

"artist's date" Julia Cameron, *The Artist's Way* (New York: Penguin Putnam, 1992), 18.

"A small daily task" Anthony Trollope, *Autobiography* (New York: Oxford University Press, 2009), 120.

Johnny Cash's to-do list Phil Patton, "Johnny Cash—Our Longing for Lists," *New York Times*, September 1, 2012, SR4.

subjects made a shopping list Daniel Reed and Barbara van Leeuwen, "Predicting Hunger: The Effects of Appetite and Delay on Choice," *Organizational Behavior and Human Decision Processes* 76, no. 2 (November 1998): 189–205.

"Grant me chastity and continence" Augustine, *The Confessions of Saint Augustine* (New York: E. P. Dutton & Co., 1900), 184.

SOMEONE'S WATCHING: *Accountability*

people were asked to pay voluntarily Adam Alter, *Drunk Tank Pink: And Other Unexpected Forces That Shape How We Think, Feel, and Behave* (New York: Penguin, 2013), 77–79.

life-sized cutout of a policeman Andrew Rafferty, "Cardboard Cop Fighting Bike Theft in Boston," NBC News, August 6, 2010, http://usnews.nbcnews.com/_news/2013/08/06/19897675-cardboard-cop-fighting-bike-theft-in-boston.

The mere presence of a mirror Roy Baumeister and John Tierney, *Willpower: Rediscovering the Greatest Human Strength* (New York: Penguin, 2011), 112–13.

"When you are a free and independent writer" Irving Wallace, *The Writing of One Novel* (New York: Simon & Schuster, 1968), 37.

dog owners get more exercise Bob Martin, *Humane Research Council,* "Average Dog Owner Gets More Exercise Than Gym-Goers," February 15, 2011, http://bit.ly/1sfRSK3.

older people walk more regularly Tara Parker-Pope, "The Best Walking Partner: Man vs. Dog," *New York Times*, December 14, 2009.

popular snack item's loyal buyers Brian Wansink, *Mindless Eating: Why We Eat More Than We Think* (New York: Bantam, 2006), 199.

IT'S ENOUGH TO BEGIN: *First Steps*

Comedian Jerry Seinfeld advised Brad Isaac, "Jerry Seinfeld's Productivity Secret," Lifehacker, July 24, 2007, http://bit.ly/1rT93AB.

TEMPORARY BECOMES PERMANENT: *Clean Slate*

36 percent of successful changes Todd Heatherton and Patricia Nichols, "Personal Accounts of Successful Versus Failed Attempts at Life Change," *Personality and Social Psychology Bulletin* 20, no. 6 (December 1994): 664–75; see also Chip Heath and Dan Heath, *Switch: How to Change Things When Change Is Hard* (New York: Crown Business, 2010), 208.

Marriage and divorce can affect people's weight Jeff Grabmeier, "Large Weight Gains Most Likely for Men After Divorce, Women After Marriage," *Research News*, Ohio State University, August 17, 2011, http://researchnews.osu.edu/archive/weightshock.htm.

DATA POINT OF ONE: *Lightning Bolt*

sometimes we're hit by a lightning bolt For an interesting examination of an aspect of the Strategy of the Lightning Bolt, see William Miller and Janet C'de Baca, *Quantum Change: When Epiphanies and Sudden Insights Transform Ordinary Lives* (New York: Guilford Press, 2001).

Gary Taubes's book Gary Taubes, *Why We Get Fat: And What to Do About It* (New York: Anchor Books, 2010). For an expanded discussion of Taubes's arguments, see *Good Calories, Bad Calories: Fats, Carbs, and the Controversial Science of Diet and Health* (New York: Anchor Books, 2008). It includes a helpful summary of Taubes's conclusions (p. 454):

1. Dietary fat, whether saturated or not, is not a cause of obesity, heart disease, or any other chronic disease of civilization.

2. The problem is the carbohydrates in the diet, their effect on insulin

secretion, and thus the hormonal regulation of homeostasis—the entire harmonic ensemble of the human body. The more easily digestible and refined the carbohydrates, the greater the effect on our health, weight, and well-being.

3. Sugars—sucrose and high-fructose corn syrup, specifically— are particularly harmful, probably because the combination of fructose and glucose simultaneously elevates insulin levels while overloading the liver with carbohydrates.

4. Through their direct effect on insulin and blood sugar, refined carbohydrates, starches, and sugars are the dietary cause of coronary heart disease and diabetes. They are the most likely dietary causes of cancer, Alzheimer's disease, and the other chronic diseases of civilization.

5. Obesity is a disorder of excess fat accumulation, not overeating, and not sedentary behavior.

6. Consuming excess calories does not *cause* us to grow fatter, any more than it causes a child to grow taller. Expending more energy than we consume does not lead to long-term weight loss; it leads to hunger.

7. Fattening and obesity are caused by an imbalance—a disequilibrium—in the hormonal regulation of adipose tissue and fat metabolism. Fat synthesis and storage exceed the mobilization of fat from the adipose tissue and its subsequent oxidation. We become leaner when the hormonal regulation of the fat tissue reverses this balance.

8. Insulin is the primary regulator of fat storage. When insulin levels are elevated—either chronically or after a meal—we accumulate fat in our fat tissue. When insulin levels fall, we release fat from our fat tissue and use it for fuel.

9. By stimulating insulin secretion, carbohydrates make us fat and ultimately cause obesity. The fewer carbohydrates we consume, the leaner we will be.

10. By driving fat accumulation, carbohydrates also increase hunger

and decrease the amount of energy we expend in metabolism and physical activity.

For a fascinating discussion of the role of fat in a healthy diet, see also Nina Teicholz, *The Big Fat Surprise: Why Butter, Meat and Cheese Belong in a Healthy Diet* (New York: Simon & Schuster, 2014).

in order to lower insulin Taubes, *Why We Get Fat*, 112–62.

quantity and quality of carbohydrates Ibid., 128–39, 195–98.

Meat is fine Ibid., 163–200.

FREE FROM FRENCH FRIES: *Abstaining*

"to take a *little* wine" Piozzi et al., *Johnsoniana; or, Supplement to Boswell: Being, Anecdotes and Sayings of Dr. Johnson* (London: John Murray, 1836), 96.

"The only way to get rid" Oscar Wilde, *The Picture of Dorian Gray* (Thorndike, ME: G. K. Hall, 1995), 29.

"It is much easier to extinguish" François de la Rochefoucauld, *Collected Maxims and Other Reflections*, E. H. Blackmore and A. M. Blackmore, trans. (New York: Oxford World Classics, 2008), 187.

"The sacrifice of pleasures" Muriel Spark, *Loitering with Intent* (New York: New Directions, 1981), 95.

the less we indulge in something Omar Manejwala, *Craving: Why We Can't Seem to Get Enough* (Center City, MN: Hazelden, 2013), 141.

"It is surprising how soon" William James, *Writings 1878–1899: Psychology: Briefer Course* (New York: Library of America, 1992), 148.

One study of flight attendants Reuven Dar et al., "The Craving to Smoke in Flight Attendants: Relations with Smoking Deprivation, Anticipation of Smoking, and Actual Smoking," *Journal of Abnormal Psychology* 119, no. 1 (2010): 248–53.

IT'S HARD TO MAKE THINGS EASIER: *Convenience*

ice-cream cooler's lid was left open Brian Wansink, *Mindless Eating: Why We Eat More Than We Think* (New York: Bantam, 2006), 87–88.

According to *Consumer Reports*, more than 30 percent *Consumer Reports*, August 2011, http://bit.ly/1oiPAUB.

70 percent of people who belong to a gym Piers Steel, *The Procrastination Equation: How to Stop Putting Things Off and Start Getting Stuff Done* (New York: Harper, 2010), 23.

office workers spend a staggering 28 percent Michael Chui et al., "The Social Economy: Unlocking Value and Productivity Through Social Technologies," McKinsey Global Institute, July 2012, http://bit.ly/1d4fPbE.

a subway station in Sweden Claire Bates, "Scaling New Heights: Piano Stairway Encourages Commuters to Ditch the Escalators," *Daily Mail*, October 11, 2009.

the image of a housefly Michael Pollak, "A Dutch Innovation," *New York Times*, June 17, 2012, MB2.

CHANGE MY SURROUNDINGS, NOT MYSELF: *Inconvenience*

"Eat all the junk food you want" Michael Pollan, *Food Rules: An Eater's Manual* (New York: Penguin, 2009), rule no. 39.

A key for understanding many bad habits? Piers Steel, *The Procrastination Equation: How to Stop Putting Things Off and Start Getting Stuff Done* (New York: Harper, 2010), 13–14; see also Terrie Moffitt et al., "A Gradient of Childhood Self-Control Predicts Health, Wealth, and Public Safety," *Proceedings of the National Academy of Sciences* 108, no. 7 (2011): 2693–98.

people at high risk for smoking Sheena Iyengar, *The Art of Choosing* (New York: Twelve, 2010), 249.

make shopping as inconvenient as possible For this, and a useful look at how convenience influences shopping, see Paco Underhill, *Why We Buy: The Science of Shopping* (New York: Simon & Schuster, 1999).

employers can use the Strategy of Inconvenience For a thorough discussion, see Richard Thaler and Cass Sunstein, *Nudge: Improving Decisions About Health, Wealth, and Happiness* (New York: Penguin, 2008).

going trayless cut food waste Lisa Foderaro, "Without Cafeteria Trays, Colleges Cut Water Use, and Calories," *New York Times*, April 28, 2009, A1.

three armed men burst into the home Michael Shnayerson, "Something Happened at Anne's!" *Vanity Fair*, August 2007.

A STUMBLE MAY PREVENT A FALL: *Safeguards*

the wily Greek hero Odysseus Homer, *The Odyssey*, Robert Fagles, trans. (New York: Penguin, 1996), Book 12.

people spend about one-fourth of their waking time Wilhelm Hoffman et al., "Everyday Temptations: An Experience Sampling Study of Desire, Conflict, and Self-Control," *Journal of Personality and Social Psychology* 102, no. 6 (June 2012): 1318–35.

people given sandwiches in nontransparent wrap Brian Wansink, "Environmental Factors That Increase the Food Intake and Consumption Volume of Unknowing Consumers," *Annual Review of Nutrition* 24 (2004): 455–70.

Hospitality expert Jacob Tomsky Jacob Tomsky, *Heads in Beds: A Reckless Memoir of Hotels, Hustles, and So-Called Hospitality* (New York: Doubleday, 2012), 58.

"The infancies of all things are feeble" Michel de Montaigne, *The Complete Essays* (New York: Penguin Classics, 1993), 1154.

"implementation intentions" Peter Gollwitzer, "Implementation Intentions: Strong Effects of Simple Plans," *American Psychologist* 54 (1999): 493–503; see also Chip Heath and Dan Heath, *Switch: How to Change Things When Change Is Hard* (New York: Crown Business, 2010), 290.

People who use if-then planning See Heath and Heath, *Switch*, 290; Heidi Grant Halvorson, *Succeed: How We Can Reach Our Goals* (New York: Hudson Street Press, 2012), 173–81; Peter Gollwitzer and Paschal Sheeran, "Implementation Intentions," http://bit.ly/1lKxCtU.

"Plans are worthless, but planning is everything" Dwight Eisenhower, remarks at the National Defense Executive Reserve Conference, November 14, 1957.

People who feel less guilt For a helpful review of relevant studies, see Kelly McGonigal, *The Willpower Instinct: How Self-Control Works, Why It Matters, and What You Can Do to Get More of It* (New York: Avery, 2012), 147–48.

"retail therapy" to feel better Karen J. Pine, "Report on a Survey into Female Economic Behaviour and the Emotion Regulatory Role of Spending," University of Hertfordshire, Sheconomics Survey Report, 2009.

when people were trying to form habits Phillippa Lally et al., "How Are Habits Formed: Modeling Habit Formation in the Real World," *European Journal of Social Psychology* 40 (2010): 998–1009.

when dieters figure that they've blown their diet Roy F. Baumeister, Todd F. Heatherton, and Dianne M. Tice, *Losing Control: How and Why People Fail at Self-Regulation* (New York: Academic Press, 1994), 177–78, 190; Roy Baumeister and John Tierney, *Willpower: Rediscovering the Greatest Human Strength* (New York: Penguin, 2011), 222.

"People do tend to self-regulate day by day" See C. Peter Herman and Janet Polivy, "The Self-Regulation of Eating: Theoretical and Practical Problems," in Kathleen Vohs and Roy Baumeister, eds., *Handbook of Self-Regulation: Research, Theory, and Applications*, 2nd ed. (New York: Guilford Press, 2011), 525.

NOTHING STAYS IN VEGAS: *Loophole-Spotting*

people who plan to start dieting tomorrow Dax Urbszat, Peter C. Herman, and Janet Polivy, "Eat, Drink, and Be Merry, for Tomorrow We

Diet: Effects of Anticipated Deprivation on Food Intake in Restrained and Unrestrained Eaters," *Journal of Abnormal Psychology* 111, no. 2 (May 2002): 396–401.

"apparently irrelevant decisions" Warren K. Bickel and Rudy E. Vuchinich, eds., *Reframing Health Behavior Change with Behavioral Economics* (Mahwah, NJ: Lawrence Erlbaum, 2000), ix; see also Roy F. Baumeister, Todd F. Heatherton, and Dianne M. Tice, *Losing Control: How and Why People Fail at Self-Regulation* (New York: Academic Press, 1994), 250.

strange, brilliant skeleton of a book J. M. Barrie, *The Boy Castaways of Black Lake Island*, General Collection, Beinecke Rare Book and Manuscript Library, Yale University.

"Those faults which we cannot conceal" Samuel Johnson, *Selected Essays* (New York: Penguin Classics, 2003), 76, first published in *The Rambler*, No. 28, June 23, 1750.

Fast-food joints exploit this loophole Sarah Nassauer, "Restaurants Create New Seasons as Reasons to Indulge; Limited-Time Shakes," *Wall Street Journal*, March 6, 2013.

"argument of the growing heap" Desiderius Erasmus, *The Praise of Folly*, Clarence Miller, trans. (New Haven, CT: Yale University Press, 1979), 31, n. 4 (also called the "Sorites paradox").

WAIT FIFTEEN MINUTES: *Distraction*

research shows that with active distraction Jeffrey Schwartz and Sharon Begley, *The Mind and the Brain: Neuroplasticity and the Power of Mental Force* (New York: ReganBooks, 2002), 84.

Author Jean Kerr spent half her writing time Jean Kerr, *Please Don't Eat the Daisies* (New York: Doubleday, 1957).

NO FINISH LINE: *Reward*

the more I thought about rewards For an extensive and fascinating discussion of the use and pitfalls of rewards, see Edward Deci, *Why We Do What We Do: Understanding Self-Motivation* (New York: Penguin, 1996); Alfie Kohn, *Punished by Rewards: The Trouble with Gold Stars, Incentive Plans, A's, Praise, and Other Bribes* (New York: Houghton Mifflin, 1999); Daniel Pink, *Drive: The Surprising Truth About What Motivates Us* (New York: Riverhead, 2009).

Organizational theorists Thomas Malone and Mark Lepper Thomas W. Malone and Mark R. Lepper, "Making Learning Fun: A Taxonomy of Intrinsic Motivations for Learning," in Richard Snow and Marshall J. Farr, eds., *Aptitude, Learning, and Instruction: Conative and Affective Process Analysis* (Hillsdale, NJ: Lawrence Erlbaum, 1987), 223.

children who got a reward for coloring Mark Lepper, David Greene, and Richard Nisbett, "Undermining Children's Intrinsic Interest with Extrinsic Reward: A Test of the 'Overjustification' Hypothesis," *Journal of Personality and Social Psychology* 28, no. 1 (1973): 129–37.

as soon as the reward stops Deci, *Why We Do What We Do*, chaps. 2–4; Pink, *Drive*, chap. 2; Kohn, *Punished by Rewards*, 82–87.

within six months of delivery Michele Levine et al., "Weight Concerns Affect Motivation to Remain Abstinent from Smoking Postpartum," *Annals of Behavioral Medicine* 32, no. 2 (October 2006): 147–53.

about one in five American adults NPD Group, "Report on Eating Patterns in America," http://bit.ly/1zHGeu1.

According to a review of studies Traci Mann et al., "Medicare's Search for Effective Obesity Treatments: Diets Are Not the Answer," *American Psychologist* 62, no. 3 (2007): 220–33.

JUST BECAUSE: *Treats*

One of the secrets of a happy life Iris Murdoch, *The Sea, the Sea* (New York: Penguin, 1978), 8.

people who got a little treat Dianne Tice et al., "Restoring the Self: Positive Affect Helps Improve Self-Regulation Following Ego Depletion," *Journal of Experimental Social Psychology* 43 (2007): 379–84.

"Constructive destruction" Jan Struther, *Mrs. Miniver* (New York: Mariner, 1990), 213.

'All severity that does not tend' James Boswell, *The Life of Samuel Johnson* (New York: Penguin Classics, 2008), 497.

women are more likely to eat chocolate Sonia Rodriguez et al., "Subjective and Physiological Reactivity to Chocolate Images in High and Low Chocolate Cravers," *Biological Psychology* 70, no. 1 (2005): 9–18.

Americans spend about half their leisure hours "American Time Use Survey: 2012 Results," Bureau of Labor Statistics, June 20, 2013, http://www.bls.gov/news.release/atus.nr0.htm.

Immanuel Kant permitted himself only one pipe Manfred Kuehn, *Kant: A Biography* (Cambridge: Cambridge University Press, 2002), 222.

SITTING IS THE NEW SMOKING: *Pairing*

In the acquisition of a new habit William James, *Writings 1878–1899: Psychology: Briefer Course* (New York: Library of America, 1992), 147.

average American sits for at least eight hours James Vlahos, "Is Sitting a Lethal Activity?" *New York Times Magazine*, April 14, 2011; Marc T. Hamilton et al., "Too Little Exercise and Too Much Sitting: Inactivity Physiology and the Need for New Recommendations on Sedentary Behavior," *Current Cardiovascular Risk Reports* 2, no. 4 (July 2008): 292–98.

I visited my friend A. J. A. J. Jacobs, *Drop Dead Healthy* (New York: Simon & Schuster, 2012), 63–74. For another account of life with a treadmill desk, see Susan Orlean, "The Walking Alive: Don't Stop Moving," *The New Yorker*, May 20, 2013.

CHOOSE MY BALE OF HAY: *Clarity*

"From the day I got my driver's license" Tory Johnson, *The Shift: How I Finally Lost Weight and Discovered a Happier Life* (New York: Hyperion, 2013).

People who use language that emphasizes Vanessa M. Patrick and Henrik Hagtvedt, "How to Say 'No': Conviction and Identity Attributions in Persuasive Refusal," *International Journal of Research in Marketing*, 29, no. 4 (2012): 390–94.

several of the top reasons for this failure "Take Meds Faithfully," *Shopper's Guide to Prescription Drugs*, No. 7, Consumers Union, 2007, http://www.consumerreports.org/health/resources/pdf/best-buy-drugs/money-saving-guides/english/DrugComplianceFINAL.pdf.

I'M THE FUSSY ONE: *Identity*

One regrets the loss Oscar Wilde, *The Picture of Dorian Gray* (Thorndike, ME: G. K. Hall, 1995).

people eat and drink more or less For a helpful discussion of how we regulate our eating according to other people's consumption and presence, see Brian Wansink, *Mindless Eating: Why We Eat More Than We Think* (New York: Bantam, 2006), chapters 5 and 8; C. Peter Herman and Janet Polivy, "The Self-Regulation of Eating: Theoretical and Practical Problems," in Kathleen Vohs and Roy Baumeister, eds., *Handbook of Self-Regulation: Research, Theory, and Applications*, 2nd ed. (New York: Guilford Press, 2011), 522–36.

one group of registered voters was asked Christopher J. Bryan et al., "Motivating Voter Turnout by Invoking the Self," *Proceedings of the National Academy of Sciences* 108, no. 31 (August 2011): 12653–56.

Haruki Murakami, an avid long-distance runner Haruki Murakami, *What I Talk About When I Talk About Running* (New York: Knopf, 2007), 104.

"I had to train myself" Janet Malcolm, *Forty-one False Starts: Essays on Artists and Writers* (New York: Farrar, Straus & Giroux, 2013), 36.

In their invaluable book *Made to Stick* Chip Heath and Dan Heath, *Made to Stick: Why Some Ideas Survive and Others Die* (New York: Random House, 2007), 195–99.

38 percent of readers *always* finish a book "The Psychology of Abandonment," Goodreads, http://www.goodreads.com/blog/show/424-what-makes-you-put-down-a-book.

NOT EVERYONE IS LIKE ME: *Other People*

Associate with people who are likely to improve you Lucius Annaeus Seneca, *Letters from a Stoic,* Robin Campbell, trans. (New York: Penguin, 1969), 43.

"health concordance" Deanna Meyler, Jim Stimpson, and M. Kristen Peek, "Health Concordance Within Couples: A Systematic Review," *Social Science and Medicine* 64, no. 11 (June 2007): 2297–310.

If one partner has type 2 diabetes Aaron Leong, Elham Rahme, and Kaberi Dasgupta, "Spousal Diabetes as a Diabetes Risk Factor: A Systematic Review and Meta-Analysis," *BMC Medicine* 12, no. 12 (2014), http://www.biomedcentral.com/1741-7015/12/12.

quite susceptible to "goal contagion" Kelly McGonigal, *The Willpower Instinct: How Self-Control Works, Why It Matters, and What You Can Do to Get More of It* (New York: Avery, 2012), chap. 8.

"I stand on one foot" Gretchen Reynolds, *The First 20 Minutes: Surprising Science Reveals How We Can Exercise Better, Train Smarter, Live Longer* (New York: Hudson Street Press, 2012), 256.

I agree with Andy Warhol Andy Warhol, *The Philosophy of Andy Warhol (From A to B and Back Again)* (New York: Harvest, 1977), 96.

Van Halen famously required bowls of M&M's David Lee Roth, *Crazy from the Heat* (New York: Hyperion, 1997), 109–11.

EVERYDAY LIFE IN UTOPIA: *Conclusion*

There is no more miserable human being William James, *Writings 1878– 1899: Psychology: Briefer Course* (New York: Library of America, 1992), 147.

About the Author

GRETCHEN RUBIN is one of the most thought-provoking and influential writers on the linked subjects of habits, happiness, and human nature. She's the author of many books, including the blockbuster *New York Times* bestsellers *Happier at Home* and *The Happiness Project*. Rubin has an enormous following, in print and online. Her books have sold more than a million copies worldwide in more than thirty languages. On her popular daily blog, gretchenrubin.com, she reports on her adventures in pursuit of habits and happiness. Rubin started her career in law and was clerkng for Justice Sandra Day O'Connor when she realized she wanted to be a writer. She lives in New York City with her husband and two daughters.